ON THE FAULT LINE

MANAGING TENSIONS AND DIVISIONS WITHIN SOCIETIES

Edited *by* Jeffrey Herbst, Terence McNamee *and*
Greg Mills

with Joel D. Barkan, Chris Brown, Christopher Clapham,
Pierre Englebert, Peter Lewis, Joseph Chinyong Liow,
J. Peter Pham, Tom Porteous, Anna C. Rader and Asher Susser

P

PROFILE BO

First published in Great Britain in 2012 by
Profile Books Ltd
3A Exmouth House
Pine Street
London EC1R 0JH

www.profilebooks.com

A 1,600-word article based on the Introduction was previously published by permis-
sion in *Foreign Policy* (online edition), 15 August 2011, as Jeffrey Herbst and Greg
Mills, 'The Fault Lines of Failed States: Can social science determine what makes one
state fail and another succeed?'

A CIP catalogue record for this book is available from the British Library.

ISBN 978 1 84668 588 0
eISBN 978 1 84765 813 5

Typeset in Bembo by MacGuru Ltd
info@macguru.org.uk

Printed and bound in Great Britain by Clays, Bungay, Suffolk

DISCLAIMER

CONTENTS

INTRODUCTION: MANAGING FAULT LINES IN THE TWENTY-FIRST CENTURY

Jeffrey Herbst and Greg Mills

S TATES EVOLVE SLOWLY, sometimes, but one of the most dramatic events of the twenty-first century was the independence of South Sudan, achieved after years of bloodshed along racial and religious fault lines and a referendum whereby the population voted overwhelming to secede from Sudan.

A few weeks before the referendum a senior official from the South explained to the authors why southern Sudanese favoured secession despite the almost impossible economic circumstances it faces: 'The state has been built around excluding [us] … Khartoum has failed to build a state to manage our diversity. In this sense the [current] Sudanese state is a failed state.' The South's president, Salva Kiir, was under no allusions about the challenge of building a new state, however. 'We have over sixty tribes in South Sudan. It is not easy with such diversity. We must accept ourselves as one nation and use different tribes to build that one nation which we can be proud of.'[1] To emphasise the point, he added: 'There has been no development in South Sudan – everything is at zero.' The southern Sudanese decided that there was no way of solving their societal divisions other than by leaving the state.

While Sudan's evolution is particularly dramatic, all countries possess innumerable and at times dramatic social, economic and political fault lines, nowhere more so than in Africa. The continent's colonial history has given rise to often fragmented and weak states, made up of many nations and cutting across geographic, racial and religious boundaries. Additionally, the post-independence state has been virtually bereft of legitimacy in the eyes of large segments of its own population. Efforts to shore it up more often than not have degenerated into neo-patrimonial or other regimes that have further eroded its legitimacy. The shorthand for these divisions is catastrophic African failure: the Rwandan genocide and Nigerian civil war (which each cost a million lives), the Sudanese civil war and Darfur conflict (another million), various Congolese conflicts (anywhere between one and five million) and so on.

However, Africa is far from alone. From Yemen to India, Brazil to China, Israel, Palestine, Afghanistan and Iraq, Sri Lanka to Guatemala, fault lines exist. In many countries they produce conflict; in others they are better managed. India, for example, a state of many nations, categories, castes and religions, with twenty-one classical languages, has generally managed its fault lines well. Canada also has a clear linguistic fault line that it has diffused, while Northern Ireland has a sectarian one that has been overcome through negotiations (albeit after a long period of violence). The nature of violence around societal fault lines is dynamic and that means the contours of domestic mass violence will continue to evolve. With war between states having become exceptionally rare (with the notable exceptions of the Great Lakes and Horn of Africa regions in Africa), the violence within nations is today the chief manner in which people kill each other in large numbers. It is therefore a phenomenon that must be understood.

In order to analyse the evolution of societal fault lines, the Johannesburg-based Brenthurst Foundation, working with Germany's Konrad Adenauer Stiftung and Israel's Dayan Center for Middle East and African Studies, commissioned more than two dozen experts to reflect on their countries or regions of expertise. The authors were given a common template with which to structure their writings so that we could get the maximum leverage from their collective work. While no study could encompass all of the different conflicts that revolve around societal fault lines, we were able to garner a wide variety of cases. Studies included rich countries (e.g., Canada) and the many poor ones (including the Democratic Republic of Congo, Kenya, East Timor) that have societal fault lines; conflicts seemingly arrayed around religion (e.g., the Balkans, Israel, India, Lebanon, Sri Lanka); race (South Africa); ethnic claims (e.g., Kenya, Rwanda, Uganda); and indigenous rights (e.g., Guatemala).[2] The case studies they produced are extremely rich and subtle.

Although we would have wished to reproduce all of them in this volume, we have selected thirteen of the papers which we think best reflect the diverse range of fault lines that can impact upon nations' stability and prosperity. While adhering to the same general template, the style and emphases of the chapters vary. The chapter on Ethiopia, for instance, delves further into the foundation of its societal fissures than others. The very fluid nature of events in Sudan in 2011, by contrast, demanded a strong focus on the 'here and now', though the chapter still captures the historical factors which triggered the fatal eruption of its main fault line. The chapters present a wealth of detail but we hope that complexity is seen as a virtue rather than a hindrance; societal divisions in these countries and elsewhere rarely lend themselves to easy characterisations. Another unique feature of this volume is the different backgrounds of the contributors, some of whom are writing about their own countries – in the case of Canada, South Africa, Israel and the UK. Most of the authors have an academic background, though the chapters on Iraq and Northern Ireland are written from the perspective of a top military commander with first-hand operational and policy-making experience in both. We believe that these different approaches in the book are an asset, as are the at times conflicting interpretations that arise among the authors on the same topic. The recent history of Iraq, perhaps not surprisingly, is a case in point.

Understanding Societal Fault Lines

No country is destined to suffer conflict because of its societal divisions and no nation is guaranteed to be at peace. France, Japan and the United States are today viewed as durable, and perhaps inevitable, nation states, but their modern tranquillity belies brutal fights in the past over societal divisions, not least the American Civil War. Indeed, for those impatient with developing countries that, like most of Africa, received independence in the last fifty years, it is important to remember that the American Civil War – notable for the extraordinary bloodletting in its day given the technology available – was fought eighty-five years *after* the Declaration of Independence.

At the same time, it is often surprising when dire conflict breaks out. Lebanon, Somalia, Sri Lanka and Yugoslavia – to cite only countries in our original survey – were all at different times hailed for their success in nation-building or for creating a national identity, only later to become exemplars of the long-term violence that societal divisions can induce.

Similarly, Liberia, a country that has been destroyed by fault-line conflicts that have produced extraordinary examples of man's inhumanity, was not an obvious candidate for self-destruction. In contrast, South Africa, which seemed destined to be submerged by an apocalyptic race war, has become, despite its many problems, a symbol of how leadership can avert what appeared to be inevitable catastrophe.

To add to the confusion, it is clear, especially when going beyond the headlines, that mass conflict over fault lines is actually extremely rare. Despite the many divisions in the vast majority of societies, most of the time people do not resort to killing, much less to large-scale violence. David Laitin estimates that only five in 10,000 paired ethnic groups in Africa are fighting each other at any one time.[3] There is widespread agreement in the academic literature that cultural differences by themselves are not enough to ignite conflict. Daniel Posner makes the simple but compelling point: 'The mere presence of cultural differences cannot possibly be a sufficient condition for the emergence of political or social strife for there are far more cultural cleavages in the world than there are conflicts.'[4] Wimmer and Cederman go one step further in their new analysis of ethnic conflict by stating that, 'more diverse states are not more war-prone, in contrast to the expectations of the diversity-breeds-conflict school'.[5]

When violence does break out, the sources of conflict are often confused, hard for insiders (much less outsiders) to understand and continually shifting. Over and over again, our authors reported that the nature of the fault lines was far more complicated than the simple headline assigned to a country. Writing on Northern Ireland, presumably one of the easiest conflicts to describe, Chris Brown notes: 'Northern Ireland's fault lines are on the one hand relatively simple: a bipolar society where religious, economic, political, cultural and social divisions tend to be mutually reinforcing. On the other hand this makes for difficult, temptingly simplistic, categorisation that ignores the more complex contributing factors …' Similarly, writing on Iraq, he finds: 'As with many states forged on the anvil of imperial cartographic neatness, Iraq is riven with fault lines: economic, political, cultural and social.' Peter Lewis notes of Nigeria: 'Ethnic and linguistic rivalries, regional assertion and religious tensions have made for contentious national politics and social instability.'

In Congo, where more people have died from domestic conflict than in any other country over the last few years, Pierre Englebert finds an extraordinarily complicated picture where the most important fault lines are not big regional or sub-national divisions but 'multiple and overlapping local fissures, widely distributed across the country, which contribute to a fragmentation of identities and networks at the local level and increased polarisation of social life'. Finally, Clapham writes that Ethiopia 'is riven by conflicts along almost every fault line – ethnic, religious, ecological, class, ideological, political – many of which are broadly aligned, though not totally commensurate, with one another. Conflicts within Ethiopia itself spread across state frontiers – especially those with its three most important neighbours.'

While every country and societal division is unique, the project identified four important issues across the many cases studied: governance, the democratic context, globalisation and external intervention and the need for flexibility of response.

Governance and the Spark of Economic Grievance

Good governance – especially the relative equitable distribution of resources by government across societal divisions – has long been understood to be essential to economic growth. The case studies reveal that good governance is also absolutely critical to preventing societal fault lines from becoming violent.

The primary preventive measure that national leaders and the international community can take to prevent fault-line violence is to prevent too powerful a 'constituency of losers' from developing. That is, if the number of people who feel aggrieved because resource allocation is unfair, biased and corrupt is relatively low, they will usually be unable to initiate violence which is self-sustaining. This is usually irrespective of the level of wealth overall in the economy. No other measure found by our group promised to be nearly as powerful or consistent in preventing fault-line violence.

In Indonesia, Joseph Chinyong Liow finds that 'during the New Order administration of President Suharto (1966–98), policies implemented by the central government in resource-rich regions like Aceh and Irian Jaya that essentially took over many of the local resources (e.g., oil, gas and gold) without giving anything substantial back to the local communities were met by strong anti-Jakarta resentment in these areas'. Similarly, while investigating Northern Ireland, Brown finds: 'The trigger for the eruption which occurred in the late 1960s was social and political: Catholics, particularly those in the poor [housing] estates of Belfast and Londonderry, saw themselves as second-class citizens, denied the perceived advantages of Protestantism and oppressed by a police force which was predominantly Protestant.' Likewise, Anna Rader writes of Sudan: 'Economic and political marginalisation has been the principal driver of conflict in Sudan, built around the two main grievances of lack of political influence and disproportionate revenue allocation, specifically from oil wealth.' Finally, Lewis writes of Nigeria: 'For decades, the key medium for securing state resources has been access to political power, and ethnic clientelism has been the central mechanism in distributional politics. It is estimated that 90 per cent of Nigerians manage on two dollars a day or less, indicating the vast gap between those at the pinnacle of the system and those further down the ladder.'

While the base of many fault lines may be a sense of relative economic dispossession, these divides are rarely defined in terms of economic grievance. Religious and other differences are regularly the overlay to the abrasion of economic resentments. Certain extraneous, global trends might exacerbate fault lines: for example, environmental change and the impact on forced migration and conflicts over shrinking resources.

Institutions and practices that ensure checks and balances, accountability and transparency are essential so that no group believes that resorting to violence is the only alternative. There may be particular opportunities to improve good governance – including the creation of capable institutions encouraging transparency and accountability, security-sector reform, independent media, effective local policing – given the spread of democracy worldwide. Critical in building state capacity and improving conditions of governance is the creation of a domestic tax system and base, which simultaneously serves to strengthen the link of accountability between electorates and leadership. Democracy is one means of asserting this link.

The Democratic Context

Democracy is an important means of resolving fault lines through instilling conditions of good governance. It is, however, a long-term process in which elections are not the only prerequisite for the successful management of fault lines.

In the vast majority of cases societal fault lines are played out in a democratic context or at least where regularly scheduled elections are held, albeit of enormously varying quality. As recently as 1989, elections, much less democracy, were uncommon in the developing world and especially rare in highly divided societies. Today, elections are held almost everywhere in the developing world, with only a few holdouts like Eritrea. Even authoritarian leaders like Robert Mugabe in Zimbabwe and Omar al-Bashir in Sudan hold elections, although their validity is usually challenged. Indeed, elections are commonly seen, as in the Democratic Republic of Congo, Sudan and East Timor, as part of the solution to societal faultiness, a sharp contrast to previous notions that fault lines had to be solved before elections and democratic institutions could gain traction. As a case in point, elections were recently held in Afghanistan and Iraq in the midst of hostilities. Tellingly, in the project's sample of countries, chosen in good part because they exemplify conflicts over societal fault lines, every single country now has regularly scheduled elections.

There are few areas where the divide between observers and practitioners has been greater than in assessing the value of elections to heal societal divides. There is no doubt that institutionalised democratic structures can play a critical and constructive role in healing divides. Terence McNamee makes clear that the democratic structures and culture of Canada allowed it to address the fundamental issues raised by francophone Quebec, including substantial transformation of how government interacted with French-speaking Canadians and massive transfers of power and money to Quebec's provincial government, which made any gambit to leave Canada a losing (if only just) proposition.

However, democratic structures are not institutionalised in much of the world that currently suffers from societal fault lines and is at risk from violence. These countries usually have weak parliaments, courts that often do not function well, a media which may only partially be free and real fears among the populace that whoever 'wins' the election (itself often of contested legitimacy because of poor procedures and ruling-party interference) will never give up power. Democratic institutions may be ill-formed, not least because the country has not had enough experience to know what kind of democratic institutions and processes are best for it. For instance, citizenship laws – a vital part of any country where votes count – in Africa often reflect colonial practices of fifty years ago, even if London and Paris have subsequently changed the way they define the polity. Indeed, in some African countries (e.g., Ivory Coast, Zambia) citizenship laws have been used to keep politicians from campaigning and thereby enrage certain groups which suddenly find themselves disenfranchised.

The authors in our project are in general sceptical about the immediate utility of elections to address societal fault lines, for a number of reasons. First, elections have an 'us versus them' dynamic which will often aggravate societal conflicts as politicians try to mobilise supporters around differences. If the elections are viewed as fraudulent, as they often are in divided societies, societal conflicts are aggravated. Inevitably, the elections are fought on one or relatively few dimensions and therefore cannot address the complexity of the divisions in society.

For external, especially Western, actors, elections can appear as a quick deliverable: one which is aimed at satisfying domestic Western consumption as much as making real progress in the target country. Precipitous elections can in practice legitimise weak governments, unsuited to the challenges of ameliorating fault lines, while at the same time limiting the subsequent influence of the international community; a comparison between the installation of a High Representative in Bosnia-Herzegovina and attempts to replicate the process in Afghanistan, as well as the examples of Congo and Nigeria described below, are cases in point.

It is also often the fact that in the rush to hold elections, not enough attention is given to the most appropriate form of voting. There are difficult choices to be made between proportional representation and systems which tie legislators directly to a geographically defined piece of land. As no system is perfect for every country, considerable time and effort must be expended to develop the best possible system, including efforts to mitigate the inevitable drawbacks of any particular set of choices. For instance, proportional representation allows parties to be represented roughly according to their share of the vote but may produce weak governments unable to deal with their country's most significant problems. Countries with first-past-the-post elections may have majority governments but may have significant groups without explicit representation in the legislature. There are numerous other aspects to elections that have also to be considered, including, for example, the enfranchisement of refugees.

Further, given the prominence attached to elections, political contests may actually allow leaders to continue to hold on to power and distance themselves from the population and the violence that is happening on the ground. Englebert notes in Congo, where the international community devoted more than a billion dollars to the election that led to victory for Joseph Kabila in 2006: 'The 2006 election has not led to an increase in domestic accountability. Instead, it has promoted an attitude of government intolerance and an unwillingness to bargain with social forces. Electoral legitimacy has fostered the regime's authoritarian tendencies. Local groups, whose grievances are long-standing and which hoped to use

the democratic opening to find a voice, have faced increased repression.'
Peter Lewis raises the same concern: 'Nigeria's political and economic life
has been dominated by an elite cartel that comprises politicians, military
officers, senior bureaucrats, traditional rulers, local notables and leading
business people. A cartel is a form of industrial organisation, formed to
manipulate markets and to share out the rents from such collusion. Cartels
are adaptable to shifting membership and strategies, guided by the purposes of market control and rent-seeking.'

While elections and democratic institutions are one possible source of
legitimacy, others are possible. In Afghanistan, it was the *loya jirga* (important meeting or assembly) that gave its approval to the new state order after
the overthrow of the Taliban regime and not vice versa. In Somaliland, it
has been the *guurti* rather than the elected organs of state (the presidency
and the House of Representatives) that has brokered compromises with
respect to the elections.

None of this is to say that elections have no value or always aggravate the problem. In India, democracy has managed the fault lines of that
extraordinarily complicated and divided society. However, India is the
rare third world country that has been democratic since independence
(except for the brief emergency engineered by then Prime Minister Indira
Gandhi in 1975) and therefore now has over sixty years of experience with
democratic structures. India was also the rare developing country that successfully devolved significant power to sub-national units.

In particular, the regular rotation of leaders promised by viable elections does have some important positive ramifications for solving fault-
line conflicts over the long term. For instance, elections may serve to
bring new leaders to power who have different visions and political tools,
and are more willing, to address the fault lines. Just such a phenomenon
occurred in Indonesia, as Joseph Chinyong Liow notes.

Other aspects of democracy are arguably more important than elections. Federalism, the devolution of power to regional or local authorities,
is cited by several authors as an important structural innovation that might
promote peace in Congo and other African countries. Barkan notes in
East Africa that federalism is 'an idea "whose time has come"'. Of course,
federalism is created by complicated negotiations between national and
sub-national leaders and only comes into effect over a long period of
time. It therefore lacks the immediate drama of elections, but may be more
important over the long term, at least in the management of fault lines. In
Africa, the greater the variety of ethnic divisions within states, the greater

the dissipation of such forces as national fault lines. Countries with a small number of large ethnic groups – Burundi, Rwanda, Nigeria and Ethiopia are four notable examples – have had to invent complex federalist structures to balance power. Federalist constitutions are preferred, too, as a management scheme in other cases, such as India and Canada. In countries with a largely monolithic ethnic make-up, such as Botswana or Lesotho, or a large number of smaller groups, such as in Tanzania, Mozambique and even South Africa, ethnic stability has proved less problematic.

Rather than elections and democracy, our authors repeatedly note that basic grievances were often addressed by other political arrangements. McNamee argues that in Canada, for instance, bilingualism was the critical innovation that diffused the crisis and deprived francophone separatists of their key mobilising grievance, although many anglophones probably saw the language policy as an imposition, if not undemocratic.

Sustained democracy with durable institutions to address societal conflicts has traditionally taken countries many decades to develop, often after several bouts of failure. Expecting elections, the iconic aspect of democracy, to solve in the short term profound and extremely complicated societal fault lines is misguided. Indeed, it should not be surprising that elections often fail and that they sometimes make the situation worse, especially when they fool international observers into believing that an elected government actually has an interest in addressing the fault lines that threaten the citizenry. Thus other political arrangements must be looked at that might address the central points of political discord more directly, even if they perhaps lessen the priority attached to voting.

The international community has not reached a consensus on prioritising elections and good governance. Or, rather, the international community has often given elections a very high priority and then wondered why good governance does not automatically follow. In the long term, it is almost certainly the case that democratic regimes are less corrupt and allocate resources less politically than alternative forms of government. However, again, that is not the situation in the developing world where both democracy and governance are first being instituted. Indeed, the international community has been repeatedly disappointed when elections do not lead to good governance. This was demonstrated most markedly in President Obama's fruitless attempt during a visit to Kabul to pressure President Karzai to improve governance, a demand that counted for little in the Afghan leader's mind because he had, after all, just been elected again as his nation's president (albeit in a disputed process).

The disagreement between the international observers' and the African Union's verdict on the quality of the various Zimbabwean elections and the Ethiopian election in May 2010 shows that Karzai's attitude is widely supported in Africa. The international community are themselves often torn between a desire to promote democratic norms in elections and otherwise, and their support for governments that are autocratic but effective – especially in states that have broken down and are being repaired, such as Uganda, Rwanda and Ethiopia. Indeed, elections run the risk of legitimising those whose governance is poor, especially if the international community's limited political capital has been exhausted promoting elections.

Globalisation and External Intervention

Globalisation is now recognised as a near-universal process. But its effect on domestic fault lines has not been fully understood, in part because each of these conflicts is usually driven by domestic factors. Despite globalisation's spread, external agents have to recognise the limits of their power in managing fault lines.

Part of the problem is that the sheer speed of globalisation has overtaken analysis. For instance, only a few years ago it was considered noteworthy that the Zapatista Army of National Liberation in Chiapas, Mexico, had a digital media strategy including use of the Internet. Today any competent fourteen-year-old with access to a parent's credit card can establish a website.

Yet there is still a lag among many in the West in particular in understanding the penetration of the technologies of globalisation throughout the developing world. For instance, Western newspapers and many observers noted with seeming amazement that Iranians used Facebook, text-messaging, tweets and other technologies to protest against the fraudulent elections in 2009, although the children of these writers use precisely those technologies all the time.

One consequence of the continuing easy flow of information is that those in the developing world know the West much better than the West knows the developing world.[6] Again, globalisation among Westerners is usually seen as a one-way street allowing greater Western penetration of the developing world, hopefully with greater understanding. However, it also means that the protagonists of conflict in the developing world understand what pushes Western buttons much better and makes it easier for those involved in conflicts to adroitly play Western audiences. Thus autocrats are quick to embrace elections and other symbols familiar to Washington, Paris and London because they know that such contests give them a certain amount of legitimacy, even if the actual execution of the political contests leaves much to be desired. Former president Daniel arap Moi of Kenya was said to have wanted to hold a 'C' election, just enough so that Westerners could not demand his removal but still allowing the fix to be in. Of course, sometimes, as subsequent Kenyan leaders found, it is difficult to control the forces unleashed by an election.

Paradoxically, the changes to the global environment have not paralleled greater influence of external actors in shaping internal dynamics to positive ends. Interveners have unsurprisingly struggled to conduct the job that more knowledgeable and invested internal actors themselves have battled with – if Kabul, for example, cannot find the political means to bring its restive southern Afghan provinces under its writ, how are the international forces going to achieve this? External powers cannot manufacture internal consensus. Change has to come from within. We also know that the international community seldom has the will, finances and strength to impose its solutions on international problems as varied as those in Cyprus, Afghanistan, Iraq and across the Middle East, in spite of an enormous amount of effort and expense, and in spite of, at times, only minimal and non-violent resistance. So 'why court failure', asks Asher Susser in his chapter on Israel, Jordan and Palestine, by trying to coerce locals to do what they have no intention of doing?

With those limitations in mind, how might global approaches to conflicts, like the underlying fault lines themselves, be better managed?

Military solutions where one side simply annihilates the other are increasingly rare, although Sri Lanka provides a recent example. Instead, most societal conflicts seem to immediately involve a host of international mediators who attempt to avoid a military solution. Indeed, one of the most important consequences of globalisation is the *over*supply of mediators. It seems that every country in the world threatened by conflict has one or more esteemed individuals, a country, a set of countries, one or more international organisations and a plethora of NGOs that are willing to intervene as part of the solution. Partially, this reflects an increasingly technocratic view that there are solutions to almost all domestic fault lines.

However, the amount of influence that outside mediators bring to bear varies enormously from country to country. In the case of Iran, Tom Porteous writes, the government is not interested in external help in managing its fault lines, so the 'tools at their [the West's] disposal, whether economic and diplomatic sanctions or military action, are blunt and could produce unintended consequences'. In cases where there is more appetite for assistance, the problem is not the availability of would-be mediators but the supply of peacekeepers – one of the most important levers that outsiders bring to countries that are in conflict or at the brink. In peacekeeping, the supply of troops and civilian officials is much lower than the demand. For instance, using the CIA's 2009 estimate of 68.7 million Congolese, it would take about 1.4 million peacekeepers to supply the same density of peacekeeping in Congo as was provided in Kosovo. No one, of course, is going to provide anything like that, or even one-tenth of that number.

In addition, while wanting to intervene, the international community is not clear on what it wants. Writing on Ethiopia, Clapham argues that there is a difference between managing fault lines and removing them. He does not believe that they can be eliminated in Ethiopia. He goes even further and argues that resolving one fault line may simply exacerbate another, an unforeseen consequence that appears reasonable given the complexity of most societal divisions but not one that is often considered by outside interveners. Similarly, while Indian democracy has been a great success in managing the fault lines of a complicated society, it has not solved those divisions. Nor should it be judged by that standard. If foreign actors interested in intervening in a country were to set their sights at helping to manage conflicts, as opposed to solving them, they might be able to align ambitions with the available political resources.

It is in the area of governance and the promotion of economic reform that the international community has struck on a set of initiatives – from Doing Business indicators to Transparency and Corruption indices – that may have the most impact on conflict over fault lines. As the analysis above makes clear, many societies have potentially dangerous fault lines, but it seems, in case after case, that disputes become notably violent when governments are corrupt and when the allocation of important resources – especially when they are scarce – is thought to be unduly influenced by political power considerations, to the detriment of some populations. Promoting good governance is therefore especially important if the world is to address societal fault lines before they become violent. Of course, only national governments can institute good governance practices, but international pressure can help.

Flexibility of Response

Dealing with the divisions – the fault lines – within societies that often give rise to the violence in the first instance is not easy from within, and even more difficult from without. Papering over these underlying differences seldom offers a permanent solution, but often a temporary aberration, postponing the inevitable collapse of government and resurgence in violence.

The international community's inability to react in a flexible manner to the particularities of certain crises and also its insistence on operating within traditional templates may mean that outside interveners not only do not solve the problem but actually make it worse. For instance, because the international community insists that the colonial boundaries in Africa (and elsewhere) be respected in all instances, it has been unable to recognise the breakaway state of Somaliland, despite the fact that it has created a viable government while the rest of Somalia is essentially lawless. Peter Pham notes the inevitable result: 'The now decades-old crisis in Somalia may have at its origin the collapse of a "failed state", but blame for the prolongation of the misery would be more accurately attributed to a wholesale failure of imagination on the part of the international community and its local clients.' Somaliland's relative success in forming its own government may, however, be precisely because it is not subject to international intervention, whim and procedure.

How might external actors best assist in managing fault lines apart from intervention?

Africa's colonial inheritance has included borders which in some cases are a source of division and violence. While the reconfiguration of borders and the creation of new states might create new problems, they could also serve – as in the case of South Sudan or Somaliland – to remove seemingly obdurate differences.

One pointer for Sub-Saharan Africa might be provided by the 2011 referendum on the creation of a South Sudan state, which could open the way for other African nations to attempt the same. States staying together is not necessarily the best solution – not just in Sudan, but also in a number of other countries. Of course, border changes are fraught with difficulty. The recreation of the Eritrean state out of Ethiopia or East Timor from Indonesia has created new issues – over boundaries, resources and the absence of capacity.

Somewhere between rigidly maintaining the borders inherited from the colonial period, as the OAU (Organisation of African Unity)/AU (African Union) preference has been, and formally redrawing political boundaries, there is the de facto solution such as in the eastern Congo. There, economically and otherwise, areas tend to look east to nearby Rwanda, not west to the capital, Kinshasa, some 1,300 kilometres away. Somaliland, to take another example, irrespective of the recognition question, has literally nothing to do with the rest of the former Somali state (no trade, no transport links, etc.) but is a vital link for Ethiopia to the world.

As Sudan to Somaliland illustrate, external interveners should examine what is possible on a case-by-case basis rather than go in with a one-size-fits-all approach. Each case and every solution is unique, and this might include the redrawing of certain boundaries. In some situations, strengthened regional union and deepening integration might also ameliorate the destructive nature of fault lines.

Conclusion: Management is Imperative

While being respectful of the differences between countries, we are able to draw some conclusions about the nature and management of fault lines. Certainly, it is clear that fault lines are universal. All countries suffer, and benefit, from cultural divisions. There is no such thing as a 'natural' nation state with a homogeneous population, because people and politicians seek out differences at every level of societal interaction. Violence around fault lines usually breaks out in the context of poor governance and the spark of economic grievance. In particular, if deprived populations perceive that the government distributes goods in a patently unfair and corrupt manner, they are more likely to protest by violence. A fundamental means of preventing societal violence is to promote good governance so that the 'constituency of losers' is never large or powerful enough to threaten social order.

However, we find that too much weight is often placed on elections as a means of addressing fault lines. Elections in divided societies that do not have democratic traditions have their role – especially in making clear societal preferences – but by themselves will neither manage nor solve fault lines in the short term. The construction of other democratic institutions, including federalism, the appropriate set of voting rules, free media, control of the military and, above all, rule of law (and unfettered access to it), is often more important than the act of holding elections. It is important for national and international policymakers to manage expectations (theirs and those of others) regarding solutions to fault lines. In particular, in a great many cases, the realistic aim should be to manage fault lines in order to minimise violence rather than to solve them, without prejudicing internal, longer-term aspirations to solve them.

The international community's response to fault-line violence has generally not become more effective over time. External actors can rarely successfully re-engineer societies. Peacekeeping, and especially peace-enforcement, remains a rare and problematic response, likely to be used less often in the future in light of rising budget deficits in the West. This means that there is a real need for the international community to show greater flexibility in developing responses to fault lines, including becoming more creative in the remaking of boundaries outside of Europe (which has seen a large number of recent boundary changes, mostly as a response to fault-line violence, as in the Balkans).

The map of the world changed in 2011. The independence of South Sudan created Africa's fifty-fourth state and, one earnestly hopes, paved the way to a more peaceful future for this new country and what remains of the old, which has not known peace for nearly half a century. But this region is still riven with fault lines. The more intractable cleavages will not be resolved by separate statehood; some fault lines could even deepen. But the momentous events of 2011 in this benighted corner of Africa may cause the international community to confront the issue of societal fault lines more directly, and more honestly, than it has in the past.

PART ONE:
THE CONSEQUENCES OF FAILURE

1

BOUNDARIES AND BARGAINS: MANAGING NIGERIA'S FRACTIOUS SOCIETY

Peter Lewis

NIGERIA'S TURBULENT SOCIAL LANDSCAPE poses deep challenges of governance and stability. Throughout the post-independence era, communal competition, polarisation and recurring violence have defined political life in Africa's most populous state. Ethnic and linguistic rivalries, regional assertion and religious tensions have made for contentious national politics and social instability. A pivotal moment in the country's history was the 1967–70 civil war, sparked by a failed bid for secession, in which more than a million Nigerians perished. Since that cataclysmic event, Nigerian elites have tempered their rancour and worked to provide mechanisms for national accommodation. However, communal insecurities, economic inequalities and distributive politics continue to foster dissension. In the wake of the transition from military rule to civilian government in 1999, at least 700 incidents of communal violence have erupted across the country, with a cumulative toll of more than 15,000 casualties and tens of thousands displaced. There is a sharp tension between Nigeria as a 'geographic expression' and a durable national idea.[1]

And yet Nigeria endures with a resilience that often surprises outside observers and even many citizens. Amid the violence, acrimony and grievance, the country has not fractured along ethnic, regional or religious lines. Nigeria may be regarded as a polarised and fractious society, but not a 'deeply divided' situation that mobilises large groups along central cultural or geographic fault lines.[2] The sources of resilience are manifold. The country's diverse social map fosters cross-cutting divisions that often blur agendas of separation, exclusion or dominance. The fragmentation of groups is closely related to a process of institutional engineering deliberately pursued by Nigerian elites. The structures of federalism have been employed to divide major ethnic blocks, devolve power and resources, and compel diverse political alliances.[3] Alongside these formal institutional arrangements is a domain of bargaining over power, representation and the allocation of resources. Much of this hinges on the distribution of petroleum revenues, political patronage and other state-mediated rents.[4] In consequence, Nigeria's tenuous stability has been secured through a combination of legal delineation – the negotiation of boundaries – and distributional politics, an arena of informal elite bargains. Bargaining and boundaries are intimately related, and serious transgressions in either domain can potentially upset the fragile equilibrium of the system.

The following section outlines the complex social landscape of Nigeria and the formation of boundaries from the colonial era through the early years of independence. The succeeding discussion will cover institutional changes in Nigeria since independence, focusing on state formation, revenue allocation, electoral arrangements and the balancing of regional representation. I will then elaborate the nature of informal political bargaining in Nigeria, emphasising the central role of elite cartels and the distributional accommodation among these strata. The conclusion offers a summary and raises key political implications.

History and Divisions

Nigeria's current population is approximately 150 million, estimated to include at least 250 distinct ethnic or linguistic communities. This exceptional diversity has been a defining factor in national life. Although quite heterogeneous, Nigeria's ethnic divisions foster a relatively concentrated pattern of identity and competition, since three groups together comprise about two-thirds of the population. The northern Hausa-Fulani (a 'hyphenated' identity among these two groups) account for about a quarter of the country, the south-western Yoruba represent approximately a fifth and the south-eastern Igbo about 18 per cent.[5] Other minorities (including Ijaw, Efik-Ibibio, Edo, Tiv, Nupe and Kanuri) do not individually exceed 5 per cent of the population and few approach that level. Hence national politics have been shaped by the three-way contention among these larger groups, as smaller communities are frequently subordinated or marginalised in the political calculus.

The ethno-linguistic landscape is overlaid by a broad religious distinction, as Nigeria is nearly evenly divided among Muslims and Christians.[6] Migration, trade and urbanisation have made for a relatively diffuse religious demography. The northern region of the country is predominantly Muslim, though threaded with Christian minorities and enclaves. The south-west encompasses both traditions. At least 40 per cent of the Yoruba are Muslim and the balance largely Christian. Intermarriage and conversion are common, and many Yoruba families include members of both faiths.[7] The Igbo and most other south-eastern communities are overwhelmingly Christian. Enclaves of Muslim traders and migrants can be found in Lagos and other cities throughout the southern portions of the country. Among the central states of the 'Middle Belt', Christian and Muslim communities are roughly balanced. There is no central geographic or cultural divide that distinguishes Nigerians along religious lines, since ethnic and faith identities are broadly dispersed.

Regionalism is a third dimension, substantially rooted in the colonial formation of Nigeria. British interests established piecemeal control over present-day Nigeria, first annexing the colony of Lagos in 1861, expanding control over the Niger Coast Protectorate at the end of of the nineteenth century and encroaching on the rulers of northern Nigeria a few years later. In 1914 the colony of Nigeria was amalgamated from these elements, with separate administrative divisions for Lagos, Northern Nigeria and Southern Nigeria.[8] Under Lord Lugard's doctrine of indirect rule, the presiding emirs in the north retained much of their authority, along with core Islamic legal, religious and educational institutions. External influence was more pronounced in the southern areas under the sway of missionary activities, more intensive colonial administration and burgeoning commerce.

In the later years of colonial rule, British authorities created a federal arrangement for self-government which designated Northern, Western and Eastern Regions in addition to a partial devolution of legislative and revenue authority. The 1959 constitution, which framed the transfer to independence, codified this structure, along with a Westminsterian parliamentary system. These institutions unfortunately served to entrench regional identities, foster inter-ethnic competition and ultimately erode the foundations of both parliamentary democracy and national cohesion. Each of the three regions was electorally captured in the 1950s by a political party linked to the locally dominant ethnic group. The Hausa-Fulani-controlled Northern People's Congress (NPC) won the Northern

Region, the Yoruba-led Action Group (AG) held sway in the Western Region and the Igbo-dominated National Council of Nigeria and the Cameroons (NCNC) governed the Eastern Region. The northern NPC, by virtue of its parliamentary majority, attained control of the federal government at independence in 1960. The largest linguistic groups emerged as salient political coalitions embroiled in a mutual rivalry for power and central resources. Sectional elites jealously guarded control of their ethnic heartland while manoeuvring for influence at the federal level.[9]

This ethno-regional competition fuelled growing political misconduct, violence and corruption throughout the short-lived First Republic. The parliamentary regime was beset by a series of crises centring on regional boundaries, the national census (which determined regional representation in parliament) and the 1964–5 elections.[10] The growing rancour and disorder eventually prompted the military to step in and civilian rule was violently terminated at the beginning of 1966. The new regime was controlled by Igbo officers, which provoked a July counter-coup by rival elements and incited anti-Igbo pogroms in the north. Igbo civilians and soldiers soon fled to their Eastern Region heartland and attempted to break away as the Republic of Biafra. Nearly three years of bitter fighting and a humanitarian blockade of the region yielded a federal victory at the beginning of 1970. At least a million people died in the conflict, the majority from starvation and disease. For succeeding generations, the conflict has influenced agendas of communal competition, political reform and institutional change.

Context and Triggers

The overlapping crises of the 1960s established lasting challenges for a workable national compact. Sweeping economic change and a turnover of regimes shaped these efforts. The emergence of large-scale oil production in the wake of the civil war transformed Nigeria's political economy. The cessation of hostilities allowed a rapid increase in petroleum production and the OPEC-inspired price increases of 1973 created a windfall for the federal treasury. In the course of the initial decade-long oil boom, the competition over resources became firmly centred on access to the central state. Beginning in the 1980s, boom-bust cycles and economic austerity aggravated this competition and undermined the economic security of most Nigerians.[11] Economic policy errors, mismanagement and endemic corruption have worsened problems of inequality and poverty.

Parallel cycles of military and civilian rule shifted the political and institutional landscape. After the coups of 1966, Nigerians embarked on three efforts to re-establish civilian rule, giving rise to a failed democratic Second Republic (1979–83), an abortive Third Republic in 1993 and the most recent (and lasting) transition to electoral rule in 1999, inaugurating the Fourth Republic. Electoral politics have continually animated ethnic and regional competition. These democratic experiments were framed by lengthy, often unstable periods of military control. Communal tensions were evident in military factionalism, several failed coup attempts and repressive actions directed at particular communities.

The deteriorating quality of governance has acted as a catalyst to further instability. Problems of scarcity are aggravated by sparse public services and general economic malaise. Criminality and violence have flourished amidst the failure to develop a rule of law. These circumstances sharpen communal competition while heightening possibilities for conflict. In the past decade a profusion of militias and vigilante groups, commonly organised along ethnic lines, have created natural outlets for strife.[12] More confrontational streams have also emerged among some religious communities, whether we consider Saudi links among Muslims or evangelical and Pentecostal inroads among Christians. Volatile demographic pressures arising from the youth bulge, migration and internal displacement often aggravate these tensions and serve as channels of tension. As groups and factions are mobilised, small incidents can readily escalate and conflicts may persist.

In recent decades, a varied landscape of conflict has encompassed different forms of division and strife. First, ethnic assertion is clearly manifest in communal organisations, vigilante groups and militias. Ethnic agendas find expression through public discourse, legal mobilisation and sporadic violence. Second, religious identities are reflected among numerous denominations and sectarian groups, national associations for Christians and Muslims, as well as coercive groups such as the Islamic *hisbah* in several northern sharia states or Christian vigilantes in Middle Belt and southern localities. An emerging Islamist militant group, Boko Haram, has been active in several northern states. Third, regional assertion frequently parallels ethnic or religious allegiances, evident particularly in the movement for the expansion of sharia law among twelve northern states and the regionally skewed voting patterns in the 2011 elections. Fourth, pervasive tensions among so-called 'indigenes' and 'settlers' in numerous states and localities focus on land, rights to services and political representation. Fifth, partisan rivalries often incite violence, as political leaders and parties regularly recruit militias during electoral seasons and periodically for other roles. Sixth, a widening insurgency in the Niger Delta takes a distinctive form, in which ethnically constituted militias have targeted foreign companies and the central government. The militants in the Delta have pursued nominal goals of regional equity and representation, often interwoven with economic agendas and illicit activities.

Formal Institutions and the Management of Fault Lines

In the pursuit of stability, Nigerian elites have sought to reduce the political salience of large ethnic units, to balance communal interests and to regulate the distribution of centralised revenues. The experimentation with institutions has played out in four areas: the creation of new sub-national political units, the fiscal relations of the federal system, the design of electoral and party mechanisms, and the selection of public sector personnel.[13]

Federal Institutions

Beginning with political geography, changes in the federal map were already under way prior to the civil war. The military regime of Yakubu Gowon initiated far-reaching reform in 1967, with the division of the country into twelve states under a revised federal structure.[14] The proliferation of states was intended to remedy the political dominance and corrosive rivalries of the major ethnic elites by subdividing them among new political units. This also furnished some administrative and fiscal representation for smaller minorities, with a view to further offsetting the hegemony of larger groups. Once set in motion, the logic of state creation exerted a potent influence on successive regimes, as numerous communities lobbied for separate boundaries and revenue allotments.

The demarcation of boundaries became the prerogative of military regimes, which could act by fiat and manage residual grievances. In 1976 Murtala Muhammad's regime increased the number of states to nineteen and introduced a uniform lower tier of local government. During the civilian Second Republic, economic decline and political bottlenecks stymied the implementation of proposed new states. Major-General Ibrahim Babangida increased the number of states twice, to twenty-one and then thirty, in the late 1980s and early 1990s. His military successor, Sani Abacha, added six more in 1996. The current division of thirty-six states, a separate Federal Capital Territory and 774 Local Government Areas (LGAs) is specified in the 1999 constitution and had not been seriously debated in the previous decade. This changing administrative landscape has shaped Nigerian politics in several ways: by segmenting elites and localities; shifting electoral districts and revenue distribution; furnishing new networks for channelling resources; and providing symbolic recognition of numerous communities and groups.

Revenue Allocation

Changes in boundaries have been paralleled by a separate process of shifting fiscal relations among units. When British colonial authorities introduced a federal structure after the Second World War, they included a formula for the allotment of resources among the constituent regions. Since that time, a string of commissions, agencies and decrees have amended the revenue allocation formula. Major revisions have been put forward shortly before independence, late in the civil war, in the midst of the oil boom, under successive military regimes after 1985 and through the current civilian regime. Some adjustments to these broad formulas have been introduced almost annually, making for a highly contentious fiscal regime.

The emergence of a petroleum-led economy constitutes the central factor in this fitful course of change. Prior to the imposition of military rule, revenue distribution strongly favoured the regions. The federal government retained just 40 per cent of total public revenues, with the balance going to the separate units. Further, a principle of derivation permitted the regions to capture half of all revenues generated within their boundaries. Nigeria's economic structure of the 1950s and 1960s, based primarily on export agriculture and solid minerals, offered a relatively diversified resource base. The separate regions, and their ethnic political elites, could draw upon substantial revenues from local cash-crop activities, including cocoa and palm produce in the west, palm oil in the east and cotton and groundnuts in the north. These revenues enabled the major parties to build formidable patronage networks and electoral machinery.

With the end of the civil war and an emerging petroleum industry in prospect, the Gowon regime radically altered the revenue allocation formula, doubling the federal take to 80 per cent of total revenues and slashing the derivation share for states to 10 per cent. By 1975 receipts from oil exports constituted more than four-fifths of government revenues and over 95 per cent of foreign exchange. Federal government control over centrally collected resource rents marked a fundamental and lasting transition in economic structure and fiscal relations. The natural corollary was the loss of any degree of fiscal autonomy on the part of states and local governments, especially as these units proliferated while federal largesse increased.

Pressures for rebalancing soon emerged, especially among states which possessed abundant natural resources, or those with other significant revenue-generating potential, such as Lagos. Northern states argued for the redistribution of revenues on the basis of population and equity. Beginning in the late 1970s, a series of commissions reduced the federal take to 75 per cent, then 55 per cent and then about half, where it has hovered (with some variance) for some two decades. States are currently allotted nearly a third of revenues and local governments about 15 per cent, while the derivation formula has been increased to 13 per cent. This latter measure greatly affects the oil-rich but underdeveloped states of the Niger Delta, which have agitated consistently for a larger share of resource revenues. Although the increase in derivation falls short of regional demands, it has dramatically raised the flow of funds available to state governments in the area.

Controversies over the fiscal formula have also raised perennial questions about transparency and accountability in the management of revenues. Nigerians harbour well-founded concerns that the central government has often failed to remit its obligations to the states, and that state governments have hoarded or misallocated funds intended for distribution to lower tiers. During the past decade, initiatives to increase the transparency of budgetary affairs have improved the flow of funds through the tiers of the federal system and permitted some degree of accounting for central revenues. Nonetheless myriad critics, especially among the communities of the Niger Delta, regularly assert that they see little benefit from the prodigious revenues supposedly accruing to their governments.

Electoral Rules and the Party System

The arena of competitive politics constitutes a third area for managing diversity. Following the collapse of the First Republic, a decade passed before the military actively contemplated a return to democratic rule. The civilian Constituent Assembly that drafted the 1979 constitution discarded the parliamentary system in favour of an American-style presidential design, including a two-tier legislature (House of Representatives and Senate) elected from single-member districts. All officials were to be elected directly on a first-past-the-post basis among multiple political parties. The most significant innovation was the geographic distribution requirement for the president, requiring not only the highest proportion of the vote but also a minimum level of support (25 per cent) in at least two-thirds of the existing states. This rule largely precluded the success of a candidate with narrow regional or ethnic appeal, since it was unlikely that a parochial figure could accrue sufficient votes across the country. The first president elected under this system, Shehu Shagari of the National Party of Nigeria (NPN), narrowly cleared the bar of distribution and was confirmed by a judgement of the Supreme Court. The victors in subsequent elections (1983, 1993, 1999, 2003 and 2007) have all clearly met the threshold of distribution. A similar provision has applied since 1979 to state governors, who have to gain sufficient votes across two-thirds of the local governments in their state.

While this design was intended to dissuade ethnic mobilisation, the parties that formed during the Second Republic carried strong echoes of the sectional groupings of the previous regime. Among the parties of the Second Republic, the ruling NPN, though substantially led by northerners, proved uniquely adept at expanding its base to gain multi-ethnic and cross-regional support. This was not sufficient to dispel the sectional character of politics. The Unity Party of Nigeria (UPN) was headed by the former Action Group leader Obafemi Awolowo and polled upwards of 90 per cent of the vote in the Yoruba-majority south-western states. The Igbo politician and former NCNC leader Nnamdi Azikiwe led the Nigerian People's Party (NPP), which garnered strong support among the eastern states. Much of the truculent contention of the Second Republic elections was marked by the communal loyalties evident in the preceding civilian regime, as the corruption and fractiousness of the political class ultimately induced another military intervention in 1983.

When General Babangida staged elections for a new civilian regime a decade later, he sought to eliminate communally based competition by mandating a two-party system with ideological features. One party was designated 'slightly to the right' and the other 'slightly to the left', with party programmes handed down by the military authorities. Although these artificial constructs were lacking in democratic foundations, they did serve as vehicles for diverse clusters of politicians seeking access to the transition process. Despite the achievement of a peaceful and credible presidential election in June 1993, Babangida annulled the results and then handed power to a civilian caretaker government, which was quickly overthrown by General Sani Abacha. Abacha's repressive and corrupt five-year rule ended with his death (reportedly by natural causes), opening the way to a new political transition process under his successor, General Abdulsalami Abubakar.

When political activity was reopened in 1998, the new parties were drawn largely from the multi-ethnic leadership of the former organisations under Babangida. The People's Democratic Party (PDP) was founded by the so-called Group of 34, a cluster of veteran politicians and political entrepreneurs from various parts of the country. The PDP established electoral machinery throughout the country, quickly emerging as the leading national party. Their main competitor, the All People's Party (APP), also had a broadly national profile, although it held greater strength in the northern states. The Alliance for Democracy (AD) had a stronger sectional appeal around Lagos and the south-west, but aspired to a wider presence among different ethnic and regional segments. By 1999 the party system reflected a significant transition towards diversified national leadership and more heterogeneous electoral appeals. The PDP was a dominant competitor in the transitional elections and consolidated its control over all tiers of government in succeeding polls.

The ruling party has steadily expanded its ability to incorporate disparate elites, manage patronage and capture elections. In the process, a dominant party system has emerged, often tainted by limited competition and diminishing legitimacy. The 2011 elections were held in more transparent circumstances that permitted greater pluralism. The PDP's majority was eroded in the polls, though it remains the largest party. Sectional parties gained ground in the legislature and state governments.

Federal Character

Another element of formal communal balancing is the constitutional rule regarding 'federal character' in public sector personnel and allocation decisions. This calls for a broadly representative profile of hiring and appointments in government institutions. Public departments, state enterprises, the military and related entities are required to have staff from across the federation, roughly proportional to the general population. This official principle of ethnic arithmetic has also modelled standards for much of the private sector, and many companies seek a diverse ethnic and regional profile among their employees. Federal character is above all a symbolic measure, but it does affirm a public ethos and frequently influences the staffing and budgeting decisions of government.

Informal Bargaining and the Management of Fault Lines

Nigeria's political and economic life has been dominated by an elite cartel that comprises politicians, military officers, senior bureaucrats, traditional rulers, local notables and leading businesspeople.[15] A cartel is a form of industrial organisation, formed to manipulate markets and to share out the rents from such collusion. Cartels are adaptable to shifting membership and strategies, guided by the purposes of market control and rent-seeking. This provides a model for understanding the composition and strategic behaviour of Nigerian ruling groups.

The contemporary Nigerian 'political class' and associated groups form a thin stratum with special access to governing institutions and state resources.[16] The national elite are built around a cohort of notables, entrenched networks and a few dynastic elements among political families and traditional rulers. While there is limited entry to elite status, ruling groups are nonetheless permeable and fluid. Aspirants regularly move into influential economic or political roles even as other individuals and factions may be sidelined or defeated. Alongside the most prominent individuals and networks there is also a regular circulation of entrants drawn from new professional and business activities, various ethnic and religious backgrounds, and an emerging younger generation. The inchoate party system encompasses these elements. This narrow yet flexible establishment forms the central arena for bargaining over authority and resources. Nigeria's chronic violence and political volatility testify to the limited capacities of national elites to reach accommodation over core tensions in the polity. While these elements can exert political leverage and influence distributional outcomes, they rarely have firm institutional control or durable influence over their constituencies.

Core Issues of Contention

Contention among Nigerian elites centres on three concerns: the balance of authority among civilian and military groups; the distribution of power among ethnic, regional and religious segments; and the allocation of state-mediated rents. For more than three decades, the political intervention of the armed forces and the viability of democratic rule formed the focus of national controversy. Since the 1999 transition to civilian rule, there has been cautious optimism that the military era has now been transcended and that civilian government is becoming regularised. While concerns about military intervention linger (especially during episodes of violence, faulty elections and succession problems in 2010 occasioned by President Umaru Yar'Adua's ill-health), there is little active debate about the nature of Nigeria's political regime. Nonetheless the turbulent politics of communal balancing and rent distribution are shadowed by concerns about military intercession in circumstances of pervasive instability or the exclusion of a major regional segment from the political process. The spectre of an authoritarian veto is vivid for many Nigerians.

A second focus is the distribution of power among Nigeria's major sectional groups. This is sometimes cast in terms of north–south regional balance, or alternatively as a rotation among Hausa-Fulani, Yoruba and Igbo, and occasionally as a concern for representation of smaller minorities such as those from the Niger Delta. Communal issues dominated the transition to civilian rule in 1999. Northern Muslims ruled Nigeria during the First Republic, and continuously for two decades after 1979, leaving southern groups aggrieved about the perceived dominance of these elites. In particular, the Yoruba were outraged by Babangida's annulment of the 1993 election, which had apparently been won by the Yoruba candidate, M. K. O. Abiola. The Abacha regime, centred on a narrow inner circle from the Muslim north, compounded ethnic resentments. With his demise, Nigeria quickly moved from its most closed regime to one of its most regionally inclusive.

This change was fraught with claims from various quarters. Southerners argued for the necessity of a 'power shift' from the north to a southern executive leadership, with the Yoruba vociferously arguing for priority to compensate for Abiola's thwarted victory. Northern elites were cautiously willing to relent on this point, though they insisted on a principle of rotation among northern, south-western and south-eastern politicians in succeeding elections. Ethno-regional rotation, or 'zoning', was a long-standing principle within political parties, and military rulers broached the practice during various transitional programmes. In the wake of the Abacha regime, politicians sought to elevate the idea as an explicit compact. In the 1999 transition elections, the leading parties fielded tickets with a Yoruba leader and a northern running mate. Olusegun Obasanjo, the former military leader and a south-western Christian, was the candidate of the PDP, winning the first two elections of the new regime. In 2007, with the completion of Obasanjo's tenure, the top parties all endorsed candidates from the north.

In a decade of rule, the People's Democratic Party has consolidated power as a dominant party with a broad reach across the federation. The PDP establishment is not controlled by a particular sectional group, as the party has developed a loose association of notables organised around the capture of elections and the sharing of spoils. With a shifting array of leaders at the apex and weak party discipline throughout the organisation, the ruling party lacks a coherent or well-regulated structure. It has prevailed by developing formidable machinery for securing elections (including substantial misconduct and fraud), while incorporating diverse networks and groups within an expansive tent.

This heterogeneous dominant party system has served to encourage accommodation among Nigerian ruling groups over elite power sharing. There is a central paradox in the costs of elite accommodation for deeper social peace. The politicians' use of ethnic appeals, coercive tactics and fraudulent electoral practices has provoked popular tension and violence across many areas of the country. There is a pronounced danger that exclusion of a major group or faction might cause that segment to defect from the bargaining process, with destabilising effects. The threshold for such instability is not clear. The escalation of insurgency in the oil-producing Niger Delta, the recent rise of attacks by extremist Islamic groups in the northern states and the recurring clashes in the Middle Belt among Christian and Muslim communities are all manifestations of fragility. Post-election violence following the April 2011 presidential election also carried strong regional and religious overtones.

The consuming focus of Nigerian elites has been contention over the distribution of state-mediated rents. These may be channelled directly from oil revenues as state expenditure, or conveyed as special economic opportunities through preferential contracts, licensing, appointments, information and regulatory favours. A permissive political and institutional setting fosters endemic corruption and the lack of transparency throughout the system gives wide latitude for self-dealing. For decades, the key medium for securing state resources has been access to political power, and ethnic clientelism has been the central mechanism in distributional politics. It is estimated that 90 per cent of Nigerians manage on two dollars a day or less, indicating the vast gap between those at the pinnacle of the system and those further down the ladder. By contrast, Nigeria is home to several billionaires and even an average member of the House of Representatives can secure over a million dollars a year in allowances and allotments. Position within the political class and access to governing elites remain the keys to attainment in this highly centralised oil state.

In consequence, political management rests on the distribution of patronage to major segments and brokers within the system. Popular groups support politicians or organisations on an ethnic and clientelist basis, as a means of securing greater access to resources and enhancing the possibilities for brokerage. Aspiring officeholders often seek out local barons to bankroll their efforts and generate support. The dominant party system has been constructed on dispersal of political largesse and broad elite access to rents, a strategy facilitated by abundant oil revenues and, more recently, improved economic policies, allowing for some diversification of business activity.

Although the civilian government has been able to wield sufficient resources to sustain political support and develop clientelist networks, the persistence of widespread poverty and deep inequality constitutes a central liability of the system. Sectional frustrations over distribution are evident in the Niger Delta insurgency and related political demands; the desire for regional assertion and redistribution that animated popular support; the expansion of sharia law in the northern Muslim-majority states; and the spate of local-level conflicts among herders and farmers or communal groups in Plateau, Jos and other localities.

Conclusion: Boundaries, Bargains and a Fractious Democracy

This discussion has considered the broad challenges of managing Nigeria's plural and frequently divisive social terrain. In the wake of political and security crises in the first decade of independence, Nigeria elites sought to contain communal pressures through institutional engineering and informal bargaining over power sharing and rent distribution. Federalism and other changes to the political system have been directed at providing more inclusive processes of governance and fiscal relations. Agreements and implicit compacts among ruling groups are aimed at balancing interests and assuring a degree of access to state-mediated rents in a centralised petro-state. These approaches have helped to mitigate the most polarising and destabilising impulses in the fractious Nigerian polity. However, an elite cartel under a dominant party has failed to assuage popular distributional demands or to reduce the burdens of poverty, inequality and uneven development. While Nigeria has proved remarkably resilient over the decades, hazards of failure are ever-present.

2

THE DEMOCRATIC REPUBLIC OF CONGO: FAULT LINES AND LOCAL FISSURES

Pierre Englebert

THE DEMOCRATIC REPUBLIC OF CONGO (henceforth Congo) was born of violence and violence has been a crucial component of its existence ever since. The abuses of Leopold II of Belgium, who established and personally owned the Etat Indépendant du Congo, are well known. By some accounts, they cost the lives of some 10 million Congolese.[1] Even without the worst abuses of his regime, the rest of Belgian colonisation was characterised by an oppressive labour regime and the systematic exploitation of people and resources.

Equally well known is the rapid decline of Congo into a violent quagmire only days after its independence on 30 June 1960. With expectations of radical change frustrated, the army mutinied and the country collapsed into civil war. The Katanga and South Kasai provinces seceded, Prime Minister Patrice Lumumba was assassinated and his supporters embarked upon a civil war that would last until 1967.[2]

The rule of Mobutu (1965–97) is usually seen as a period of more stability, but his regime was no less predicated upon violence and predation. In the end, it collapsed under the assaults of a patchwork insurgency, which started in the Kivu region (if not in Rwanda) and spread through the country like a brush fire.[3]

The following decade was marked by the worst violence probably ever experienced by the Congolese. Hardly a year after Laurent-Désiré Kabila's takeover, war began in the east again and spread on a massive scale, with the intervention of no fewer than nine other African countries. By mid-1999 the country was de facto partitioned in two or three zones: one under government-Angolan-Zimbabwean control; one under Rassemblement Congolais pour la Démocratie (RCD) rebels and Rwandan control; and one under Mouvement pour la Libération du Congo (MLC) rebels and Ugandan control (although 'control' is an exaggeration in each case). The war itself was rapidly stalemated, but violence continued unabated, particularly in the east, and is estimated to have since caused the death of some 4 to 5 million people.

Kabila was killed in 2001 and replaced by his son Joseph, who allowed the peace process to unfold. A national unity government was formed in 2003 and oversaw a transition to an elected regime in 2006. Joseph Kabila was elected president. Nevertheless, widespread violence continued, particularly in the east, but also in the Bakongo region and even in Equateur.

What are Congo's Fault Lines?

Conventionally, especially since the secession of Katanga from 1960 to 1963,[4] Congo has been perceived as wrecked by large fault lines that are preventing national integration. This is largely misleading, however. As this paper argues, it is local divisions that matter most, and these local divisions are not particularly natural but have been triggered by specific policies, most notably those with respect to access to citizenship, land and the right to local office.

It is nonetheless true that there are large regional differences, almost unavoidably in a country the size of Congo, which contains by some estimates about 350 ethnic groups[5] and four large linguistic groups (Lingala, Kikongo, Swahili and Tshiluba). The Katangans, particularly the populations associated with the Lunda culture, have been particularistic and in search of greater autonomy from the centre. There have been recurrent tensions, occasionally violent, between Katangans and the neighbouring Kasaians. In the east, the Kivu provinces are often seen as belonging more to the 'Great Lakes' nebula than to Congo. They have been largely severed from the rest of the country since the early 1990s and much of their trade takes place with East Africa and beyond rather than with Kinshasa. Even closer to Kinshasa, the Bas-Congo region and its Bakongo populations are fiercely autonomous and have harboured irredentist dreams with their kinsmen in Angola and the Republic of Congo since the 1950s.

More recently, following the end of the war, the country has given the impression of being split by an east–west divide, which was made

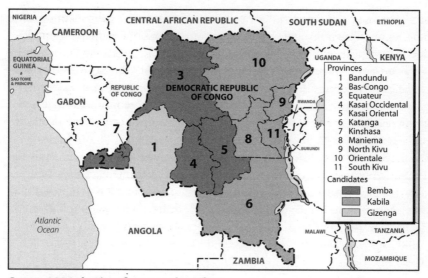

Congo: 2006 election, first-round results

particularly salient by the results of the 2006 presidential elections (see map above, showing results of the first round by province).

Congolese of the eastern provinces are the ones who experienced the war and its atrocities first-hand. They blame most of it on Rwanda, Uganda and their rebel proxies. As a result, they saw Joseph Kabila as the peacemaker and rewarded him with astronomical percentages of votes (above 90 per cent in the Kivus). The west never suffered to quite the same extent, but witnessed the corruption of the transition regime of which it grew tired. There is, however, also a regional element that cannot be denied, although it must be tempered and one cannot impute too much to it: Kabila is from the east (north Katanga by his father), while his main opponents were from the west (Jean-Pierre Bemba from Equateur, Antoine Gizenga from Bandundu and Etienne Tshisekedi – who ended up boycotting the elections – from Kasai).

While all these differences can occasionally be salient and feed narratives of grievances among many Congolese, they are not as important or as rigid as they may seem. In fact, they contrast with the remarkable sense of national unity that pervades Congo, irrespective of the region.[6] Thus they do not necessarily constitute fault lines in the sense of obstacles to national integration.

More important, in fact, are multiple and overlapping local fissures, widely distributed across the country, which contribute to a fragmentation of identities and networks at the local level and increased polarisation of social life. This polarisation has shared responsibility for the failure at state reconstruction in Congo as much as anything else. It has undermined the social fabric to the point of debilitating collective action. Yet, rather than being a pre-existing societal impediment to state building, it has been intimately associated with the exercise of state power, from which it partly derives.

Indeed, the greatest fault lines in Congo are local. The Congolese do not typically complain about their integration in the nation. What feeds their grievances is the largely shared impression that their fellow Congolese cheat them and favour their kinsmen at the local level, and that they need to rely on similar solidarities to reach their own goals of safety and well-being. This is what the Congolese refer to as tribalism. Thus we see divisions between Rwandophone and Hunde populations in North Kivu, between Banyamulenge and the Vira populations in South Kivu, between Lendu and Hema in Ituri, between Lunda and Balubakat in the Katanga region, between Bakongo and Lingala-speakers around Matadi, and so on. As in many other parts of Africa, these fissures are increasingly articulated around narratives of autochthony and outsiders, in which the son-of-the-soil category has gained much currency.

Although all these groups tend to embrace the idea of Congo, they either suspect each other of manipulating the state for discriminatory purposes or tend to deny each other the right to belong to Congo (at least to a similar degree). These local divisions feed upon national politics and, conversely, feed back into national politics – in a process the Congolese refer to as the tribalisation of politics. They create circumstances of distrust where alternative agendas are always suspected and jeopardise consensus and state building.

The Underlying Contribution of Poverty

Before looking at actual short-run triggers of these local fissures and the role of the state among them, it is important to bear in mind the sheer degree of poverty of the majority of the Congolese, which conditions their behaviour and their relationship towards the state and towards each other. Since the early 1990s life in Congo has become incredibly precarious.[7] The average Congolese lives on less than a dollar a day with limited access to clean water, nutrition, health care and education. Even in the relatively more prosperous cities, like Kinshasa, deprivation is so widespread as to be visible to the naked eye. The majority of residents live day to day, spending their waking hours in search of sustenance for their families. People barter, scavenge or practise urban agriculture on little patches of dirt by the side of the street. They frequently wait hours on end for some economic opportunity, or walk long distances in and out of towns in similar searches. Students squat many to a room, without plumbing, to attend classes in dilapidated and overcrowded auditoriums. This situation is further compounded in the east, where hundreds of thousands of people have been displaced by war and violence over the last ten years, enduring lives of misery, uncertainty, fear and frequent flight.

This degree of material deprivation has had and continues to have very significant social and political consequences. Particularly, it raises the relative premium associated with access to positions of state authority and the likelihood that such positions are translated into opportunities for economic advancement. These consequences have been largely ignored in the design of the transition and post-transition and make it exceedingly hard to build functional democratic institutions in Congo.

The State and the Law as Shapers of Fissures and Triggers of Violence

Corrupt Governance

The first and overarching determinant of social conflict is the nature of Congolese governance as a regime of private appropriation. As a consequence of both its origins as an enterprise of exploitation and predation, and the material scarcity of life, the state is first and foremost an avenue of personal survival or private accumulation for those who can benefit from its authority.

While this is also true elsewhere in Africa,[8] it is a particularly extreme phenomenon in Congo, where a broad regime of impunity exists. Most politicians, military leaders and local bureaucrats maximise their time in office by plundering state resources at a rapid rate. Presidents empty state coffers; prime ministers inflate their operating budgets beyond any reasonable proportions; ministers charge for positions in their cabinets; parliamentarians sell their votes; civil servants charge for the public services they are supposed to deliver; and local policemen run rackets against civilians. The entire state is structured along a massive web of mutual predation.

There are two consequences of this regime of corruption. First, national elites set the tone for a predatory system of governance that is largely reproduced across the country at all levels of state authority. Thus the state is widely perceived by all to be a means for the private appropriation of the resources of others. In many ways, those in state power then produce rules and institutions that magnify these opportunities for appropriation. Second, given the relative material rewards associated with such local positions of governance, individuals and communities compete fiercely for access to them, which transforms mere cultural differences into violent fault lines.

Access to Land

The rules for access to land illustrate the degree to which the state dominates the regime of wealth and income appropriation. There is no free market in land in Congo (as in many other African countries). Instead, land is allocated to individuals by administrative fiat. There are by and large two ways of claiming land rights. The first is the pursuit of 'native authority', to borrow Mamdani's expression.[9] In this instance, access to land is predicated upon control of local chieftaincies, which are legally entitled to allocate it to people in their jurisdictions. Although the land is not the private property of the chief, he assigns plots to families in exchange for tribute. This customary form of allocation was largely maintained through colonisation, when it was codified as chiefs became agents of indirect rule. It was maintained and reinforced in the post-colonial era, when chieftaincies increasingly became extensions of state administration, which frequently appoints them. The three smallest units of Congolese territorial administration – the *localité*, the *groupement* and the *collectivité* – are in fact managed by customary chiefs. Chiefs of *collectivités* – the level usually referred to as chieftaincies – have particularly important prerogatives with respect to land.

In the Kivu regions, for example, where conflict has been endemic, local competition for land, necessary for economic survival, has often translated into competition for control of these chieftaincies and thus polarisation along 'ethnic' lines. Since these were historically in the hands of 'autochthonous' populations, Rwandophones who have migrated to the area in waves over the last century have 'persistently [called] for a Native Authority of their own'.[10] They have typically chosen one of two ways to go about this quest, both of which have promoted local fault lines and conflict. One way has been to authoritatively remove 'autochthonous' chiefs in existing chieftaincies and replace them with Rwandophones.

Grass-root attempts to implement this option in the early 1990s contributed to the explosion of local conflict in North Kivu. Indeed, Hutu leaders had tried in 1993 to forcibly remove Hunde chiefs in Masisi and replace them with Hutu authorities, leading to retaliatory violence by Hunde gangs against Rwandophone populations. Once the RCD-Goma rebel movement was in control of the region after 1998, it returned to this approach, forcibly removing several Hunde chiefs in the territories of Rutshuru and Masisi and appointing Rwandophones in their stead.

The other way to seize control of chieftaincies has been to promote the creation of new chieftaincies by higher levels of state authority. This approach has a long history in the region, dating back to the creation of Rwandophone chieftaincies by the colonisers in South Kivu between 1906 and 1933 and in North Kivu from the late 1930s. Soon after independence, the Rwandophones of South Kivu lobbied to recreate their colonial administrative autonomy. All they managed to get, however, was the small *localité* of Bijombo, which remained under the authority of an Uvira *collectivité*. In North Kivu, the Hutus of Rutshuru retained their chieftaincy, but those in the Masisi lost it on the eve of independence. Their lack of control over local state authorities until the 1990s prevented the Rwandophones from re-establishing the chieftaincies they had lost or creating new ones. After 1997 the Banyamulenge of South Kivu called again for a territory of their own, to be protected by their own troops and located along the border with Burundi in the Ruzizi plains. In 1999 the RCD-Goma, acting as the Congolese sovereign over that region, carved the new *territoire* of Minembwe from the existing *territoires* of Fizi, Mwenga and Uvira.

The second approach to land acquisition is what Mamdani refers to as 'civic politics'. Here, traditional chieftaincies are bypassed and access to land is obtained through control of political and administrative power in national or local branches of the state. This was the approach followed for a while by Kivu's Rwandophone elites, for example. Several Rwandophones rose in the Mobutu administration from the mid-1960s onwards. The careers of others unfolded in provincial administrations. There, however, they still faced considerable obstacles from 'autochthonous' groups. In fact, the splitting of the Kivu province in 1962 into three provinces (North Kivu, Central Kivu and Maniema) resulted from the lobbying of 'autochthonous' representatives from Beni, Lubero and Masisi and took place without agreement of the Rwandophones from Rutshuru and Goma. The advantage of North Kivu for the former was that it produced a majority Nande population, whereas all groups had previously been minorities in the larger Kivu province. The Rwandophones thus became a minority to the Nande and were crowded out of administrative power in the province – undermining their quest for civic citizenship. Notice how administrative and institutional manipulations thus raise the salience of local fault lines. 'Autochthonous' populations of Nande, Hunde and others subsequently used their control of the North Kivu province to push back the rights of Rwandophones, reappointing, for example, Hunde chiefs in districts where they had been displaced during the colonial era. After its takeover in 1998, however, the RCD-Goma proceeded to undo the consequences of this earlier development, with the widespread appointment of Rwandophones to positions of provincial authority in North and South Kivu.[11]

Access to Citizenship

Whichever strategy of access to land is pursued, it first necessitates access to citizenship. And here too the laws of the state induce local societal polarisation and promote local ethnic divisions. Indeed, Congolese law is oddly indirect when it comes to citizenship. Instead of conferring citizenship to people who resided in its territory at the time of colonisation or independence and their descendants, it confers it to people who belong to 'groups' which did. This is an odd formulation. It makes Congolese nationality both colonial and ethnic. One of its implications is the possibility to reject individuals en bloc. If one can demonstrate that a group was not present in today's Congolese territory at a specific date, its descendants have no claim to citizenship. Thus it encourages autochthony/allochthony distinctions. Another consequence is that it reinforces the ethnic identification of people, making it a matter of legal benefits. Thus, to be a Congolese national, one must first be a Congolese tribal. The law does not, however, specify a list of these ethnicities and nationalities, maintaining a level of uncertainty that opens the door to endless manipulations.

So, whether one pursues the 'native' or 'civic' approaches to land control, one must first establish one's ethnic identity. In summary:

- **Track One:** Recognition of ethnic group as historically Congolese → access to nationality → access to chieftaincy → access to land
- **Track Two:** Recognition of ethnic group as historically Congolese

→ access to nationality → access to political power/administrative functions → access to land

The definition of Congolese citizenship in ethnic terms is closely related to the history of violence in the Kivus and other regions of Congo. The ethnic definition by the state of conditions for access to land and chieftaincy has promoted the local salience of ethnicity and the polarisation of communities. The very fact that 'communities' appear as the main agents of conflicts is related to the legal definition of Congolese nationality as 'tribal' and to the sovereign prerogatives awarded to ethnically defined local chieftaincies in terms of land allocation. Ironically, the state has thereby promoted local communal conflicts. Yet, in waging these conflicts, local communities have embraced sovereign instruments which have in turn reproduced the state.

Electoral Legitimacy

Against this background of instrumentalisation of the state and local polarisation, the Kabila government's electoral legitimacy has ironically represented an additional driver of instability and might have increased the fault line between state and society rather than diminishing it, as one would expect of elections. The 2006 election has not led to an increase in domestic accountability. Instead, it has promoted an attitude of government intolerance and an unwillingness to bargain with social forces. Electoral legitimacy has fostered the regime's authoritarian tendencies. Local groups, whose grievances are long-standing and which hoped to use the democratic opening to find a voice, have faced increased repression.[12] Societal grievances have been repressed as illegitimate, as illustrated by the brutal putdown of the Bundu Dia Kongo movement in Bas-Congo in 2007 and 2008, which left more than 200 dead,[13] or by that of the Dongo insurgents of Equateur in late 2009.

Outside Intervention

The preceding focus on the creation of local fault lines by state laws and policies should not obscure the role of outsiders in creating and reinforcing fault lines. At the time of colonisation already, differential exposure to the state and to modernisation produced local polarisations, as between the Lulua and Luba in the Kasai region, or the Bakongo and Ngala in and around Kinshasa.[14] Yet the most important foreign interventions in recent times in terms of promoting fault lines have been the Rwandan invasions of 1996 and 1998. Not only have these two invasions exacerbated fissures between Congolese of Rwandophone and non-Rwandophone ancestry – to the point of widespread anti-Rwandan racism in Congo – but they also share responsibility for the broad east–west schism that has developed as a function of differential suffering during the war. Moreover, the presence of former Hutu *génocidaires* in the Kivu provinces to this day – the infamous Forces Démocratiques pour la Libération du Rwanda (FDLR) – is the direct if protracted consequence of the exportation of Rwandan politics into Congo, a feature that dates back to 1994. It is a mistake to equate eastern Congolese problems with the FDLR, as there are many other local fault lines inimical to stability. Yet they do represent an obstacle to peace and state reconstruction in the short run.

Managing Congo's Fault Lines

Unfortunately, post-conflict reconstruction efforts by donors in Congo have done little to mitigate existing fault lines and reduce social polarisation. In general, reconstruction in Congo has been an excessively top-down exercise that has taken little account of complex local dynamics.[15] Promoting the restoration of the authority of the Congolese state has been problematic to the extent that it remains an unreformed enterprise of predation and exploitation. From Leopold II to Kabila II, Congo has never been a benevolent or developmental state. Although the current Congolese state cannot dream of the 'integral' powers of its Mobutist predecessor,[16] it remains deeply authoritarian and is worse in some sense, to the extent that numerous additional shady characters have been integrated into it through the peacemaking and reconstruction processes. The armed forces (FARDC or Forces Armées de la République Démocratique du Congo), for example, have become a dreadful hotbed of criminals and marginalised youths. Quickly and poorly integrated, full of recent and former rebels, unpaid, poorly trained, prone to corruption and collaboration with rebels, predatory to civilians, largely incompetent – the army itself is an important factor of violence and a wedge between the state and society. Denis Tull[17] appropriately calls it a 'force of disorder'. Yet post-conflict efforts undertaken by MONUC (the UN Mission in Congo) have understandably attempted to promote the authority of the state, which has translated into the spread of FARDC and increased social dislocations which carry the seeds of future grievances and conflict.

Aside from donor-supported pacification and reconstruction efforts, the greatest hope for Congo during its transition back to democratic rule in 2003–6 was the promise of decentralisation. Although the 2005 constitution had steered clear of the full-fledged federalism that some wanted, it nevertheless formally ushered in a 'strongly decentralised' unitary regime. Even though the idea that decentralised authority is necessarily closer to the people can be naive, there is little doubt that locally elected and locally financed government structures might have been better able than the Kinshasa government to address local fault lines and to negotiate local social contracts among communities. To this effect, the 2005 constitution provides for the increase of the number of provinces from eleven to twenty-five, and for the retention by these provinces of 40 per cent of the tax revenue they generate. These provisions have yet to be implemented, however, and an increasing number of observers doubt that they will under a Kabila regime. Fearful of lack of fiscal control, donors seem supportive of this violation of the constitution. Currently, Kinshasa appropriates all revenue and returns a meagre 2 per cent to the provinces. Moreover, the government also widely manipulated the elections of provincial executives in 2007 to stack up provincial authorities with central government supporters and further alienate peripheral groups. Yet the constitution was the outcome of one of the rare true processes of social bargaining in Congo during the transition. Its neglect undermines the democratic nature of the state and reduces opportunities for the local management of fault lines.

A bona fide land reform would be another important step towards resolution of local fault lines. The necessity of land for survival among many Congolese communities makes it an overwhelmingly crucial resource. The fact that its allocation relies on political mechanisms in a state as corrupt and dysfunctional as Congo makes it an explosive and divisive issue. Any land reform would have, first and foremost, to curtail the authority of chiefs and the state in allocating land. Second, it would have to operate some initial redistribution of land among individuals – not communities – to level the playing field and redress past injustices. This would require a massive series of local consultations and a huge documentation effort, which donors and MONUC could help with. Finally, with the land titled and distributed, liberal market principles of freeholding, supported by a strengthened judicial system, ought to be introduced. If the regular court system cannot be reformed to perform, a parallel land-specific system of arbitration could be developed. At any rate, whatever mechanisms of land distribution and subsequent adjudication are elaborated, they must be careful to focus on the rights of individuals and not on the demands of communities, the political significance of which must be deflated by institutional design.

Conclusions and Boundary Speculations

Congo is a crime of a country. It has been from the beginning. Outside observers and analysts then occasionally think that the crime cannot be stopped without first putting an end to the country. Hence the occasional suggestions for the partition of Congo.[18]

While I am sympathetic to these suggestions, boundary changes are not ex ante the obvious solution to Congo's problems (as, incidentally, they might prove not to be for South Sudan either). For one thing, even if as a result of false consciousness, they would be fiercely resisted by a large majority of the Congolese themselves. It is indeed a painful irony of the Congolese state that its victims embrace its domination.[19] More importantly, however, there are no meaningful ways to partition Congo. A sovereign Katanga or Kivu would be just as post-colonial, arbitrary and rife with its own fault lines.

Yet these objections do not mean that the solution to Congo's problems might not imply, ex post, some significant boundary changes and even a complete disappearance of Congo as we know it now. What they do mean, however, is that this is not for any outsiders to decide but for the Congolese. The impetus to reform that is currently necessary is one whereby the presence and the authority of sovereign Congolese institutions across the territory are deflated and diluted so as to give local communities (defined here regionally and not ethnically) a voice and a chance to settle their conflicts. They must be given the tools to produce their own sovereign institutional solutions, based on local social contracts.[20] The state must then be the aggregate result of these exercises, their institutional sum. But for such an exercise to be genuinely democratic, it must be agreed at the onset that local communities retain among their institutional options the right to opt out. Allegiance to Congo cannot be demanded; it must be given. An amputated Congo might be the eventual outcome, but it would most likely be a more accountable one with greater citizen ownership and a better chance at fostering security and development.

3

OVERCOMING THE PAST: WAR AND PEACE IN SUDAN AND SOUTH SUDAN

Anna C. Rader

UNTIL JULY 2011, Sudan was the largest country in Africa, one surrounded by volatile neighbours in a region beset by conflict. Sudan's history of domination, marginalisation and underdevelopment had been underscored by a fault line running between north and south, a consequence of external interference and internal dynamics that has now been formalised with the partition of the country into the rump state of the Republic of the Sudan and the new state of the Republic of South Sudan: an extreme fault-line management option. Both countries retain the legacy of their shared history of conflict, and are riven by the fault lines that criss-crossed 'old' Sudan which, overlaid on to political flashpoints, were not effectively taken into account by attempts to construct a holistic peace. Optimistic observers will hope that partition brings peace to both Sudans. But formalising the north–south fault line with an international border has activated and energised new fault lines – grievance-led and identity-based – that will dictate the pace of progress in both countries, each of which also retains old wounds and tensions which, particularly in Darfur, remain potent challenges.

This chapter revisits Sudan's history, examining the political and economic factors that led to the emergence and consolidation of the fault line between the colonially administered northern and southern regions. It reviews the subsequent manipulation of the country's resource and organisational disparity by a Khartoum-based political elite that prompted sustained resistance from a southern opposition in the form of two civil wars. It then gives an overview of Sudan's principal fault line, arguing that neither the north nor the south was a monolithic entity, and that each still contains its own divisions and fault lines. It considers the flashpoints for renewed conflict and how the inability of either government to address grievances along internal fractures means that both states now face a core-periphery dilemma – the historical conflict driver. It concludes by arguing that the end of the Comprehensive Peace Agreement was a milestone in regional politics and international diplomacy, but that both countries will nevertheless find it difficult to overcome their past.

A Divided History

Early Sudan was a patchwork of tribal kingdoms.[1] Conquest by a Turco-Egyptian regime in the 1820s conglomerated the many small states, giving shape to a unified country. However, slave raiding and agricultural exploitation of the southern Sudanese hinterland by northern merchant tribes (so-called 'Arabs') led to the emergence of a regional imbalance in wealth and power: the nascent north–south rift. The Turco-Egyptian dominion was overthrown by an indigenous Islamist rebellion that began around 1883 and established an emirate under the Mahdi, Muhammad Ahmad, in a period that has been considered an example of proto-Sudanese nationalism. After the death of the Mahdi, a new administration emerged under Khalifa Abdullahi that distinguished between the *Ansar* (followers of the Mahdi – predominantly Muslim northerners) and 'unbelievers', reinforcing existing racial attitudes and erecting an exclusive nationalism.[2] This period of Sudanese history is notable for the development of a politicised religious identity (militant Islam) that overlapped with the culturally defined notion of 'Arabness', and for the consolidation of formerly coincidental attributes (Arabic-speaking, Islam-practising and north-living) into an explicit 'northern' identity, at the expense of a racialised 'other' in the south.

The Mahdiyya came to an end in 1898, defeated by an alliance of alienated northerners, Nubian dissidents and the British and Egyptian colonial powers. The resulting Anglo-Egyptian Condominium entrenched northern privilege through preferential treatment including economic investment in infrastructure and governance, while 'native administration' in the south, a form of indirect rule, prioritised 'tribal' structures over complementary institutions or capacity for self-rule. These separate colonial administrations led to divergent state-building trajectories in the north and the south that perpetuated Sudan's core-periphery imbalance – a dynamic that would underwrite most of Sudan's modern conflict.

Independence on 1 January 1956 came amidst civil war. Though there had been almost a decade of advance joint administration, the true scale of combining north and south was overwhelming. Both had been governed separately for nearly half a century, on top of decades of unequal relations, meaning that they lacked a common framework within which to communicate. Unlike other post-colonial states that fell back on shared ascriptive characteristics after independence, Sudan was riven with fault lines – economic, religious, tribal, cultural, geographic – that cross-cut and pre-dated the north–south dichotomy. Moreover, the pace of Sudanese decolonisation was dictated more by the fact of shared colonial administration than by the maturity of nationalist movements or the strength of indigenous institutions.[3]

The state quickly became the object of political elite competition:[4] northern riverine groups wanted to continue favourable economic policies towards the core (Khartoum and the Nile regions), while southern, eastern and western groups demanded retribution for past political and economic marginalisation. A southern resistance movement known as Anya Nya had been gaining momentum since the 1955 Torit mutiny, in which southern soldiers refused to transfer to the north: an early rebellion against proposals for a united post-independence Sudan.[5] The guerrillas objected to the 'cultural colonialism' of the north, viewing Arabicisation as a deliberate effort to deny non-Arabic speakers national power;[6] the result was the targeting and murder of northern public servants in the south.[7] Tensions escalated with the establishment of a military regime under General Abboud in 1958, which declared a state of emergency and abandoned parliamentary democracy. The central government became characterised by overt Islamic symbolism and continued the preferential treatment of northern Arab Sudanese, refusing calls to recognise Christianity as a state religion. During the 1960s it became increasingly clear that attempting to cultivate a Sudanese nation based on the Arab language and Islamic faith would not succeed – instead of national concord, it fed division.[8] As the Anya Nya rebellion gathered pace, Sudan descended into a civil war that cost half a million lives, displaced tens of thousands of people and sidetracked the requisite post-independence nation building.

In 1972 the first civil war ended with the signing of the Addis Ababa Agreement (AAA). But the unsteady peace was dissolved by the outbreak of new fighting, triggered by the failure to fully implement the peace accord, the discovery of oil in the south in the late 1970s and the attempted extension of sharia law across Sudan by the Khartoum government in 1983 – three issues that would be recurring sources of conflict in Sudan's future. This second civil war, prompted by an army mutiny in 1983, ran until 2005. Fought between the Khartoum-based government and the Sudan People's Liberation Movement/Army (SPLM/A), a southern-based opposition movement, it would be one of the world's longest-running wars, leading to the displacement of an estimated 4 million Sudanese and the deaths of 2 million from famine, disease and conflict: one of the greatest civilian death tolls of any war of the twentieth century.[9]

Under the leadership of Colonel John Garang, the SPLM/A strove for a culturally diverse but united Sudan. The SPLM's early manifesto specifically repudiated separatism, not least because of the difficulty of articulating 'the south' as a geographic entity, but also because the SPLM/A saw the so-called 'problem of Southern Sudan' as a symptom of the broader nation-wide problem of 'Backward Areas'.[10] The Organisation of African Unity's and the United Nations' commitment to colonial borders, together with the reservation of neighbour and backer Ethiopia towards instability, also mitigated secessionist sentiments. Committed to unity, the SPLM did not see itself as a potential future government and thus developed neither a mode of governing nor sustainable civil institutions,[11] meaning that, although the SPLM fought for 'the south', there were few shared conceptions of a southern political community that could unite the fractious southern tribes. Garang was a strong factor in maintaining political coherence, but the SPLM coalition nevertheless splintered into secessionist (SPLM-United) and unificationist (SPLM under Garang) strands in the early 1990s, leading to bloody inter-tribal strife underwritten by post-Cold War small arms proliferation.[12]

Meanwhile, in the north, a comprehensive Islamicisation of the state was taking place under a militant Islamist group led by Omar Al-Bashir, a Sudanese military officer who had overthrown the civilian government in June 1989. Bashir's Revolutionary Command Council for National Salvation used patronage, purges and an appeal to religious orthodoxy as a substitute for political legitimacy and secular nationalism.[13] Bashir would continue to lead Sudan as head of the National Congress Party (NCP) for over twenty years, becoming a controversial figure and one of Africa's longest-ruling heads of state.

Elusive Peace

The brief period of post-independence peace had been unable to generate collective norms on conflict resolution, political community and justice, or to overcome the colonial legacy of divide and rule. The subsequent years of civil war postponed the opportunity to mitigate Sudan's regional and sub-regional fault lines and instead focused on conflict resolution between the principal adversaries – north and south. Discussions of peace in Sudan hence tended to centre on this relationship through a narrow lens of issues such as power sharing, revenue allocation and boundary making. Though these issues are triggers for violence, Sudan's peace processes have generally not addressed the complex interplay of structural and ethno-political factors that inform the range of Sudanese fault lines.[14] Early peace agreements such as the AAA in 1972 failed because they did not – or could not – address the entirety of the inequitable status quo at the root of Sudan's history of violence.[15] The AAA, for example, worked within the framework of the north–south dichotomy and sought to give the south better governing structures; but the attempted federalism unravelled because of perceived economic and political inequality between southern tribes[16] – sub-regional fault lines that revealed the disunity of the south.

The 1990s were characterised by failed peace agreements between the irreconcilable parties of north and south, entrenching the fault line further. Efforts to resolve the second civil war were stonewalled by a powerful Khartoum, despite mediation by regional powers. The ongoing violence between government forces and SPLA fighters could not be contained within the ceasefire, and fighting depleted trust between the negotiating parties. Another opportunity expired in May 1992 at the Abuja Conference, when the Khartoum government, on the offensive in southern Sudan, was unprepared to make concessions, while the joint SPLM/SPLM-United delegation was unable to reconcile competing positions on an independent southern state. More progress was made by the regional development organisation IGADD[17] in 1994, although the resulting Declaration of Principles, calling for a secular state, recognition of diversity and self-determination, was composed by the mediators, not the negotiating parties, and was unsurprisingly rejected by Khartoum.[18] Ultimately pre-Comprehensive Peace Agreement (CPA) efforts faltered because the inclusion of the full range of regionally delineated political interests within a national framework required a 'radical restructuring' of Khartoum's power base,[19] something early agreements were unable to deliver. Moreover, the peace conferences failed to be fully inclusive: while the south fielded a range of representatives from both factions, the 'north' was only ever represented by the NCP, which did not reflect the spectrum of northern peoples or interests.[20]

Nevertheless, after over a decade of mediation by international and regional actors, negotiations sponsored by the Intergovernmental Authority on Development (IGAD) and a consortium of Western powers began promisingly in 2001.[21] All major parties agreed to the principle of self-determination for southern Sudan, signing the Machakos Protocol on 20 July 2002. After two more years of tough negotiations, the NCP and the SPLM agreed to protocols on the sharing of power and wealth, and a referendum on the future status of the south to be held in 2011.[22] The final peace agreement, the CPA, was signed at Naivasha on 9 January 2005, ending twenty-one years of war. A United Nations Mission in Sudan was established under UN Security Council Resolution 1590 on 24 March 2005 in order to support the CPA's implementation and protect human rights.[23]

Comprehensive Peace?

Unlike previous efforts to manage the north–south fault line, the CPA focused on explicitly restructuring relations between the two main loci of power. Though the CPA was designed around South Sudanese autonomy, the restructuring of the state suggested by the power-sharing arrangements raised expectations in Darfur and east Sudan, two marginalised regions in the north, about the CPA's national dividend, not least the possibility of curbing what they saw as the excessive power of the central government.[24] However, disregarding Garang's insistence that South Sudan's grievances were part of a broader challenge of uneven and underdevelopment, there were few or no specific arrangements in the CPA for other regions, bar political changes for enhanced representation. All regions were supposed to benefit from a government of national unity and a national assembly put in place to govern Sudan during the six-year interim period; legislative and executive elections were designed to inject political legitimacy into the whole system, replacing political appointees with elected representatives.

For Sudan, a massive country with a widely dispersed population of 40 million, poor infrastructure outside the major cities and a deficit of democratic culture, the holding of general elections – the first since 2000 – was a serious logistical challenge. Presidential and parliamentary elections were originally scheduled for April 2009 but pushed back to February 2010 and then April 2010. The elections set the scene for the final year of the interim period and, as a dry run for the 2011 referendum, there was obvious apprehension about both process and outcome. Incidents of violence broke out in the days that followed, particularly in Jonglei State in the south, where tensions had been running high since January and where allegations of vote rigging in the gubernatorial race inflamed inter-tribal relations. As the first experience of multi-party democracy in over twenty years, the elections were a considerable achievement, but concerns about electoral malfeasance demoralised relations between the north and south, particularly in light of President Bashir's reinstatement amidst his indictment by the International Criminal Court for war crimes. Though they were generally considered free and fair by observers, there were electoral irregularities and the elections were, moreover, not nationally inclusive, exposing Sudan's fault lines, in particular in Darfur, where problematic voter registration, instability and intimidation impeded voting.

The electoral milestone demonstrated that much more needed to be done in Sudan to identify gaps in CPA implementation and build capacity at the national government level. The south, however, was quickly consumed by the looming referendum, an undertaking replete with challenges, while the north turned to the consolidation of power and attempted to manipulate its desired referendum outcome through bribes and informal pressure. The CPA, and especially the elections, was designed to make unity attractive – but the elections were predominantly an authentication of Sudan's 'competing nationalisms',[25] affirming Khartoum's and Juba's separate trajectories.

International Relations

The CPA was also an experiment in regional and international mediation. Sudan's size, natural resources and 'Arab-African' character made it a focus for regional heavyweights such as Ethiopia, Egypt and Kenya, for whom a conflict-ridden Sudan was the black hole on the edge of which teetered the wider stability of East Africa. The period of prolonged civil war had drawn on Cold War-era alliances, characterised by counterbalancing and proxyism, implicating a number of neighbouring powers in Sudan's conflict economy. Sudan had been the single largest recipient of US development and military assistance in Sub-Saharan Africa during the 1980s, but by the 1990s the relationship was strained by the implication of

Sudan in the fortunes of al-Qaeda.[26] However, by the turn of the millennium, the US and Sudan had renewed relations, with a bilateral dialogue on counter-terrorism in 2000 and cooperation in the wake of 9/11. The US, together with other regional and Western powers – notably the UK, Italy and Norway, and the IGAD member states – invested considerable time and energy in the CPA negotiations, and it is an unlikely coincidence that such a concerted push happened during the so-called 'War on Terror', in which the US and its allies sought to deny sanctuary to al-Qaeda. The quartet of international countries helped hold the CPA parties to account and break deadlocks during the tough negotiations, but external appetite waned during the crucial implementation phase. In the words of the International Crisis Group, the international community had its 'eyes wide shut' in the months that followed: engagement and interest effectively disappeared after the peace talks were wrapped up at Naivasha, with donors turned off by the inexperienced diplomacy of the Garang-less SPLM,[27] distracted by the disintegrating situation in Darfur and at cross-purposes over aid, monitoring and leadership responsibilities.[28] The US was also increasingly consumed by its wars in Iraq and Afghanistan,[29] and until the run-up to the referendum in 2011, when international pressure was once more required, CPA implementation was led by the unstable partnership of a 'strong but unwilling' NCP and a 'weak but committed' SPLM.[30]

Towards Partition

The CPA's most significant provision was for a referendum on the future status of South Sudan, scheduled for 9 January 2011, six years from the date of signing. In the months preceding the vote, most southern Sudanese made it clear that they would be voting for partition. It was plain, however, that neither unity nor secession was the easy way out for Sudan: while the former would have required a wholesale renegotiation of the national social contract, for which neither side had the requisite political appetite, the latter was likely to open fissures in the rump and expose the government of South Sudan to myriad developmental pressures. Amidst last-minute deal making and concessions, the referendum did take place as scheduled. With around 3.8 million votes cast, 98.8 per cent of registered southern voters chose secession. Khartoum and other regional states acknowledged the result without obfuscation and the international community endorsed the world's newest prospective state.

Though the holding of the South Sudan referendum was widely

considered a vindicating moment for the CPA, overall the peace agreement has had a mixed report card. Commendably, it brought peace, ending decades of civil war. But its political settlement was also unable to generate the social capital required to overcome entrenched perceptions of inequality and injustice that have long driven instability along Sudan's national fault lines. Written within the framework of north versus south, the ongoing brinkmanship between the two political elites not only delayed needed reform but perpetuated the politics of exclusion. By focusing on the top level, the CPA did not establish participatory mechanisms to encourage Sudanese to invest in a shared conception of political community, or develop the civic space or transitional justice mechanisms needed to settle disputes without resorting to arms. Moreover, in subscribing to the story as told by political elites in Khartoum and Juba, efforts to manage Sudan's fault lines have overlooked the complex stratifications within each state. In failing to engage with issues such as land rights and local governance, even the CPA was unable to engage with those flashpoints that cause Sudanese to take up arms along entrenched ethnic lines.

Fracture and Fault Lines

A review of Sudan's history highlights the multiple drivers of conflict and discord that have been at work for a century, if not longer. It is little wonder that modern Sudan became deeply disfigured by its internal fault lines, the intractability of which provoked responses ranging from subjugation and repression to full-scale civil war. Many of these fracture points and fault lines have shaped both countries' development and remain relevant today.

As observed above, Sudan's principal and most prominent fault line historically ran between the north and south of the country, an artefact of unequal economic relations between the primarily nomadic, trading tribes of the north and the pastoralists of the more verdant south. The formalisation of the divide came in 1930 with the colonial Civil Secretary's 'Southern Policy' speech, in which he distinguished between 'Arabs' (northern Muslims) and 'Africans' (Christian/animist southerners). This inaccurate conceptualisation of emergent Sudanese identities became the dominant framework for colonial interpretations of Sudan. By perceiving the 'north' as a cultural and political entity, the British reinforced boundaries around the dominant group – the Arab Muslims – to the exclusion of other ethnic, religious or cultural groupings in the north. It also gave credence to the

narrative promulgated by the north that the 'south' was tribalistic, culturally and confessionally distinctive, and a territorially described zone. While
the south under colonialism remained heterogeneous, with 'tribes' becoming increasingly politicised, the dominant Arab Muslim group in the north
developed a corporate awareness.[31] Over time, subjective identifications in
both regions became vested with national symbolism by political elites,[32]
embedding structural sources of conflict into the fabric of Sudanese identity and creating a fundamental rift between north and south.

The Sudanese state has historically been a vehicle for exploitation
and division, unable to provide a national framework for the resolution of
grievances. Economic and political marginalisation has been the principal
driver of conflict in Sudan,[33] built around the two main grievances of
lack of political influence and disproportionate revenue allocation, specifically from oil wealth. This activated regionally articulated identities –
most spectacularly in South Sudan and Darfur – undercutting the idea
of 'the nation' in Sudan.[34] Though Garang's vision was one of a united
Sudan, by the turn of the millennium both the north and the south had
become robust identity categories with a hard 'inside/outside' boundary.
North and south identities were deeply entrenched, historically embed-
ded and politically deployable, but the north south fault line obscured
their internal complexity. Moreover, though it was hoped that the CPA
would address marginalisation across Sudan, in reality it entrenched existing power dynamics. Data from the 2009 census estimated that the Sudanese population contained more than fifty ethnic groups, subdividing into
at least 570 distinct peoples[35] – when mapped on to political and economic grievances, each of these was, and is, a potential fault line along
which both negotiation and dispute is possible. As Mohamed Suliman has
observed:[36]

> Most violent conflicts are over material resources, whether actual
> or perceived. With the passage of time, however, ethnic, cultural and
> religious affiliations seem to undergo transformation from abstract
> ideological categories into concrete social forces. In a wider sense, they
> themselves become contestable material social resources and hence
> possible objects of group strife and violent conflict.

Regional Divisions in Sudan

Despite the narrative of Arab supremacy, the 'north' has never been a coherent ethno-cultural unit. The dominance of self-identified Arabs in Sudanese life – politically and geographically – suppresses, for instance, the nomadic Bedouin and tribes such as the Fur and Beja who want to maintain their indigenous 'African' culture together with their Islamic faith.[37] In fact, many northern groups used by Khartoum's National Congress Party as proxies in conflict, such as the Baggara Arabs in South Kordofan, are themselves marginalised minorities.[38]

Such northern groups – who had neither special arrangements nor a referendum out of the CPA – continue to be omitted from the equation. Oppression by successive Islamist administrations has fractured traditional conflict resolution mechanisms in the north and drought has taken its toll on livelihoods; the growth of Islam at the heart of the state also excludes non-Muslims. The encampments of thousands of displaced people around large northern towns constitute Sudan's 'invisible citizens';[39] those who can may return to South Sudan, but others will need to be incorporated into the Sudanese social contract. The mismanagement and exclusion of northern minorities is a recipe for possible fracture along an intra-north fault line. Throughout the CPA period, Sudanese President Omar Al-Bashir continued to maintain considerable support in the north through infrastructure and investment projects funded by oil money. In the aftermath of partition, this privileged core based in Khartoum and Omdurman will want to see a return for continuing to back the NCP – which, according to some reports, is weakened and fractious – and Bashir himself, whose position has been made more vulnerable by the revolutions of the 2011 Arab Spring.

These politics will also need to be balanced against the appeasement of Sudan's periphery in order to consolidate the rump state. The outbreak of conflict along the border in May 2011 is suggestive of the deep splits in northern 'coherence'. Prompted by the Abyei dispute (see below), the upturn in violence in South Kordofan and Blue Nile State revealed another hidden seam along which the predominantly Muslim Nuba erupted. Their grievances are strikingly similar to those that activated the southern, western and eastern rebellions: economic and political disenfranchisement from the centre, lack of religious and civic freedom, poor governance and few or no returns on the promised development dividend.[40]

Another such region is Red Sea State, part of the very poor eastern region. Despite being host to Sudan's largest gold mine and a major pipeline, the state has suffered persistent drought and famine, acute poverty and unemployment, with a sustained, though largely invisible insurgency in the late 1990s. The conflict was settled in 2006 with the Eastern Sudan Peace Agreement built around a development dividend, but the scale of the challenge, coupled with ongoing environmental degradation, means that the area remains a potential flashpoint. After the loss of South Sudan, Khartoum will want to ensure that this region does not follow the path of Darfur and generate a profound ethno-geographic identity along which conflict could be articulated.

Darfur remains the principal testament to the impact of economic underdevelopment, political marginalisation and ethnic mismanagement in Sudan. Government-led efforts to counter Darfurian demands for political representation and economic reparation for decades of core-periphery oppression fed a low-intensity insurgency synchronous with the civil war in the south. As peace appeared possible on the southern front, Darfur escalated into bloody conflict in February 2003. Fighting between the main rebel groups, the Justice and Equality Movement (JEM) and the Sudan Liberation Army (SLA), and Khartoum's proxy militia, the 'Arab' horsemen known as the Janjaweed, has claimed hundreds of thousands of lives and led to an acute human security crisis with national and regional ramifications. Sudan observers have been divided over whether a settlement for Darfur should have been incorporated into the CPA or whether a separate agreement was appropriate. Nevertheless, it is significant that representations of the conflict in the Western media and by foreign policymakers have internationalised what began as a local insurgency driven by economic and political marginalisation, raising the stakes for both sides in a situation that was termed genocide by the Bush administration, but which has more generally been mischaracterised as a struggle between 'African farmers and Arab herdsmen'.[41] Darfur remains a serious fault line in Sudan and, as discussed below, one whose resolution will no doubt be influenced by the trajectory of both Sudans after 2011, as well as by international appetite for African conflicts.

South Sudan

South Sudan is also riven by fault lines. The period of colonial indirect rule hardened lines between historically fluid groups such as the Dinka, Nuer and Equatorians, 'ethnicising' southern tribes by explaining away massive geographical differences within the south in terms of 'culture'. Although the SPLM has been the south's primary political vehicle for a quarter of a century, a plethora of political affiliations based on tribal entities exists and these have been both aggravated and enunciated by conflict, leading to chronic intra-south instability.[42] In particular, tribal violence between the Nuer and Dinka has been based in part on perceptions of 'Dinka domination' of the SPLM/A, which led to the fracturing of the SPLM in the early 1990s and was a prevalent charge made against the SPLM in the late CPA period. Enduring insecurity, poverty, land disputes and the absence of the promised peace dividend continue to provoke contemporary conflict in the south – conflict that is increasingly explained in 'tribal' terms although much of it is intra-tribal or political feuding with little relationship to tribal lines.[43] Cattle raiding and counter-attacks have long been part of southern Sudanese life, but these disputes now escalate along ethnic lines and are triggers for violence. In Jonglei State, for instance, the Lou Nuer have traditionally occupied a band of territory that is largely waterless; their seasonal migration therefore brings them into conflict with neighbouring Dinka, Jikany Nuer and Murle.[44] The proliferation of small arms and wider insecurity has led to serious fighting between ethnic militias that has claimed hundreds of lives. These centrifugal forces are now encapsulated within the new state of South Sudan, which also has its own 'periphery' at a geographic and psychological distance from the core of Juba.

Ongoing insecurity and conflict have hardened boundaries between ethnic groups in the region, but they have also led to the pronunciation of ethnicity – for instance, the multiple hill-dwelling tribes of the Nuba Mountains in contested South Kordofan developed a sense of self-awareness as a sub-national group that was a relic of the conflict, having been sharply defined in contrast to the Baggara Arabs of Kordofan, with whom they previously lived in harmony.[45] Conflict over competing land claims led the Baggara to participate in the pro-Khartoum paramilitary group, the Popular Defence Force, and the Nuba in the SPLA, meaning that local grievances were pursued as part of broader political agendas. This articulation of ethnicity in the context of perceived injustice has led to multiple inter-tribal conflicts within South Sudan that threaten future peace there. Though these disputes tend to be conducted in a tribalist framework, in fact much of the enduring instability in the south is due to political marginalisation: the government has little penetration beyond Juba and there is insufficient local governance or engagement. South

Sudan faces a number of flashpoints and fault lines that will complicate its efforts to unite the country in the aftermath of independence.

Flashpoints and Future Conflict Drivers

The Comprehensive Peace Agreement period ended on 9 July 2011 and with it came the internationalisation of the Sudanese north–south fault line as the country formally became two. After nearly fifty years of continuous conflict and less than a decade of peace since colonial independence, force has been the default strategy at all levels of Sudanese society. Prevailing insecurity, as well as unresolved or unimplemented CPA provisions, complicates the peace. Sudanese on both sides of the border want security, which means armed militias in the south and west are unlikely to lay down arms until there is confidence in the civilian government and army to ensure stability. The heavily brutalised population suffers an acute security dilemma – no villages will disarm until their neighbours do so, and while ongoing problems such as cattle rustling and land grabs continue, that is not likely to change. The climate of instability is ripe for exploitation by ethnic entrepreneurs, political elites and warlords. Disarmament and demobilisation were painfully slow during the interim period, and the required integration of northern and southern armies was a complicated distraction. Security sector reform is urgently needed in both states. Additionally, though the incursions from Chad may have ceased for the time being, ongoing conflict overspill from Uganda in the form of the Lord's Resistance Army and from the Central African Republic destabilises the south and south-western borders, a particular problem for newly independent South Sudan.

Sudan's civil conflicts were driven by core-periphery inequality and contested natural resources, together with the systemic failure of the political class to build an inclusive national community, in particular around issues such as the role of religion in the state. South Sudan's independence was an effort to ameliorate these conflict drivers. But these three factors will continue to be long-term dynamics within both the Sudanese states and between them. There are also other simmering issues around land ownership, displacement and return, and justice that may further ratchet up tensions in the new states and be proximate causes of short-term conflict. Both states face an uphill struggle to meet expectations and improve the quality of life for ordinary citizens, since Sudan's history has shown that even banal grievances and demands have the potential to create a self-perpetuating conflict complex of distrust, low-intensity violence and the invocation of ethnic identity. Both are large countries and the lack of development in South Sudan in particular means that such conflict may be heavily localised and viewed as apart from the concerns of the government elite. However, the low-grade erosion of the fringes is a critical threat to the nation building that is urgently required in both countries.

In particular, there are three clusters of flashpoints that will challenge not only the new Republic of South Sudan, but also Sudan and by implication the wider region. Sudan–South Sudan peace turns on their resolution.

Border Demarcation, Oil and Abyei

It is of profound significance that what had been a soft border, even during colonial times, has now become a 'hard' international one. Borders are highly symbolic expressions of the nation, defining the in-out boundary and acting as physical embodiments of the state. The Sudan–South Sudan border is politically supercharged because it reflects the victory of South Sudanese self-determination and also therefore the loss of the south for Khartoum. Border demarcation will alter the lives of countless families at the fringes of Sudanese society who, through inter-tribal marriage, will find themselves separated from their kinsmen; it will also affect seasonal migratory routes and tribal pasturelands.[46]

The border has long been a site of contestation for Sudan and South Sudan, and its demarcation was one of the unimplemented CPA requirements of the interim period. The border runs to over 2,000 kilometres, a little less than that between Afghanistan and Pakistan, a notoriously difficult to secure frontier. Aside from the enormous logistical challenge, demarcating the border necessitated describing the extent of both states, which inflamed tensions during the CPA period. The 2002 Machakos Protocol defined the boundary of South Sudan as the 1956 independence line, excluding Abyei, South Kordofan and Blue Nile State – former SPLA strongholds and areas of considerable natural wealth. To assuage both sides, the CPA provided for special power-sharing arrangements for the contested Three Areas during the interim period, with a separate referendum for Abyei on whether to retain its status in the north or become part of Bahr el Ghazal in the south, and popular consultations for Blue Nile and South Kordofan in order to legitimise their status within a future political settlement.[47]

However, neither the Abyei referendum nor the popular consultations took place in January 2011 and, as analysts and observers predicted at Naivasha, the Abyei issue threatened to derail the CPA. An oil-rich region, it was long the fulcrum of the north–south contest. During the CPA period, oil was described as a structural reason for peace;[48] indeed, the location of Sudan's best oil reserves in the south was one of the factors that brought the NCP and SPLM to the negotiating table. Though the conflict limited exploration, Sudan is estimated to have 5 billion barrels of proven oil reserves, mostly in South Sudan; in 2008, the IMF reported that oil represented 65 per cent of Khartoum's revenues and 98 per cent of total revenues for the Juba government.[49] During the CPA period, South Sudan agreed to share 50 per cent of its oil receipts with the central government; until it develops an autonomous capability, South Sudan will be dependent upon Sudan for its refinery and transit infrastructure, an arrangement that diplomats had hoped would tie both countries together.

Prior to partition, the stagnation of the border demarcation process stultified progress on oil negotiations as Khartoum resisted efforts to include oil-rich border areas in the south. In particular, the NCP failed to accept the findings of the Abyei Boundaries Commission in 2004, claiming that it had exceeded its mandate. The inability to agree Abyei's border led the SPLM to suspend its participation in the government of national unity, and northern proxy forces reportedly mobilised in the area.[50] The case went to the Permanent Court of Arbitration at The Hague in 2008, which found in 2009 that the Abyei commission had exceeded its mandate only in certain respects. Its ruling assigned Khartoum control of the lucrative Heglig oilfields and Nile oil pipeline.[51] Despite this, agreement on the boundary, and hence the population, of Abyei was not forthcoming, and Khartoum was resolute that Abyei was a non-negotiable prerequisite for the referendum.[52] Under enormous international pressure, the South Sudan referendum went ahead as planned, with Juba expending considerable political capital to ensure its own future – possibly at the expense of the Abyei referendum. Without advance resolution, the Abyei issue derailed relations in the succeeding months, and briefly appeared to be Khartoum's ace card when in May 2011 it made recognition of the new state of South Sudan contingent on border demarcation.

For Khartoum, Abyei assumed enormous symbolic resonance – not least because, despite oil-sharing agreements, losing the principal oilfields and associated oil revenue (estimated to be as much as two-thirds of its former oil reserves) was considered a serious threat to the power base of the Sudanese elite.[53] The human security situation in Abyei deteriorated in February 2011 following clashes between armed Misseriya and southern police units, leading to a build-up of forces on both sides of the border. Following the ambush and murder of a unit of Sudanese Armed Forces (SAF) at the border, the SAF invaded Abyei with tanks, heavy artillery and air cover on 21 May 2011, seizing control of the town and contravening the CPA. At this time, the frontier was still populated by large numbers of SPLA and Sudanese military – many on the wrong side of the border. The stand-off cost civilian lives (northern aeroplanes reportedly conducted strafing and bombing raids) and put both capitals on the defensive; the gravity of the situation led the UN Security Council to sanction a six-month force of Ethiopian peacekeepers for Abyei.[54] The two governments had earlier agreed to a jointly patrolled demilitarised border, but the border became militarised as both states sought to establish their respective zones of control. Fighting also broke out between Sudanese government forces and rebel groups in the northern states of South Kordofan, the Nuba Mountains and Blue Nile, most notably led by members of SPLA-North who had been allied to the south during the civil war but found themselves in the north after the CPA. UNMIS, the UN peacekeeping force deployed to Sudan during the CPA period whose mandate expired on 9 July 2011, was unable to intervene. As SPLM-North fighters reportedly allied with Darfurian groups, Khartoum began to face the prospect of a war on three fronts.[55]

The issue of Abyei, and more broadly of oil relations and the border zone, was the CPA's Achilles' heel. The humanitarian crisis that erupted along the border following the mobilisation of Sudanese forces in spring 2011 proved how much the CPA had rested on Khartoum's restraint. Even more significant, the violent clashes throughout the summer that spread through Blue Nile and South Kordofan made clear that those provisions that had been conveniently considered optional in the pre- and post-referendum negotiations – self-determination for the Three Areas and border demarcation – were critical to peace. The resultant civilian fatalities, displacement, food insecurity and reports of ethnic cleansing in Abyei, South Kordofan and Blue Nile revealed that the north–south fault line remained immensely brittle after independence. Most alarmingly, it suggested that separation was insufficient to heal the decades of marginalisation and underdevelopment in forgotten regions of the north and south, and that unresolved issues over the border could bring old enemies back to war.

Land Ownership and Displacement, Return and Resettlement

With large swathes of the population nomadic pastoralists, land holds a symbolic place in Sudanese culture; the insecurity fomented around land issues is therefore particularly flammable. In both Sudan and South Sudan, conflict has changed land use and ownership, destroying local natural resources and aggravating food insecurity. Millions of displaced people have yet to return to their former homelands. When they do, they often find their land occupied by other internally displaced persons (IDPs) or former soldiers, who claim their territorial rights stem from their role in the 'liberation';[56] others remain in transit areas or move to new parts of the country where tribal politics hinders integration. The hardening of tribal lines and the history of brutalisation mean land disputes are ripe for political manipulation and are increasingly a source of violent ethnic conflict in South Sudan.

The land regime has been seriously upset by years of conflict, absence of the rule of law and perceived inequality. In the north, creeping desertification and persistent drought have led to southwards encroachment, upsetting the land ownership equilibrium. In the Nuba Mountains, for instance, the settlement of formerly nomadic Baggara Arabs in the pasture lands of the Dinka has been a recipe for tension; in other parts of South Sudan such as Magwi County, however, it is the Dinka that have displaced Madi farmers. The spread of mechanised farming in South Kordofan also led to widespread displacement as well as changing livelihoods; and in Unity State, the state forcibly moved thousands off their territory in order to grant oil exploration concessions. In Darfur, the lack of agricultural land, with the concomitant ineffective land management system, has been one of the main drivers of conflict and has yet to be satisfactorily addressed.

Historically, inter-tribal agreements regulated pastoral movement across Sudan, ensuring that primary land rights of access and tenure were observed. In the south, tribal courts continued under native administration, but were replaced with northern administrators after independence. The SPLM's civil administration reinstated the use of tribal chieftain power, but the politicisation of local ethnicity, together with the proliferation of the rule of the gun, has undermined customary law.[57] Renewed efforts to build a civil authority structure in the mid-1990s went some way towards creating independent judicial arrangements, but there was little in place prior to the CPA to ameliorate this serious flashpoint.

The CPA did not directly address the issue of land ownership, but postponed it to the post-agreement phase. The creation of three principal land commissions – National, Southern Sudan and Darfur – was intended to resolve disputes, assess compensation and advise on reform; state land commissions in South Kordofan and Blue Nile were also established. However, the commissions' constitution and mandate were subject to wrangling between the main parties, delaying their creation for over two years. By centralising the dispute resolution mechanism, the CPA made the land issue into a political football. What is more, by failing to engage sufficiently with the local governance level, few institutional provisions were made for the equitable distribution of both usable land and development resources that are not subject to political manipulation and can be 'owned' by local Sudanese. This is particularly important in cases of group rights – for instance, communal customary claims by nomadic tribes – since individual disputes can quickly escalate into group conflict along ethnic lines.[58] NGOs in Sudan have attempted to document land rights and disputes, but this needs to be done in a comprehensive way by government agencies. Effective and fair land management is one of the most problematic but important tasks facing the South Sudanese government. As violence in Jonglei has attested,[59] the potency of land conflict in South Sudan could underwrite a return to war.

In addition, the fraught issue of IDPs will take a long time to resolve. All over South Sudan, widespread displacement due to conflict has created an estimated 4.9 million IDPs who will need to be returned and reintegrated into society. The mass repatriation of IDPs has the potential for intra-south conflict if issues such as land ownership, distribution and reconstruction are not carefully managed.[60] In Darfur, 2.7 million IDPs remain in camps, unable to return home or develop economic activities to support themselves. The sense of injustice and abandonment may be expressed in ethnic terms, leading to destabilisation along existing fault lines, as well as the emergence of a new one – displaced versus settled – that needs to be managed as a matter of urgency. In addition, Sudanese refugees are also based in camps in neighbouring countries; and Sudan hosts refugees from Eritrea, Chad, Ethiopia and Central African Republic, adding to the problem of return and integration.

The issues of land ownership, displacement, integration and return are complex, not least for a nascent state. Moreover, they are intimately bound up with questions of rights and justice, key considerations for both Sudan and South Sudan, not least the citizenship question which, at the time of writing, had not been resolved and risked creating 'stateless' people, particularly in the nomadic communities along the borders.[61] In some respects, two new nations were born on 9 July 2011, both of which require new conceptions of citizenship and national identity, reinforced by respect for human rights and robust justice regimes. Left unresolved or sidelined, such issues could give succour to existing narratives of marginalisation, articulated along both countries' sizeable fault lines.

Uneven Peace in Darfur

Massive international concern at claims of genocide ensured that Darfur was centre stage diplomatically in the mid-2000s, just as the Naivasha peace process was winding down. Although the UN and other humanitarian organisations disputed the allegations of ethnic cleansing and genocide,[62] the strong international reaction (particularly by the US) spurred peace negotiations between Khartoum and the largest opposition group, the Darfur SLA led by Minni Minawi, at Abuja in 2006. But the Darfur Peace Agreement (DPA) was a hasty settlement based on the CPA but which did not include agreement from all the principal factions, let alone reflect the interests of wider civil society, particularly Darfur's displaced communities. The international mediators' commitment to extracting a settlement amounted to 'deadline diplomacy' that muddled the timelines and failed to build trust and good faith between the parties.[63] Rather than forging peace, the DPA accelerated the fragmentation of the opposition into smaller ethnic groupings that were more difficult to work with.[64] The DPA's major flaw was its focus on the outcome rather than the process of making peace, neglecting the need to repair trust and find common ground between enemies.

Formal fighting did subside in the aftermath of Abuja, and Darfur's conflict was subsequently described as 'frozen',[65] but the reality was protracted insecurity, banditry and inter-tribal raiding. Partly this was because historical enmity and local tensions between and within nomadic and farming communities had now been subsumed into a politicised conflict: in many respects, Darfur become a battlefield upon which power struggles between a host of actors – Khartoum and the international community, Khartoum and its opponents, the central government and the rebel groups, and between the rebel groups – were played out.[66] According to some observers, the international community's 'megaphone diplomacy' was also to blame for alienating Khartoum and fuelling rebel intransigence.[67]

Diplomatic efforts to bring together the warring parties in 2010 seemed to signal progress. A framework ceasefire deal signed between JEM and Khartoum was brokered by Chad and signed in Qatar in February, giving JEM political recognition and seats in government. However, the absence of principal rebel groups such as Abdel Wahid's SLA faction from the talks jeopardised what some commentators had called a major break-through. By May 2010 JEM had withdrawn from the agreement following disputes over the April general elections: Darfur, still under emergency rule, was the scene of serious electoral fraud. Although most election-monitoring missions were unable to observe voting due to the security situation, it was clear that many people in the populous Darfur states, particularly IDPs, had been disenfranchised in advance by patchy voter registration.[68]

The intensity and duration of conflict in Darfur have shown that the DPA is insufficient for peace. The humanitarian crisis remained severe during late 2010 and into 2011, with ongoing displacement and violent raids, despite the presence of an African Union/United Nations peace-keeping force, UNAMID. Khartoum felt that it received insufficient credit for the peace process with the south,[69] but its implementation of both the CPA and DPA fluctuated according to international attention: when eyes were on the south, Darfur wobbled; when Darfur demanded con-sideration, progress on CPA milestones wavered. The proposed referen-dum for Darfur was delayed during 2011, suggesting that the international community will have to focus hard to demand peace in Darfur following South Sudanese independence as Khartoum seeks to consolidate power within its new reduced borders, and in the face of new rebel demands on the back of the success of the CPA. For South Sudan, Darfur is also problematic: Southern Darfur borders two of its own states, threatening conflict overspill; and Juba will be weary of anything that complicates Khartoum's negotiating appetite. For the time being, Darfur's fault line is neither managed nor stabilised, and remains a critical stumbling block in Sudan's future.

Prospects for South Sudan

Unresolved CPA issues and tense relations with Khartoum are just some of the challenges facing the new state of South Sudan. Despite large oil receipts, the government focused on meeting CPA benchmarks and prepar-ing for the referendum over capacity building. Social welfare, infrastructure and administration have all been neglected, and South Sudan ranks at the bottom of nearly all human development indicators. In the west and south in particular, expectations of an economic peace dividend have not been met. The government also faces an aggravated political climate. Political allegiances in South Sudan are complex: many groups felt that their interests were better met by a distant government in Khartoum than one in Juba. Without the north to balance against, intra-south fracture along sub-national fault lines is possible. Indeed, violent internecine fighting erupted throughout 2010: a multi-agency report found that 2,500 people had been killed and 350,000 displaced in the previous twelve months.[70] Civilian deaths were also caused by renegade army units loyal to General George Athor Deng Du, who clashed with the SPLA following his failure to win the Jonglei gubernatorial race, and with whom armed confrontations continued into the spring of 2011.[71] Athor was just one of many who felt that their political aspirations had not been met by the administration in Juba in the aftermath of the general elections. Those excluded from the independence windfall may prove similarly impedimental, of particular concern given that it will take months if not years for the South Sudanese government to exercise its monopoly on violence, a Weberian criterion of statehood.

South Sudan now faces a period of nation building and political consolidation. The SPLM must leave behind its military structures and identity as a liberation movement, and become an inclusive national political party that can capture the imagination of the country. Other political parties must also be given the opportunity to grow, and civic space preserved for institution building by civil society. Sudanese history demonstrates how the inability of a central state to reconcile competing claims results in the rabid localisation of conflict. The South Sudanese government will need enormous sustained political will to repair the fabric of society and ensure that peace, so hard fought for, is not discredited. Just as John Garang recognised in his vision for 'New Sudan', multiculturalism, inclusive citizenship and political representation will all be needed to create a lasting political settlement.

On security, South Sudan also faces considerable challenges. As discussed above, security sector reform, disarmament and demobilisation will be urgent priorities in the early years. It will also need to build its own diplomatic and international credentials. Juba has some long-standing allies, particularly Uganda, Kenya and Ethiopia, who have expended political capital on resolving their neighbour's civil war and who seek to benefit from the economic opportunities of a new state.[72] Uganda hopes that South Sudan can provide a security bulwark against the Lord's Resistance Army, which is still implicated in cross-border raids; and all of South Sudan's neighbours will be invested in ensuring that it becomes a viable state, not a failed one. And Juba may now find allies in Libya and Egypt, two states formerly opposed to the South's self-determination, whose changes of government during the Arab Spring may have positive implications for regional relations. The South Sudanese government will also have to build a new diplomatic relationship with Khartoum as former colleagues in the government of national unity become foreign dignitaries; and the resolution of bilateral challenges, such as the establishment of cooperative mechanisms for border and oil management, requires credibility and trust. The government in Juba will be tested, too, on issues such as Nile water management and the observation of international obligations associated with becoming the 193rd member of the United Nations.

Conclusion

Former Sudanese ambassador Francis Deng once described the history of Sudan's conflict as a 'war of visions' between contrasting and seemingly incompatible identities.[73] Prior to the Comprehensive Peace Agreement, attempts to manage Sudan's principal fault line between the north of the country and the south were unsuccessful either because they sought to impose a partisan nationalism atop diversity or because virulent regionalism was unable to forge an overarching narrative of Sudanese nationhood. The strength of oppositional identities – bolstered by patronage networks, economic inequality, political disenfranchisement and geographic distance – undermined attempts at parliamentary democracy, federalism and decentralisation, making conflict, elite bargaining and negotiated settlements the default tools of fault-line management. Moreover, years of conflict and undemocratic government deprived Sudan of neutral civic space in which to develop norms of political community and resolve conflict.

Ironically, both the north and south had claimed unity as their goal during the second civil war, but for different reasons and with different conceptions of what such an outcome might look like. The basic disjunction between the visions of north and south meant that there were few shared national tropes to underwrite nation building and overcome fault lines; the depth of animosity also meant that neither unity nor division had widespread legitimacy as both the NCP and the SPLM were unable to generate an inclusive and non-partisan narrative for Sudan – a realisation of 'unity in diversity'.[74]

Although the north–south dichotomy was Sudan's most politically salient fault line, its resolution alone will not guarantee peace in Sudan or South Sudan. In both countries, fault lines such as that of Darfur, South Kordorfan and Blue Nile State need to be actively managed, rather than controlled by patronage networks or suppressed by force, and legitimacy needs to be continually won in order to overcome internal schisms and centrifugal forces. Both South Sudan and Sudan are vulnerable in the aftermath of their divorce, and the scale of the border clashes of 2011 is a sober reminder that war between these new neighbours is not impossible. Their shared history bespeaks marginalisation, conflict and ethnic politicisation; but with political courage and leadership, a commitment to multiculturalism, justice and local governance, economic development and international support, the past may yet be overcome.

4

SOMALIA AND SOMALILAND:
STATE BUILDING AMID THE RUINS

J. Peter Pham

SOMALIA IS OFTEN HELD up as the example of a 'failed state'. Certainly the collapse in 1991 of the Somali state and the subsequent failure of what, to date, have been no fewer than fourteen attempts to reconstitute a central government underscore the difficulty faced by both Somalis and the international community as they try to resolve the long-running crisis. The recent flourishing of piracy off the country's coasts and the growing violence of an extremist Islamist insurgency within it lend greater urgency to the search for a solution, which this essay argues is to be found in the largely unknown positive examples which have emerged where Somali society itself has managed to bridge its fault lines in Somaliland, Puntland and other regions.

Somalia in often described in Hobbesian terms as 'the only country in the world where there is no government',[1] but instead 'a long-running, multisided battle for control'[2] by heavily armed fighters representing 'a tangled web of clans and militias'.[3] To a certain extent, the depiction is justified in so far as it is perhaps the only example in the world today of what Robert Rotberg called the 'collapsed state', that 'rare and extreme version of the failed state' that is 'a mere geographical expression, a black hole into which a failed polity has fallen', where 'there is dark energy, but the forces of entropy have overwhelmed the radiance that hitherto provided some semblance of order and other vital political goods to the inhabitants (no longer the citizens) embraced by language or ethnic affinities or borders'.[4]

However accurate the designation 'failed state' may be for the one-time

Somali Democratic Republic, it does not do justice to the complex realities on the ground. In fact, what many journalists refer to as 'Somalia' in their lurid accounts of the struggle for resources and power is really only the central and southern parts of the former national territory. Elsewhere in the Somali lands, away from the erstwhile capital of Mogadishu, alternative centres of power and stability have emerged. These emergent polities have enjoyed significant success in managing deep fault lines, thus offering not only a distinctly Somali solution to the national crisis, but also challenging a number of widely held notions about how societies and economies operate, including 'ideas about how politics operate in the absence of a government; how markets function without legal institutions and currencies; and how communities draw on customary forms of identity and organisation to tap markets and weather extraordinary levels of instability'.[5]

The Context of State Collapse

In order to appreciate both the role played by the state in Somali life and the consequences of its collapse, it is necessary to understand traditional patterns of identity and social organisation among the Somali. Somali identity is historically rooted in patrilineal descent (*tol*), meticulously memorialised in genealogies (*abtirsiinyo*, 'reckoning of ancestors'), which determines each individual's exact place in society. At the apex of this structure is the 'clan-family'. According to the usual division, the following are the major clan-families: Darod, Dir, Hawiye, Isaq, Digil and Rahanweyn. The first four, historically predominantly nomadic pastoralists, are reckoned 'noble' (*bilis*) clans, while the Digil and Rahanweyn (also known collectively as Digil Mirifle), who were cultivators and agro-pastoralists, occupy a second tier in Somali society. The latter also speak a dialect of Somali, *af-maymay*, which is distinct from the *af-maxaa* of the former. A third tier also exists in Somali social hierarchy, consisting of minority clans whose members, known collectively as *Sab*, historically carried out occupations such as metalworking and tanning which, in the eyes of the nomadic 'noble clans', rendered them ritually unclean.[6] It is notable that Muhammad Siyad Barre's vice-president and defence minister (and sometime prime minister), Mohamed Ali Samantar, was a *Sab* of metalworking background (*Tumal*). The choice of this particular officer, who was recently the defendant in a far-reaching human rights case adjudicated by the Supreme Court of the United States, for preferment undoubtedly had much to do with the fact that his origins make it highly unlikely that he could ever lead a coup against his benefactor.

The foremost living authority on Somali history and culture, British anthropologist I. M. Lewis, has noted that while 'clan-family member-ship has political implications, in the traditional structure of society the clan-families never act as united corporate groups for they are too large and unwieldy and their members too widely scattered'.[7] Consequently, the clan-families are segmented agnatically by reference to an eponymous ancestor at the head of each clan lineage. Within the clan, the most clearly defined subsidiary group is an individual's 'primary lineage', which also represents the limits of exogamy. Within the primary lineage, an individ-ual's primary identification is with what has been described as the '*diya*-paying group' (from the Arabic *diya*, 'blood-wealth'), the basic unit of Somali society. The members of a *diya*-paying group, who generally trace descent from a common male ancestor four to eight generations back, are united by formal political contract (*heer*) in collective responsibility for one another with respect to exogenous actors. If a member of a *diya*-paying group kills or injures someone outside the group, the members of his group are jointly responsible for that action and will collectively see to making reparation. Conversely, if one of its members is injured or killed, the *diya*-paying group will either collectively seek vengeance or share in whatever compensation may be forthcoming. Of course, the nature of the clan system is itself very nuanced and, while rooted in blood relationships, is also historically a consequence of nomadic pastoral life, with its need to defend scarce resources, that results, over time, in an openness to the formation of new alliances and, even later, in new identities.[8]

The pervasiveness of the clan system distinguished Somalia from the vast majority of post-independence African states, where the principal problem was the formation of a viable transcendent nationalism capable of uniting widely divergent ethnic groups who found themselves gathered together in 'states' created by colonialism. The Somali were different. They consisted of a single ethnic group with only one major internal division – that the Digil/Rahanweyn speak a distinctive dialect – and 'consid-ered themselves bound together by a common language, by an essentially nomadic pastoral culture, and by the shared profession of Islam'.[9] Nation-alism was already part of their experience in so far as it concerns national culture since they 'spoke the same language, shared the same predomi-nantly nomadic herding culture, and were all adherents of Sunni Islam with a strong attachment to the Sufi brotherhood'; all they lacked was political unity at the level of the culturally defined nation.[10] Thus Somalis formed an ethnic group or nation, but not, traditionally, a single polity. Despite fifty years of state building, urbanisation, civil war, state collapse and emigration, the bonds of kinship remain the most durable feature of Somali social, political and economic life. While ethnicity is a category with applicability vis-à-vis non-Somalis that a Somali may encounter, within Somali society it is clan that is the focus of identity, notwithstanding the fact that the latter, unlike the former, does not exhibit readily apparent formal 'markers', relying instead on genealogical criteria which, until fairly recently, were orally transmitted.

Modern 'Somalia' itself, which historically had never been a unified political entity, was born out of a union between the British Protectorate of Somaliland, which became independent as the State of Somaliland on 26 June 1960, and the territory then administered by Italy as a United Nations trust and which had, before the Second World War, been an Italian colony. The latter received its independence on 1 July 1960, and the two states, under the influence of the African nationalism fashionable during the period, entered into a union, even though, common language and religion notwithstanding, they had never developed a common sense of nationhood and had had very different colonial experiences. Consequently, by the time a military officer, Siyad Barre, seized power in October 1969, 'it had become increasingly clear that Somali parliamentary democracy had become a travesty, an elaborate, rarefied game with little relevance to the daily challenges facing the population'.[11]

A year after taking over, Siyad Barre proclaimed the Somali Democratic Republic, an officially Marxist state, and tried to stamp out clan identity as an anachronistic barrier to progress that ought to be replaced by nationalism and 'scientific socialism'. The non-kinship term *jaalle* ('friend' or 'comrade') was introduced to replace the traditional term of polite address *ina'adeer* ('cousin'). Traditional clan elders had their positions abolished or, at the very least, subsumed into the bureaucratic structure of the state. At the height of the campaign, it became a criminal offence to even refer to one's own or another's clan identity.[12] Given how deeply rooted the clan identity was, it was not surprising that *Jaalle* Siyad Barre failed in his efforts to efface the bonds. Ultimately, it was the regime itself which simply dissolved when, in January 1991, Siyad Barre – who had ironically evolved over time from a Soviet client into a US ally after President Jimmy Carter broke with the Ethiopian regime of Mengistu Haile Mariam over the latter's increasingly repressive human rights record[13]

– caught between popular rebellions led by the Isaq and Darod in the north as well as a Hawiye uprising in central Somalia, was ignominiously chased out of Mogadishu. By the time of the dictator's flight

> Somalia had fallen apart into the traditional clan and lineage divisions which, in the absence of other forms of law and order, alone offered some degree of security. The general situation now vividly recalled the descriptions of Burton and other nineteenth-century European explorers: a land of clan (and clan segment) republics where the would-be traveller needed to secure the protection of each group whose territory he sought to traverse.[14]

While, shortly after seizing power, Siyad Barre adopted 'scientific socialism' with the professed goal of uniting the nation by eliminating its ancient clan-based division, in order to maintain power the dictator soon fell back to calling on kinship ties – another example of their continuing relevance. With the exception of his previously mentioned defence chief, Siyad Barre's most trusted ministers came from his own patrilineal Marehan clan, followed by members of the Dhulbahante clan of his son-in-law Ahmed Suleiman Abdulle, who headed the notorious National Security Service, and then the Ogaden clan of his maternal kin. All three clans were part of the Darod clan-family. Siyad Barre's 'MOD' coalition of the three clans first led him into a disastrous Ogaden War (1977–8), a clumsy attempt to exploit the chaos of the Ethiopian Revolution in order to seize the eponymous territory. The resulting influx of over a million Ogadeni refugees created enormous problems for the Somali state (which became even more dependent upon humanitarian aid from its Western allies). These problems were exacerbated when half the refugees were placed in camps in the middle of the northern regions of Somaliland – the traditional home of their Isaq rivals. This led to the Isaq forming the Somali National Movement (SNM). Another result of the failed war was an abortive coup attempt by disaffected officers from the Majeerteen clan, another Darod group, against the regime; those who escaped arrest went on to form the Somali Salvation Democratic Front (SSDF) with the backing of their clansmen. Over the next decade the two new opposition groups, both born of a conflict that had its origins in Siyad Barre's own complicated political management strategy, would light the fuses that would ultimately explode not just the dictatorship but the Somali state with it.[15]

When, after the collapse of the Siyad Barre regime, the Hawiye leaders whose forces held sway over the abandoned capital, Muhammad Farah 'Aideed and Ali Mahdi, fell out with one other, the fighting and cutting off of food supplies brought about a humanitarian crisis which provoked global outrage, leading to no fewer than three successive international military interventions to secure more than ephemeral space for the flow of humanitarian assistance: the United Nations Operation in Somalia I (UNOSOM I, April–December 1992), the United States-led Unified Task Force (UNITAF, December 1992–May 1993) and United Nations Operation in Somalia II (UNOSOM II, March 1993–March 1995).[16] Following the UN's withdrawal, events in central and southern Somalia returned to the course they had been on before the brief interlude of international involvement, with armed clan factions mobilised by powerful figures – referred to by Somalis with the traditional title formerly reserved for battle leaders, *abbaanduule*, and thus quickly dubbed 'warlords' by foreign journalists – and sustained by the spoils of conflict battling each other for control of territory and such economic assets as existed, including bananas for export.[17]

Meanwhile, in the absence of effective political structures of any kind, Islamic authorities cropped up in response to problems of crime, sharia being a common denominator around which different communities could organise. The Islamic legal authorities gradually assumed policing as well as adjudicating functions, those authorities having greater (i.e., external) resources acquiring greater influence. It should be noted that the Somali traditionally adhere to Sunni Islam and follow its Shāfi'ī school (*mahdab*) of jurisprudence, which, although conservative, is open to a variety of liberal views regarding practice.[18] Throughout most of historical times up to independence in 1960, of the different movements within Sunni Islam in Somalia, the most dominant among the populace were the Sufi brotherhoods (*tarīqa*, plural *turuq*), especially that of the Qadiriyya order, although the Ahmadiyya order, introduced into Somali lands in the nineteenth century, was also influential.[19] While traditional Islamic schools and scholars (*ulamā*) played a role as focal points for rudimentary political opposition to colonial rule in Italian Somalia, historically their role in the politics of the Somali clan structure was neither institutionalised nor particularly prominent. In part this is because historically sharia was not especially entrenched in Somalia: being largely pastoralists, the Somali relied more on customary law (*xeer*) than on religious prescriptions.[20] Hence Somali Islamism is largely a post-colonial movement which became active in the late 1980s and, without the collapse of the state and the ensuing civil strife (and, some would add, the renewed US interest is terrorist linkages in the aftermath of the 11 September 2001 attacks), it is doubtful that militant Islamism would be much more than a marginal force in Somali politics.[21]

In the absence of a functioning state and amid the divisions of society, Islam came to be seen by some Somalis as an alternative to both the traditional clan-based identities and the emergent criminal syndicates led by so-called 'warlords'.[22] Religion's increased influence has been largely a phenomenon of small towns and urban centres, although increased adherence to its normative precepts is a wider phenomenon. Islamic religious leaders have helped organise security and other services and businessmen in particular were supportive of the establishment of sharia-based courts throughout the south, which was a precursor of the Islamic Courts Union established in Mogadishu in June 2006. Suffice to say the Islamists attempted to fill certain voids left by state collapse that were otherwise unattended to by emergent forces like the warlords. In doing so, they also made a bid to supplant clan and other identities, offering a pan-Islamist identity in lieu of other allegiances.[23]

Given their earlier experiences with Somali Islamism, especially al-Itihaad al-Islamiyya (AIAI, 'Islamic Union'), a group established in the early 1980s which sought the creation of an expansive Islamic Republic of Greater Somalia and eventually a political union embracing all Muslims in the Horn of Africa,[24] it was not surprising, after many of the same extremists emerged in positions of authority in the Islamic Courts Union, that neighbouring Ethiopia took a dim view of the establishment of the Islamic Courts Union in Mogadishu. The Ethiopians finally intervened in late 2006 to support Somalia's internationally backed[25] but weak 'Transitional Federal Government' (TFG), which had been established in October 2004 at a conference in Kenya promoted by the sub-regional Intergovernmental Authority on Development (IGAD).[26] Unfortunately, while the intervention ended the rule of the Islamic Courts Union in the desolate former capital, it also provoked an insurgency spearheaded by the even more radical Harakat al-Shabaab al-Mujahideen (Movement of Warrior Youth, al-Shabaab), a group subsequently designated a 'specially designated global terrorist' by the US Secretary of State Condoleezza Rice in 2008,[27] a 'listed terrorist organisation' by the Australian government the following year[28] and, in early 2010, a 'proscribed organisation' under the Terrorism Act by the British government[29] and a 'listed terrorist group' by the Canadian government.[30]

Even after Ethiopian troops withdrew in early 2009, the Shabaab-led insurgency against the TFG has continued, drawing the UN-authorised African Union Mission in Somalia (AMISOM) deployed to protect the transitional regime deeper into the conflict and causing them to suffer increasing casualties, with terrorist attacks like the suicide bombing of 17 September 2009, which killed seventeen peacekeepers, including the deputy force commander, Brigadier General Juvenal Niyoyunguruza of Burundi, and wounded more than forty others,[31] and that of 3 December 2009, which killed three TFG ministers as well as sixteen other people attending a graduation ceremony within the small enclave of Mogadishu thought to be still controlled by the beleaguered regime.[32] As it concluded its first year of existence in its current iteration under the former Islamic Courts Union leader Sheikh Sharif Sheikh Ahmed, the TFG was still 'not a government by any common-sense definition of the term: it is entirely dependent on foreign troops ... to protect its small enclave in Mogadishu, but otherwise administers no territory; even within this restricted zone, it has shown no functional capacity to govern, much less provide even minimal services to its citizens'.[33] The situation was such at the beginning of 2011 that the International Crisis Group went so far as to declare that members of the regime were 'not fit to hold public office and should be forced to resign, isolated, and sanctioned'.[34] A report from the organisation asserted that the TFG had 'squandered the goodwill and support it received and achieved little of significance in the two years it has been in office' and that 'every effort to make the administration modestly functional has become unstuck'.[35]

In fact, not only has the TFG 'failed to generate a visible constituency of clan or business supporters in Mogadishu', its very survival 'now depends wholly on the presence of AMISOM forces',[36] which were almost entirely responsible for the modest, but not insignificant, gains made against insurgent forces during a determined offensive in early 2011. Even then, despite a surge which brought the peacekeepers' troop strength to just over 9,000 and heavy fighting, the AMISOM commander acknowledged that it could claim to have secured only half of the Somali capital's sixteen districts.[37]

As for the TFG's own forces, out of the 9,000-plus troops which the three separate military missions – the United States, the European Union and France – have trained and armed for the regime over several years, no more than 1,000 remained by the end of 2010.[38] Efforts to supply this minuscule force have likewise proved counterproductive, as exemplified by the attempt by the United States to transfer some eighty tons of weapons and ammunition to the TFG in May 2009: just about the only noticeable change caused by the shipment was the collapse of prices in the arms market operating within walking distance of the government compound, suggesting that a significant proportion of the weapons were simply sold by corrupt regime officials.[39]

Alternative Centres

Fortunately, this *tour d'horizon* does not encompass the entire story of the Somali. In fact, the troubles faced by the TFG, which are sensationally generalised by journalists as those of the whole of Somalia, are more accurately those of a demographic minority. Consider the numbers: of the estimated 9 million Somalis in the world, more than 1 million of them are refugees or permanently living in the diaspora; 3.5 million live in the Republic of Somaliland and another 2.4 million in Puntland. Thus the conflicts of central and southern Somalia affect at most one-third of the national territory of the collapsed Somali Democratic Republic and directly impact the daily lives of less than one-third of the Somali population. As tragic as this is, it is still a far cry from the universal reign of endless chaos often imagined. Meanwhile, positive developments elsewhere in the former Somali state show what is possible when a 'bottom-up' or 'building-block' approach is allowed to take place instead of imposing the hitherto favoured 'top-down' strategy for resolving conflicts, consolidating peace and state building within a political space. In addition, it illustrates how a process that is viewed as legitimate and supported by the populace can also address the international community's interests about issues ranging from humanitarian concerns to maritime piracy and transnational terrorism.[40]

Although the sovereignty it reasserted has yet to be formally recognised by any other state, more than a decade and a half have gone by since Somaliland proclaimed the dissolution of its voluntary 1960 union with what was once the Somali Democratic Republic. The modern political history of Somaliland begins with the establishment, in 1884, of the British Somaliland Protectorate, which, except for a brief Italian occupation during the Second World War, lasted until 26 June 1960, when the territory received its independence.[41] Notification of the independence was duly communicated to the United Nations and some thirty-five members accorded the new state diplomatic recognition. Several days later, the Italian-administered UN trust territory of Somalia received its independence.

The two states then entered into a hasty union that a number of legal scholars have argued fell short of the minimal standards for legal validity and that the Somalilanders quickly regretted, due in no small measure to the discrimination the predominantly Isaq northerners suffered at the hands of the numerically superior members of clans from other regions.[42]

After the collapse of the Siyad Barre regime in 1991, elders representing the various clans in Somaliland met in the ravaged city of Burao and agreed to a resolution that annulled the northern territory's merger with the former Italian colony and declared that it would revert to the sovereign status it had enjoyed upon the achievement of independence from Great Britain. Unlike other parts of Somalia, conflict in the region was averted when the Somali National Movement (SNM), the principal opposition group that had led the resistance against the Siyad Barre dictatorship in the region, and Isaq clan leaders purposely reached out to representatives of other clans in Somaliland, including the Darod/Harti, Gadabuursi and Ise. The chairman of the SNM, Abdirahman Ahmed Ali 'Tuur', was appointed by consensus to be interim president of Somaliland for a period of two years by the Burao conference. In 1993 the Somaliland clans sent representatives to Borama for a national *guurti*, or council of elders, which elected Mohamed Haji Ibrahim Egal, who had briefly been prime minister of independent Somaliland in 1960 as well as democratically elected prime minister of Somalia between 1967 and the military coup in 1969, as president of Somaliland. Interestingly, while the apportionment of seats at the two conferences was done along clan lines in a rough attempt to reflect the demographics of the territory, the actually decision making was by consensus – thus obtaining the buy-in of minority clans and pre-empting the emergence of those fault lines.[43]

Egal's tenure saw, among other things, the drafting of a permanent constitution, approved by 97 per cent of the voters in a May 2001 referendum, which provided for an executive branch of government consisting of a directly elected president and vice-president and appointed ministers; a bicameral legislature consisting of an elected House of Representatives and an upper chamber of elders, the *guurti*; and an independent judiciary. After Egal's unexpected death in 2002, his vice-president, Dahir Riyale Kahin, succeeded to the presidency. Kahin, in turn, was elected in his own right in a closely fought election in April 2003 – the margin of victory for the incumbent was just eighty votes out of nearly half a million cast and, amazingly, the dispute was settled peaceably through the courts. Multiparty elections for the House of Representatives were held in September

2005 which gave the president's party just thirty-three of the eighty-two seats, with the balance split between two other parties.

Although the report of a 2005 African Union (AU) fact-finding mission led by then AU Commission Deputy Chairperson Patrick Mazimhaka concluded 'that the union between Somaliland and Somalia was never ratified and also malfunctioned when it went into action from 1960 to 1990 mak[ing] Somaliland's search for recognition historically unique and self-justified in African political history' and recommended that 'the AU should find a special method of dealing with this outstanding case',[44] no country has yet recognised Somaliland's independence. This apparent snub, while grating to Somalilanders, has not prevented them from building a vibrant polity with a strong civil society sector.

Left to their own devices, Somalilanders found the demobilisation of former fighters, the formation of national defence and security services, and the extraordinary resettlement of over 1 million refugees and internally displaced persons fostered the internal consolidation of their renascent polity, while the establishment of independent newspapers, radio stations and a host of local NGOs and other civic organisations reinforced the nation-building exercise. The stable environment thus created facilitated substantial investments by both local and diaspora businessmen, who have built, among other achievements, a telecommunications infrastructure that is more developed and varied than that in any of Somaliland's neighbours.[45]

In this context, one needs to single out the educational sector as not only a bridge between Somalilanders in the diaspora and their kinsmen at home, but also an important impetus for the reconstruction and development of the region. The showcase of this is Amoud University, the first institution of its kind in Somaliland, which opened its doors in Boroma in 1997. The school took its name from an eponymous high school that was the first institution of its kind under the British Protectorate and had been the alma mater for many distinguished Somalilanders. The university was founded as a modest joint effort by local citizens, who assumed responsibility for the initiative, and their relations abroad, especially in the Middle East, who raised money for it and sent textbooks and other supplies. The institution opened with just two academic departments, education and business administration – the former because of the dire need for teachers in the country, the latter because of the opportunities for employment in the private sector as well as the possibility of graduates starting their own businesses. Even a noted Somali critic of Somaliland's quest for independence has praised Amoud for having 'underscored the preciousness of investing in collective projects that strengthen common values and deepen peace' and 'given the population confidence that local resources can be mobilised to address development needs'.[46] Subsequently, universities have been established in Hargeisa (2000), Burco (2004) and Berbera (2009, although the institution has its origins in an older College of Fisheries and Maritime Management).

Unfortunately, Somaliland's political progress has stalled in recent years, due to the repeated postponement of presidential and legislative elections, beginning in 2008. In the author's judgement, while the crisis is 'home-grown', outside actors, especially the European Commission (EC) and the non-governmental organisation Interpeace, exacerbated the situation, however unintentionally. First, the nomination of the National Election Commission (NEC) by the president and the opposition-controlled parliament took longer than expected. Then the government in Hargeisa, the EC and Interpeace reached an agreement to undertake a new voter registration scheme throughout Somaliland that would result in the issue of a combination voter and national identification card – an admittedly important symbolic goal for a nascent state. Complicating the exercise further, the NEC, with the agreement of Somaliland's political parties, decided that the card would carry, in addition to a photograph of the bearer, biometric data. The whole process began only in October 2008 and was soon after interrupted by the suicide bombings carried out by al-Shabaab. When the process resumed, it was carried out with great enthusiasm and dispatch by both government and donors, so much so that fingerprint data was not collected from more than half of those registered and multiple registrations clearly took place in a number of localities. Eventually an internal compromise worked out in late September 2009 by all three of the region's political parties with encouragement from Ethiopia and the United Kingdom prorogued the term of the president and vice-president until one month after the holding of elections – whose date was not specified – thus preventing escalation of the crisis into violence, but still not holding elections. While the election problem is one rooted in Somaliland's internal politics, the outside actors did their local partners no favours by backing a process that was highly problematic from the outset and then, in the case of Interpeace, becoming embroiled as a party to the expanded conflict. Fortunately, good sense and some timely mediation by the traditional clan elders won the day, the internationally monitored presidential election in June 2010, which resulted in the defeat of the incumbent Kahin, the election of Ahmed Mohamed Mohamoud 'Silanyo' and a smooth transition between the two – an unheard of occurrence in the region – serving to further reinforce Somaliland's case for the international recognition that has thus far eluded it.

While they do not have the unique historical, juridical and political status that Somaliland can claim, the Darod territories in the northeastern promontory of Somalia have also demonstrated the success of the building-block model for the country and the wisdom of working with the deeply ingrained clan identities among the Somali. In 1998, tired of being held back by the constant violence and overall lack of social and political progress in central and southern Somalia, traditional clan elders of the Darod clan-family's Harti clan – including its Dhulbahante, Majeerteen and Warsangeli sub-groups – met in the town of Garowe and opted to undertake a regional state formation process of their own in the northeast, establishing in collaboration with the Somali Salvation Democratic Front (SSDF), the political faction that had represented their clan interests, an autonomous administration for what they dubbed 'Puntland State of Somalia'. After extensive consultations within the Darod/Harti clans and sub-clans, an interim charter was adopted which provided for a parliament whose members were chosen on a clan basis and who, in turn, elected a regional president, the first being Abdullahi Yusuf Ahmed, who in 2004 went on to become president of the TFG.[47] Following the departure of the region's first president for what was to be his disastrous tenure at the head of the TFG, Puntland legislators chose General Mohamud Muse Hersi ('Muse Adde') as the new head of the regional administration. After serving one four-year term of office, Muse Adde lost a bid for re-election to Abdirahman Mohamed Mohamud 'Farole', who was elected in January 2009 from a field of over a dozen candidates.

Unlike Somaliland, which has opted to reassert its independence, Puntland in its constitution simultaneously supports the notion of a federal Somalia and asserts the region's right to negotiate the terms of union with any eventual national government.[48] While Puntlanders have their share of difficulties – many of which could be said fairly to be of their own making – and their political institutions have not yet achieved the advanced level of those in Somaliland, engaging the region's leaders is nonetheless the sine qua non for achieving what should be the international community's two primary strategic objectives in Somalia: containing (and gradually weakening) the radical Islamist threat to regional security and minimising (and likewise eventually suppressing) the menace posed to merchant shipping by Somali pirates, many of whom have based themselves in the region and, short of military invasion and occupation, whose havens cannot be denied without the cooperation of the authorities in Puntland. It should be noted that, while the authorities in Puntland have been especially diligent in their efforts to root out religious extremism in their midst, their commitment to the fight against piracy is less consistent. Eyl and Garaad in Puntland, together with Hobyo and Xarardheere in central Somalia, have emerged as the primary centres of pirate activity where 'senior officials are believed to be abetting piracy networks'.[49] Some analysts go even further and worry that the region is 'becoming the pirate version of a narco-state'.[50] This development should not be surprising given that in 2008, for example, a year in which it is estimated that over 100 million dollars was paid in ransom to the pirates operating there, the entire budget for the Puntland State amounted to 11.7 million dollars.[51] Thus it remains to be determined whether or not Puntland authorities are prepared for or even capable of entering into some sort of a 'grand bargain' with the international community whereby they rein in their pirate constituents in return for political and economic engagement by the international community – an idea that was endorsed in the final report of former French minister Jack Lang, special adviser to the UN Secretary-General on Somali piracy.[52] A recent report by the Council on Foreign Relations in the United States suggests one possible direction that such engagement might take:

> Development agencies should also seek to create a partnership with Puntland's legitimate business community – probably the only social segment currently strong enough to challenge the pirate networks. The international community could focus on organizing the professional community in Puntland into a professional association, providing capacity-building support and engaging the group in a discussion about what can be done to reduce piracy. A program that explicitly ties development incentives in the coastal zones to antipiracy efforts could effectively mobilize a population tiring of pirate promiscuity and excess.[53]

Processes similar to those in Somaliland and Puntland are also being seen elsewhere among the Somali. In the central regions of Galguduud and Mudug, for example, the local residents set up several years ago what they have dubbed the 'Galmudug State', complete with its own website.[54] In 2009 they elected a veteran of the old Somali military, Colonel

Mohamed Ahmed Alin, to a three-year term as the second president of what describes itself as 'a secular, decentralised state'. A similar process is taking place in Jubaland along the frontier with Kenya, apparently with the backing of the latter, which wants a buffer between it and the anti-TFG Islamist insurgency. In 2010 local clans in the region began forming a secular administration of their own. In April 2011 it was announced that the new autonomous authority of 'Azania' had been inaugurated, with the TFG's own defence minister, Mohamed Abdi Mohamed 'Gandhi', as its first president.[55] There are similar stirrings among the Hawiye, both in the Benadir region around Mogadishu and the Hiiraan region on the Ethiopian border, and among the Digil/Rahanweyn clans further south.

In any event, vital to the relatively successful efforts by Somaliland, Puntland and other areas to avoid both major internal conflict and embroilment in the violence affecting most of southern Somalia has been the role played by their clans. It was traditional clan elders who negotiated questions of political representation in key forums. In circumstances where elections were impossible, representatives were designated by clan units from among their members through a deliberative process in which all adult males had an opportunity to participate and where decisions were made on a consensual basis. The resulting social contract is – in stark contrast to the TFG process, which emphasises the individual actor – one between groups with deeply rooted legitimacy in kinship and geographic bonds.

Interestingly, another trait which the authorities in Somaliland and Puntland share with each other, but not with the TFG in Mogadishu, has been the fact that they have largely been self-supporting with respect to governmental finances. It has been argued that one of the most significant factors undermining state formation in Africa has been a limited revenue base: that is, a dependence on foreign aid and/or natural resource extraction for revenue. Throughout the world, the experience has been that taxation as a means of raising revenue not only provides income for the state, but facilitates a greater cohesion between the state and its stakeholders. In contrast, the virtual absence of taxation in post-colonial Africa has resulted in regimes that are largely decoupled from their societies.[56] From this perspective, it is telling that the most advanced state-building project among the Somalis has been in Somaliland, where the government collects taxes and licence fees from business and real estate owners and imposes duties on the *khat* trade as well as imports and exports through the port of Berbera. Likewise, the second most successful endeavour is in

Puntland, where the reliance on customs duties and an occasional fisheries licence is perhaps more remote than direct taxes, but nonetheless requires that the government maintain certain minimum levels of efficiency (thus another reason why revenue flows from piracy, which has been centred in Puntland, are pernicious). In contrast, the TFG and its predecessors relied exclusively on foreign aid.

Perhaps most importantly in the context of the rising tide of Islamist militancy in southern and central Somalia is the fact that, as one of the most astute observers of contemporary Somali society has observed, this reliance – especially in Somaliland, but also in Puntland – on the older system of clan elders and the respect they command 'has served as something of a mediating force in managing pragmatic interaction between custom and tradition; Islam and the secular realm of modern nationalism', leading to a unique situation where 'Islam may be pre-empting and/or containing Islamism'.[57] The consequence of having an organic relationship between Somali culture and tradition and Islam appears to assure a stabilising, rather than disruptive, role for religion in society in general and religion and politics in particular. In Somaliland, for example, while the population is almost exclusively Sunni Muslims and the *shahāda*, the Muslim profession of the oneness of God and the acceptance of Muhammad as God's final prophet, is emblazoned on the flag, sharia is only one source of the three sources of the jurisprudence in the region's courts, alongside secular legislation and Somali traditional law (*xeer*). On the other hand, given the limited resources of the Somaliland government, Qur'anic schools play an important role in basic education. Yet alongside these popular institutions stand equally well-received secular charities like the Hargeisa's Edna Adan Maternity Hospital, founded in 2002 by Edna Adan Ismail, the former foreign minister of Somaliland, which provides a higher standard of care than available anywhere else in the Somali lands for maternity and infant conditions, as well as diagnosis and treatment for HIV/AIDS and sexually transmitted diseases and general medical conditions. Thanks to this integrative approach, the northern clans have largely managed to 'domesticate' the challenge of political Islam in a manner that their southern counterparts would do well to emulate.

Lessons Learned

The now decades-old crisis in Somalia may have at its origin the collapse of a 'failed state', but blame for the prolongation of the misery would be more accurately attributed to a wholesale failure of imagination on the part of the international community and its local clients. First, they have been fixated almost exclusively on southern and central Somalia, continually repeating the mistakes of their successive 'top-down' attempts at state building, while obstinately refusing to even acknowledge the largely positive experiences in other parts of the country. Second, their approach has been almost entirely centred upon the state, while ignoring the traditional clan leaders, members of the vibrant Somali business community and civil society actors – the very people whose efforts have prevented statelessness from degenerating into complete anarchy and disorder and who have repeatedly shown themselves to be the best-positioned to bridge the deep fissures in Somali society. Third, when they do deign to intervene through proxies like the brave, but perhaps hapless, Ugandan and Burundian troops deployed in the beleaguered AMISOM peacekeeping force, instead of husbanding those scarce resources to contain the spread of the instability from Somalia and prevent additional foreign fighters and supplies from fuelling the conflict in the country, they expend them in a vain effort to prop up an unpopular and illegitimate regime and impose a peace where one does not exist.

In this regard, the comments of that remarkable scholar of the Somali I. M. Lewis are worth reporting:

> If further progress is to be achieved in state-formation, Somali politicians will surely have to come out of 'denial' and start seriously exploring how clan and lineage ties can be utilised positively. Perhaps they could learn from their nomadic kinsmen who unashamedly celebrate these traditional institutions. Here a less Eurocentric and less evolutionary view of lineage institutions by Western commentators, social scientists, and bureaucrats might help to create a more productive environment for rethinking clanship (i.e. agnation) positively.[58]

In contrast, the creation of the current version of the 'Transitional Federal Government' at the beginning of 2009 was an exercise in political management which, while it made the requisite bows to Somali bonds of kinship, was more designed to impose a certain preconceived notion. Since an Islamist insurgency was perceived to be the chief challenge, a supposed 'moderate' Islamist was installed at the head of the TFG through the extra-legal machinations of a group of ersatz parliamentarians designated for that purpose by the Special Representative of the United Nations Secretary-General, doubling the size of the already bloated legislature. The parliament also extended its own term by two years, although by what legal authority no one knows, although the matter is largely irrelevant as it has not in fact been legally convened since April 2009 for want of a quorum.[59] As for the new president, it was simply assumed that because he was an Islamist, he would be able to win over other Islamists. As it turns out, his backers failed to take into account the clan dynamics and soon learned that Sharif Ahmed had trouble rallying his own Abgaal kinsmen.[60] By year's end, the current TFG controlled even less of Mogadishu than its unpopular predecessor did, despite the presence of an AMISOM force of what was then more than 5,000 troops. The regime's few forces are regarded as just another armed faction – and quite justifiably so since they behave like one – while the TFG itself has done little to establish its bona fides. A March 2010 report by the United Nations Monitoring Group on Somalia was especially damning in its assessment of the interim regime and was, for all intents and purposes, a scathing indictment not only of the TFG, but of any policy built on it:

> The military stalemate is less a reflection of opposition strength than of the weakness of the Transitional Federal Government. Despite infusions of foreign training and assistance, government security forces remain ineffective, disorganised and corrupt – a composite of independent militias loyal to senior government officials and military officers who profit from the business of war and resist their integration under a single command. During the course of the mandate, government forces mounted only one notable offensive and immediately fell back from all the positions they managed to seize. The government owes its survival to the small African Union peace support operation, AMISOM, rather than to its own troops ...[61]
>
> The security sector as a whole lacks structure, organisation and a functional chain of command – a problem that an international assessment of the security sector attributes to 'lack of political commitment by leaders within the Transitional Federal Government or because of poor common command and control procedures' ... To date, the Transitional Federal Government has never managed to deploy regimental or brigade-sized units on the battlefield.
>
> The consequences of these deficiencies include an inability of the security forces of the Transitional Federal Government to take and hold ground, and very poor public perceptions of their performance by the Somali public. As a result, they have made few durable military gains

during the course of the mandate, and the front line has remained, in at least one location, only 500 metres from the presidency.[62]

While the security situation has evolved to be somewhat less dire – thanks largely to improved training for AMISOM, as well as the outbreak of famine in 2011, which weakened al-Shabaab – it remains precarious. Even when al-Shabaab retreated from Mogadishu in August 2011, the failure of the TFG to fill the space the insurgents vacated led, in little less than a month, to their return in several districts, while others fell under the control of warlords. The inescapable conclusion to be drawn from the evidence the Monitoring Group exhaustively mustered is that about the only thing members of the TFG do well – aside from letting foreign forces fight battles and suffer casualties for them – is to engage in criminal activity, ranging from simple theft of resources to visa fraud. A more viable course than anything hitherto adopted by the international community will be one that, by adapting to the decentralised nature of Somali social reality and privileging the 'bottom-up' approach, is better suited to buy Somalis themselves the time and space within which to make their own determinations about their future political arrangements, while at the same time being flexible enough to allow their neighbours and the rest of the international community to protect their legitimate security interests. Supporting governance at the level where it is accountable and legitimate – whether in the context of the nascent states like Somaliland and Puntland in the northern regions or the nascent polities, local communities and civil society structures in parts of the south – is the most effective and efficient means of both managing the societal fault lines and countering the security threats that have arisen in the wake of the collapse of the Somali state.

If the failure so far of all internationally backed attempts at establishing a national government and the uncertainty surrounding the current effort indicate anything, it is the futility of the notion that outsiders can impose a regime on Somalia. The Somali crisis can be resolved only by an approach that is rooted in Somali culture, especially those organic links which bind Somalis of all backgrounds to the social identities that have been their ultimate refuge amidst the vicissitudes of their recent turbulent history.

PART TWO:
PEACE THROUGH POLITICS

5

FROM BOMBS TO BALLOTS: THE RISE OF POLITICS IN NORTHERN IRELAND

Chris Brown

'The Irish never forget and the English never remember'

William Gladstone

M OST OF THE STUDIES in this book concern states. Northern Ireland, geographically connected to what since partition in 1921 has been the Free State and subsequently the Republic of Ireland, remains a part of the United Kingdom, albeit physically separated from Great Britain. It was a political compromise at the time of partition: a seemingly pragmatic solution to the demands of the Nationalist majority on the island of Ireland for independence from the United Kingdom, while appeasing the overall minority Unionist community, whose concentration in Ulster gave them a majority in the six counties which now comprise Northern Ireland. There are other examples[1] of such geographical entities, but Northern Ireland has proved to be a microcosm of the fault lines which caused the original partition of the island of Ireland.

Northern Ireland's fault lines are on the one hand relatively simple: a bipolar society where religious, economic, political, cultural and social divisions tend to be mutually reinforcing. On the other hand this makes for difficult, temptingly simplistic, categorisation that ignores the more complex contributing factors which require analysis in order to offer mitigation strategies addressing specific issues, rather than combating the entire hydra.

Attempts to deal with this complexity during the forty years of the current 'Troubles' have spawned a multitude of structures; for that reason alone, Northern Ireland makes an instructive case study.

Northern Ireland illustrates, moreover, the importance of differentiating between conflict prevention, which attempts to stop a fault line from erupting in the first place; conflict termination measures, which aim to halt an existing eruption while not necessarily addressing the underlying cause; and conflict resolution measures, which seek reconvergence.[2] Partition in 1921 was arguably a conflict termination rather than a conflict resolution strategy; the challenge is foresight, not hindsight.

Religion: Root Cause or Pretext?

It is simplistic, indeed untrue, to lump Catholicism with nationalism and Protestantism with unionism, but the religious divide was the original fault line which lay at the heart of Ireland's troubles from the Protestant settlement of the sixteenth and seventeenth centuries. It is not a neat fault line: although the Protestant settlers concentrated in the north of the island, there remained a minority Catholic population in what is now Northern Ireland. More significantly, there has always been a significant minority of Catholic Unionists and an increasing number of Protestant Nationalists. Religion per se has decreased as a fault line over time; however, it reinforces many of the Province's social and economic challenges, not least education, housing and employment. It has therefore frequently been used as an excuse for all Northern Ireland's woes.

Eruptions of this main fault line have arguably never, at least since partition, been solely religious in their cause. The trigger for the eruption which occurred in the late 1960s was social and political: Catholics, particularly those in the poor estates of Belfast and Londonderry, saw themselves as second-class citizens, denied the perceived advantages of Protestantism and oppressed by a police force which was predominantly Protestant. Bringing in the British Army for internal security was therefore seen by both London and, at least initially, Catholics as an admission of failure of civilian policing and as a conflict termination strategy, designed to provide impartial security. In itself, however, it did little to address the underlying social and political fault lines. True, the Royal Ulster Constabulary (RUC) was reformed with the disbandment of the Special Constabulary, the almost exclusively Protestant reserve force which had been mobilised as unrest had increased, but if anything the barriers, both the physical ones erected by the army to quell unrest and the psychological ones created by the increasingly mono-sectarian existence of respective communities, deepened the divide. As so often happens, the intervention of a third force perpetuated, indeed cemented, the fault line with two consequences: both sides could increase the rhetoric with relative impunity and the intervening force became an alternative target for the frustrations of both sides. The underlying levels of unemployment provided a ready source of agitators; the underlying housing dereliction provided a ready source of bricks for the agitators to hurl at each other. Inevitably bricks fell short. Soldiers who thought they were there to protect the population became the target, deliberate or otherwise, of increasing levels of rioting throughout the early 1970s. Their predictable reaction was interpreted by the Catholics as a lack of impartiality. This was a tipping point. The Catholic community sought an alternative source of protection: the IRA, the military wing of Republican Sinn Fein, added the political dimension to the fault line. Internal splits within the IRA saw the emergence of the Provisional IRA (PIRA) as the self-proclaimed guardian of the Catholic community. Those who had hitherto thrown bricks were easy prey to the intoxicating brew of hero worship bestowed on those who took up arms in defence of their community. In reaction to sectarian attacks, Protestants also developed their own means of providing security for their communities with organisations such as the Ulster Volunteer Force, harking back to the origins of the armed struggle that had surrounded the 1921 partition. In addition to attacks on security forces and the opposite sect, both sides applied 'community justice' to those who infringed their own rules. The more the level of violence increased, the more the army and police concentrated on defeating the perpetrators rather than protecting the population, the more the situation deteriorated, the more British forces became the manifestation of British oppression. In the eyes of the Nationalist community, the British Army had lost its legitimacy, marked by incidents such as 'Bloody Sunday' in January 1972 and international condemnation of security force interrogation tactics.[3] The year 1972 saw a peak in both members of the security forces killed and barricaded communities, such as the Bogside and Creggan estates in Londonderry, which became no-go areas for security forces. Operation MOTORMAN in the summer of that year saw the largest concentration of military forces to remove the barricades.[4] At the same time as the unofficial barricades were being removed in order to restore law and order, barricades were being erected by the security forces around city centres to stem the ingress of bombs. As the military regained some degree of stabilisation in urban areas, so the manifestation of the fault line mutated from mass public order to a terrorist campaign, using the porous border with the Republic as a safe haven.

An important step in the re-establishment of legitimacy was the transfer from the mid-1970s to police, rather than military, primacy for security. Police officers routinely accompanied army patrols to provide an important degree of community policing, even where this was resented. Wherever the security situation permitted, the Republican narrative of the British Army as an occupying force was countered by utilisation of the Ulster Defence Regiment (UDR), volunteers drawn from the community, albeit largely Unionists, which increasingly took responsibility for security in their respective counties. The UDR[5] had the added advantage of continuity – some served on active duty for more than thirty years – which created far more awareness of the situation than could be achieved by regular army units rotating through the Province on six-month tours of duty. Continuity in British security forces was enhanced by the adoption of two-year tours of duty for formation (brigade and above) headquarters staff and by intelligence continuity staff attached to regular rotational battalions.[6] Rather than sallying forth from large isolated bases into the community, security forces were based as far as possible in the community. This provided security which the IRA could not replicate and also steeled the RUC to operate as a community police force where they otherwise would have been too vulnerable. From the 1990s until the end of military operations in 2007, the intelligence network was reinforced by observation towers along the border with the Republic. Legitimisation of the military's increased powers of arrest, detention and so on was enshrined in law, including the Justice and Security (Northern Ireland) Act 2007 and its predecessor Terrorism Act 2000, which also proscribed fourteen terrorist groups and established an Independent Assessor of Military Complaints Procedures, a unique step which further engendered confidence in the military's role.

From the mid-1970s the IRA dual track of 'ballot box and Armalite' was used by the UK government to encourage their reliance on the former rather than the latter. Negotiation with the Republican leadership eventually led to their reconciliation and political engagement.[7] Herein lay, and still lies, the key to conflict resolution. Its success required enduring commitment at the highest political level. Moreover, it required negotiation from a position of strength. The UK political leadership's relegation of Irish-related terrorism, grouped with animal rights activists, to a single reference in the 2008 version of the National Security Strategy tragically contrasts with the murders of two soldiers and a police officer in March 2009.

Ownership of the strategic narrative in Northern Ireland was in many ways as important for both sides as actual realisation of respective end states. There are as many versions of Irish history from 1689 as there are historians. In an attempt by the British government to dominate the narrative during the latest eruption, Republican leaders were precluded from speaking on British media. This backfired. The media merely dubbed the words of actors with similar accents over footage of the Republican interviewee. The solution has proved to be 'constructive ambiguity', allowing both sides to maintain its narrative. The inherent short-termism in this approach may ultimately be more difficult to reconcile, however.

The role of the Church in conflict resolution is worthy of examination in the context of Northern Ireland. Even though the triggers for eruption of the fault lines were seldom religious, healing those fault lines could be achieved only with the support of the clergy. Conversely, inflammatory remarks by clergy, particularly where the religious fault line was conflated with politics,[8] were doubly difficult to heal. The clergy's role has been broadened to include wider conflict resolution initiatives, such as Archbishop Robin Eames's chairmanship of the Consultative Group on the Past.

Sporadic terrorist incidents continue,[9] and will continue, but attack levels are now a fraction of their peak. The remaining threat emanates from Republican splinter groups[10] which split from the Provisional IRA when the latter embraced the political process. Dissident Republicanism charges PIRA and Sinn Fein of 'selling out' to the British. Key is that it has no political agenda other than the unification of Ireland by violent means, focused on attempts to regenerate sectarian violence to the extent that it undermines the existing political institutions in Northern Ireland; brings British military forces back into the policing role; and convinces Westminster that the blood and treasure costs of retaining Northern Ireland within the UK are too great. It is not therefore susceptible to a political agenda in the same way as mainstream Republicanism. It is both disavowed by most Republicans and relies for its survival on Republican communities where either fear or high unemployment outweighs the perceived advantage of turning the perpetrators over to the police. Concerted efforts to cut the dissident Republicans' supply of funds and weaponry have forced them to harness diminished resources for spectacular attacks[11] which, while attracting media attention, have not reversed the underlying downward trend in violence. Nevertheless, successful attacks do reinforce the mystique of the dissidents while, at the same time, undermining the credibility of those mainstream Republicans who are engaged in the political process. The greatest danger is therefore defection within mainstream Republicanism, individuals or groups, to the dissident cause. In countering this, there is a clear role to be played by the security forces in defeating the dissidents, but an equal, arguably more crucial, role for the political process to demonstrate progress for Northern Ireland in general, but specifically as regards the Republican agenda. In that lies danger for the Unionists in conceding ground to the Republicans to the extent either that Unionist support for the existing political process evaporates[12] or that maintenance of Northern Ireland as part of the UK is pointless, thereby gifting the Republican end state of a united Ireland.

Political Divisions

The Unionist–Nationalist divide has always been at the heart of Northern Ireland politics. Even though the vote on both sides may from time to time be split by intra-sectarian divides, the existential threat has always been sufficient to coalesce the vote along these traditional lines when push came to shove. The Unionists, traditionally with a two-thirds demographic majority, could therefore always rest assured that they would ultimately remain dominant.[13] Unionist compromise was therefore seldom necessary. Parties which attempt to bridge the sectarian divide are not new, but their popularity has always been limited.[14] Similarly, coalitions between Unionist and Nationalist elements have been attempted, but have withered when confronted with existential issues. And the divide is so bipolar as to exclude the possibility of a third-party king-maker. Faced with such intransigence, Republican inclination to eschew politics was unsurprising.

The key therefore to progressive political engagement was to find a system whereby the Nationalist community felt that politics was worth pursuing and where Republicanism could find political, rather than violent, expression. This became the goal of much of the dialogue from the mid-1970s. Various formulae were tried. The stick for both sides was the removal of power from Stormont self-rule to direct rule from Westminster; the carrot was peaceful conflict resolution.[15] The first major initiative – the 1974 Sunningdale Agreement – established a power-sharing formula between the UUP and the SDLP (Nationalist) and north–south bodies, not dissimilar to today's structures. It was opposed by both the DUP and

Sinn Fein and sank later that year on the rocks of the Ulster Workers Council strike. The current power-sharing executive, created under the St Andrews Agreement in October 2006, has a Unionist First Minister and a Republican Deputy First Minister with four ministries allocated to the DUP, three to Sinn Fein, two to the Alliance Party and one each to the UUP and SDLP, reflecting the membership[16] of the elected Northern Ireland Assembly. A further Ministry of Policing and Justice was created when those functions, previously exercised from Westminster, returned to Stormont in 2010. However, the power-sharing executive, conflict-preventive though it has proved to be, is not a system which has elsewhere been conducive to legislative efficiency or long-term conflict resolution.[17] The question is therefore when the fault line is sufficiently healed to permit a more traditional, adversarial political system. The answer is not yet, but the issue is already on the Unionist agenda.

However, Northern Ireland politics is not an isolated process: it is played out against the background of wider political engagement between London and Dublin. Traditional Irish suspicion of British agendas, char-acterised by much of the east–west politicking from partition until the mid-1980s, created a fault line which has only recently been closed as the two sides gained confidence, not least the Irish, whose economic success during the 1990s has led to a maturity, both economic and political, which has transformed the Republic's status, particularly within Europe. Dublin and London did not traditionally share the same goals. The narrowing of that divide therefore became a key, not only to unlocking the deadlock in Northern Ireland politics, but also to improved relations between the two capitals, based on equality as sovereign nations. A significant milestone was the Hillsborough Anglo-Irish Agreement in November 1985, establish-ing a north–south inter-governmental forum. Her Majesty's visit to the Republic in May 2011 – the first such visit since partition – is the most recent manifestation of the maturity of this fault-line healing process. As far as Northern Ireland politics is concerned, independence has never been a realistic option and therefore both Unionists and Nationalists have traditionally looked over their shoulders for what they see as their ultimate guarantors. Both the DUP and Sinn Fein opposed the 1985 Agreement. The DUP also opposed its successor Good Friday Belfast Agreement in 1998, which repealed Articles 2 and 3 of the Irish Constitution;[18] set up a north–south ministerial council and parliamentary forum; and agreed a common approach on symbols and emblems. However, both London and Dublin have consistently made it clear to the politicians in Northern

Ireland that their prime interest lay in peaceful conflict resolution, rather than partisan support for one or other cause. This has disabused both sides from their former predilection for sabre-rattling in the belief that reinforcement from Dublin or London was guaranteed. On the other hand this distancing has meant that London and Dublin have enjoyed decreasing influence with both sides in Northern Ireland. The Belfast Agreement also paved the way for the release of terrorist prisoners, decommissioning of terrorist weapons under the supervision of an independent international body and further reform of the police under the 1999 Patten Report. This led to the change from the RUC to the Police Service of Northern Ireland (PSNI) with its quota system of Catholic officers.[19] The success of this approach led to Sinn Fein's January 2007 pledge of support for policing in Northern Ireland and the consequent July 2007 withdrawal of the military from the internal security role.

The Economic Divide

'Ireland has been stunted in her development by the English invasion and thrown centuries back'[20]

The post-Second World War decline of Northern Ireland's shipbuilding and linen industries exacerbated the economic differential between Northern Ireland and mainland Britain, while Northern Ireland's traditional economic links with the south did little to bolster the decline in the north in the 1960s and 1970s. In the 1960s Ireland was one of the poorest countries in Western Europe, with a GDP of 60 per cent of the EU average. Different taxation regimes north and south of the border have long been a source of trade, both legal and illegal. Illegal trade funded terrorist coffers. For a long time the police were so occupied by the terrorist threat that they had little capacity to deal with 'good honest crime'. However, the accession of Ireland to the European Union in 1973 made the Republic a net beneficiary of EU structural and cohesion funding.[21] Coupled with a taxation and regulatory regime conducive to economic growth, including one of the lowest rates of corporation tax in the developed world, and a time zone which made it an ideal bridge between Irish diaspora-owned businesses in the USA and mainland Europe, to whose single market it now had access, the south's meteoric economic rise during the 1980s, 1990s and up to 2007[22] had the greatest beneficial spin-off of any of the economic measures designed to assist Northern Ireland. Always a step behind and a degree lower than its southern neighbour in growth, Northern Ireland rode the 'Celtic tiger' to huge benefit. The downside of this phenomenon is that Northern Ireland has suffered disproportionately in relation to the rest of the United Kingdom as the economic downturn bit over the last three years.

Employment in Northern Ireland was traditionally split along sectarian lines.[23] Although it is illegal to ask the religion of an employee or potential employee, the housing divide discussed below would invariably pigeonhole an employee by his or her address. Unemployment was clearly and directly related to unrest from the outset. One way in which the employment situation was conscientiously engineered to mitigate against the economic and sectarian fault lines was an increase in the size of the public sector. While this was an effective conflict prevention tactic, it has left Northern Ireland with a bloated public sector which can be sustained only by subsidy from Westminster greater than any other region of the UK. A swing to the private sector, much vaunted but as yet undelivered, would undoubtedly assist broader conflict resolution.

Social Segregation[24]

Much of the discontent which precipitated the Troubles had social underpinnings. Standards of social housing in 1960s Northern Ireland lagged behind those in the rest of the UK. Education was, and remains, largely divided along sectarian lines. Articulation of these issues, for example by John Hume,[25] and the Northern Ireland Civil Rights Association protests which triggered these fault lines in the late 1960s were in many ways Northern Ireland's answer to the social unrest across much of Europe at the time.

Perhaps the most insidious aspect of the religious divide in Northern Ireland is its application to education. The majority of schooling is split on sectarian lines. And while the role of the Church in conflict prevention is nowhere better seen than in schools, the mere institutionalisation of the fault line from an age of innocence means that most children, particularly those in areas where housing is also segregated, emerge from the schooling system with entrenched sectarian views.[26] Arguably, therefore, the greatest contribution to conflict resolution in Northern Ireland lies with reform of the education system.

As violence escalated in the early 1970s communities in which Catholic and Protestant had lived as neighbours, particularly in Belfast and

Londonderry, witnessed segregation which entrenched the lines along which housing was divided. Address became synonymous with religion. The sinister comment 'We know where you live' implied both knowledge of your religion and an ability to inflict revenge. Interfaces between Catholic and Protestant housing provided the flashpoints for rioting. The conflict termination tactic of creating 'peace lines', walls which separated one sect's housing from the other's, has proved effective in reducing levels of violence, but at the same time formalised the fault line so as to work against conflict resolution. In recent years therefore experiments have been conducted in removing the 'peace lines'; sadly, though, more are still being erected than removed. Interestingly the economic growth that Northern Ireland has witnessed in the last decade has had different effects on both communities in respect of housing. Enriched Protestants have tended to forsake their traditional inner-city enclaves for the leafy suburbs and beyond, while prosperous Catholics have frequently remained in their traditional communities at the same time as improving their housing status. Smart redevelopments of derelict sites in districts such as the Falls are proving attractive to Catholics who have 'made good'.

The fault line instilled at school and reinforced by physically divided communities is perpetuated through social activity along sectarian lines, none more so than in the Protestant Orange Lodge tradition of thinly disguised provocative marching through Catholic or interface areas. The resultant mass public order incidents of the early days of the Troubles have now been mitigated by several strategies designed to defuse the inherent tension by a process which lays down routes, timings and so on for approval by commissions representing both communities. The 2006 St Andrews Agreement also established a strategic review of parading. Nevertheless, Unionist MLA Edwin Poots, when Minister for Environment and Culture in August 2008, described the Orange Order as a 'backward-facing, history obsessed, parish-pump society'.

Sport has played a significant role in conflict resolution in Northern Ireland because of its ability to unite north and south, Protestant and Catholic. True, the Catholic sporting focus has traditionally been the Gaelic Athletic Association; and sport can be divisive, the classic example being the 'old firm' soccer rivalry between Glasgow Rangers and Glasgow Celtic, the respective colours of which flagrantly advertise the sectarian background of their supporters on the streets of Scotland and Northern Ireland, but Ireland has examples of sport's ability to heal where it is played on a combined north–south basis, not least with rugby. The pitfalls in this approach to conflict resolution are exemplified in the debate over the future of the former Maze prison site, replete with PIRA mythology, as a national stadium, but sport is worth consideration in the wider context of nation building and fault-line healing.

Rule of Law: The State v. the People

The widespread Catholic perception of discrimination or intimidation by the state, in terms of housing and employment, also applied to justice. The make-up of the civil police has been discussed above, but the wider justice system fell prey to sectarian prejudice as violence escalated. Objectivity of juries proved increasingly unreliable. Non-jury trials in so-called Diplock Courts proved a pragmatic and effective approach to this challenge. Northern Ireland has also spawned an unprecedented number of inquiries, from those set up to examine the 1972 'Bloody Sunday' incident to the public inquiries set up by the Secretary of State for Northern Ireland under Canadian Judge Peter Corey in accordance with the August 2001 Weston Park Agreement between the British and Irish governments to investigate disputed murders. In addition the PSNI Historical Enquiries Team (HET) is currently reinvestigating more than 3,000 deaths during the Troubles.[27] Inquiries have become an industry in Northern Ireland, as have the associated damage claims.

Role of External Actors

The UK government has always considered Northern Ireland to be an internal issue and therefore resisted external intervention. A UN peacekeeping role, for example, was unconscionable. Nevertheless, the considerable Irish diaspora, not least in the USA, made external interest and interference inevitable. One of the targets of Republican strategic narrative was the US Irish Catholic diaspora. This had two primary effects: under organisations such as NORAID substantial funding for the Republican cause was raised. Following the attacks on the USA in September 2001, the narrative was turned on its head in London, Washington and Dublin to stem the flow of funds, but by that stage hundreds had been killed by weaponry funded in Boston.[28] Secondly, the Irish-American vote produced sufficient leverage in Washington to apply pressure on the UK, both to resolve the conflict and to involve external actors in the resolution process. Senator George Mitchell was appointed by President Clinton as the US envoy to Northern Ireland, a successful tactic which assisted in brokering much progress in the late 1990s.[29] Mechanisms such as the Independent International Committee on Decommissioning, led by Canadian General John De Chastelain, have achieved significant decommissioning of terrorist weapons, while the Independent Monitoring Committee (IMC)[30] has provided objective assessments of progress towards conflict resolution which are respected by all sides; this in itself has converged some of the otherwise divergent strategic narrative.

Northern Ireland Fault-line Management Strategies' Applicability to Other Situations

The danger in a simplistic mutatis mutandis approach to conflict resolution is nowhere starker than in Northern Ireland. Methods which work in one situation can actually do more harm than good in another. The key is to understand the situation itself and why a particular tactic has worked. However, there are some constants. The security framework has to be sufficient to protect the population from insurgents. The military cannot provide the solution to the underlying fault lines, but they can, if strong enough, hold the ring and give time and space for politics to work. In Northern Ireland troop strengths proved strong enough, but a comparison with other missions shows a wide disparity of troop density, in relation to coverage of both ground and population:

Comparison of peak international troop strength by territory and population[31]

Location	Peak number of international troops	International troops per km^2	International troops per head of population
Kosovo	40,000	1 per 0.3 km	1 per 50
Bosnia	60,000	1 per 0.85 km	1 per 66
East Timor	9,000	1 per 1.6 km	1 per 111
Iraq	155,000	1 per 2.8 km	1 per 161
Somalia	40,000	1 per 16.0 km	1 per 200
Liberia	11,000 + 2,200 (MEF)	1 per 8.0 km	1 per 265
Sierra Leone	18,000	1 per 4.0 km	1 per 300
Haiti	20,000	1 per 1.5 km	1 per 375
Afghanistan	20,000 (OEF) + 6,000 (ISAF)	1 per 25.0 km	1 per 1,115

Nevertheless, there is a limited honeymoon period within which the underlying fault lines need to be addressed. And the security forces must retain legitimacy; rule of law 'expediency does not pay. Departing from international humanitarian law even just a little bit is like being just a little bit pregnant.'[32] This opportunity was squandered in Northern Ireland and the situation deteriorated to one in which the military became what Republicans would call 'a party to the conflict'. In order to avoid this situation, or recover from it, sustained political engagement at the highest level is required.

Conclusion: Prospects for Resolution of Northern Ireland's Fault Lines

Politics is the key to conflict resolution in Northern Ireland.[33] Failure of the power-sharing executive and Northern Ireland Assembly would be a significant setback, albeit probably not fatal: Northern Ireland has been there before. Nevertheless, an enduring political process is a clear and cathartic manifestation of the victory of jaw-jaw over war-war. But mere continued existence of a political process is not enough. Northern Ireland has yet to make the leap from voting along sectarian lines to voting for policies. The current structure of the Assembly is not conducive to such progress. Political stagnation is potentially fatal: politics must evolve if it is to lead to conflict resolution. The alternative – a return to the Armalite – evokes genuine revulsion from all community leaders at the thought of their children and grandchildren growing up in the climate of terror which they themselves experienced. Yes, there will continue to be attacks from an eroded and increasingly desperate terrorist legacy, but the vast majority of the population have no truck with dissident Republicanism and increasingly see the benefits of eschewing violence. Nevertheless, a return to violence remains the veiled threat behind failure of the political process.

But politics alone will not resolve the conflict in Northern Ireland. The economic divides between Northern Ireland and the Republic, between Catholic and Protestant, and between the island of Ireland and Great Britain are insufficiently deep to derail progress, even in the current economic climate.[34] Ultimately, however, and despite the repeal of Section 2 of the Irish Constitution calling for a united Ireland, the evolution of politics, combined with economic and social progress, in Northern Ireland makes a united Ireland less and less abhorrent to those Unionists whose fathers found the concept anathema. It remains the Republican end state; Unionist threats of a bloodbath are increasingly incredible.

6

INDONESIA: LONG ROADS TO RECONCILIATION

Joseph Chinyong Liow

CONFLICT HAS BEEN A DEFINING FEATURE of much of Indonesia's post-colonial political history. Events such as the revolution of 1945–9 and confrontation – first against the Dutch over claims to Irian Jaya (West Irian) in 1961 and later against the Federation of Malaysia, accused by Jakarta of being a bastion of insidious neo-colonialism (1963–6) – were instrumental in shaping the strategic outlook of Indonesia's central leadership in Jakarta.[1] Much in the same manner, conflicts between central government and the provinces, including separatist and secessionist movements, have been integral to national identity formation, not to mention state building and consolidation. Indeed, the past sixty years have seen the central government formulate and implement hardline policies in places as diverse as Aceh, Sulawesi, East Timor and Irian Jaya among others in order to eliminate resistance to central authority and to secure the territorial integrity of the Indonesian nation-state. The persistence of such internal conflicts was further used to justify and legitimise the authoritarian and centripetal proclivities of the Suharto government, which ruled Indonesia for thirty-two years before the president himself was unceremoniously forced to resign in 1998.

Indeed, so acute was the sense of vulnerability – indeed, impossibility – and debility of a unitary post-Dutch East Indies modern Indonesian nation-state that pundits, alarmists and naysayers confidently predicted the 'Balkanisation of Indonesia' after the demise of a New Order regime underpinned by Suhartoesque authoritarianism. As it turns out, what transpired in fact portrayed a considerably different picture. After the initial outbreak of separatist, sectarian and religiously inspired violence – no doubt manipulated and at times orchestrated by local political forces and military interests – the predicted break-up of Indonesia failed to materialise. Instead, the central government in Jakarta granted independence to one province, East Timor, and a significant amount of autonomy to another, Aceh.

This chapter examines the local and historical context of rebellion and internal conflict in Indonesia with particular reference to Aceh and East Timor, two restive provinces that lie at opposing corners of Indonesia's vast archipelago, by focusing on causes and triggers. It then compares, contrasts and analyses the conditions that made the resolution of these long-standing, seemingly intractable conflicts possible, and discusses the implications. Finally, it concludes by drawing some general lessons that may be relevant for other cases explored in this volume.

Secession and the Indonesian State

The possibilities for secession – namely, the act of withdrawal by a constituent unit of an internationally recognised state to establish a new sovereign entity – has never been far from the surface of Indonesian geo-strategic discourse and remains a constant security challenge for Indonesia. In such a situation, when leaders of both the seceding community and the state express their positions in stark uncompromising terms, the resultant effect is a struggle that may be bitter, violent and protracted, particularly when the state uses its coercive powers to settle the dispute and recalcitrant rebels privilege the use of violence to achieve their political goals.

Indonesia is a vast archipelago consisting of more than 17,000 islands and a host of different ethnic and linguistic groups. Given its geographic, demographic and ethnic configuration, it is hardly surprising that the problem of separatism and secessionism has been a source of concern for Indonesia's political leaders and policymakers since independence. Several regional rebellions that arose during the 1940s and 1950s, such as the Darul Islam Movement and PRRI/Permesta, were based on ideological, historical and economic grounds that propelled local communities to either fight for a separate state of their own or at least pressure the central government for a greater say in regional affairs. Although these movements had been officially crushed by the 1960s, remnants remain and their activities, however limited, continue to have an impact on Indonesia's internal security and domestic stability today.

Meanwhile, during the New Order administration of President Suharto (1967–98), policies implemented by the central government in resource-rich regions like Aceh and Irian Jaya that essentially took over many of the local resources (e.g., oil, gas and gold) without giving anything substantial back to the local communities were met by strong anti-Jakarta resentment in these areas. This contributed to the rise of a new wave of armed separatism led by groups such as the Free Aceh Movement (GAM) and Free Papua Movement (OPM). While there were periodic attempts at dialogue, Jakarta's response to their aspirations was for the most part defined by the use of force against these armed movements, in addition to authoritarian and iron-fisted policies to curb dissent among the larger community from which these groups drew support and sympathy.

Circumstances changed considerably after the demise of the Suharto regime in the wake of the economic crisis of the late 1990s. With Suharto's departure, laws passed on decentralisation and regional autonomy significantly affected the national and local balance of power. The fact that local officials were no longer appointed by Jakarta, and had to be directly elected, created multiple polarities of power within both the local and the national political arena. One could even argue that with significant power now shifting to the regions, the dangers of secessionism lurk at every corner of the archipelago now that they have the capacity and opportunity to secede, especially when we consider the motivation of those resource-rich areas with a history of military suppression in the past. On the other hand the potential for such sentiments to arise has been to a large extent curbed by the broader democratisation of Indonesian politics, which has created a more consultative government and expanded the political space available for the expression of regional political and economic aspirations within the parameters of Indonesian territorial integrity.

Until recent years, two of the most persistent internal conflicts that confronted the post-colonial Indonesian state could be found at the furthest corners of the country. To the east lay East Timor, the Portuguese colony annexed by the New Order regime in 1976, ostensibly to exterminate a fledgling but increasingly popular communist party, and ruled with an iron hand until independence following a referendum in 1999. To the west lay the province of Aceh, with a long and proud history of Islamic culture and political independence.

Triggering Conflict: Aceh

Among the most conservative of Muslim communities in Indonesia, the Acehnese have gained a reputation (from their struggle against Dutch colonial authorities) for being ferocious fighters for whom identity, culture and independence have always been paramount.[2] A major player in the global spice trade, Aceh provided bitter resistance to Dutch colonial authority following the latter's invasion in 1873, and it was only in the early 1900s that the region was successfully incorporated by force into the Netherlands East Indies.

The Acehnese conflict of the contemporary era had its roots in the complex political environment of Indonesia in the 1950s. Acute problems brought about by core-periphery rivalries were the result of insufficient guarantees over the rights of the provinces to maintain their cultural identities and resource base. In addition to that, rivalries that were inherent in a competitive, Javanese-centric national political culture effectively crippled governance during the Sukarno era (1945–67), thereby weakening the political resolve in Jakarta to deal with the volatile province and its secessionist ambitions. This potent combination of factors gave rise to significant disenchantment in the provinces over the political direction of the Republic of Indonesia and the unwillingness of Jakarta to recognise the unique identity of the regions, leading to a series of regional rebellions. Foremost was the rebellion led by Tengku Daud Beureueh, whose decision to cooperate with S. M. Kartosuwirjo, leader of the Darul Islam movement, effectively expanded the Acehnese revolt by drawing it into the wider orbit of a concurrent rebellion known as the Darul Islam rebellion, which had the explicit aim of forming an Indonesian Islamic state.[3]

With the resolution of conflict in 1959, Jakarta agreed to grant the province special status whereby the culture and identity of the Acehnese could be accommodated and guaranteed within a special region framework (*daerah istimewa*). In reality, however, the provisions of autonomy were never realised. Later, grievances associated with the exploitation of Acehnese resources by Suharto's New Order regime led to a resurgence of violent resistance in 1976. On this occasion, the rebellion was led by Tengku Hasan di Tiro and mobilised around GAM (Gerakan Aceh Merdeka or the Free Aceh Movement), which had the creation of an independent Acehnese state as its ultimate goal and was driven by a host of perceived political, economic and social injustices. Positioning himself as an intellectual leader of the rebellion, di Tiro accused the Indonesian government of asserting Javanese hegemony on the province. Di Tiro's call for separation did not immediately find willing listeners. Gradually, though, the narrative of resistance gained currency – in large part facilitated by the repressive response and extractive policies of the central government – and eventually peaked in the late 1990s.

The Indonesian government responded to Hassan di Tiro's movement with massive repression, notably during a period of martial law in the late 1980s. The strain and animosity in core-periphery relations reached a zenith when the province was unofficially designated as a Military Operations Region (Daerah Operasi Militer or DOM). Military operations were designed to inflict systematic violence against not only the GAM cadre but suspected supporters and sympathisers as well. According to government and NGO investigations of the martial law period, security forces acted with impunity as homes were destroyed, Acehnese civilians were often harassed, sometimes physically beaten and tortured, and occasionally killed. This policy of repression was premised on the Suharto regime's logic that if the Acehnese were going to be 'disloyal' to the republic they would be forcibly brought back into the fold – something Suharto himself was known to have called 'Shock Therapy'.

Conflict Narratives and Fault Lines

Congruent to most armed movements that agitate for self-determination, the narrative of colonial domination has been central to the interpretation of the conflict. In GAM's view the conflict stemmed from the 1873 Dutch invasion of the 'State of Acheh-Sumatra' and was perpetuated by the 'illegal transfer of sovereignty' in 1949 from the 'old, Dutch colonialists to the new, Javanese colonialists'. GAM justified its claim to territorial sovereignty through its discursive construction of a singular Acehnese national identity based on ethnicity, language, culture, history and geography.

While historical narratives proved central to perceptions of marginalisation, it was the repressive and exploitative policies of the central Jakarta government that gave these narratives currency and meaning, and that served as triggers to conflict. Even GAM agreed that Acehnese resentment towards the Indonesian state was aggravated by the latter's exploitation of Aceh's natural resources, broken promises about the province's 'special region' status and depredations committed against Acehnese civilians during military operations. As Aceh was the site of lucrative oil and gas assets, its resource wealth influenced Jakarta's decision to deploy large numbers of security forces to the province, whose aggressive response to perceived security threats not only effectively beat back GAM's armed insurgency, but also produced thousands of civilian casualties.

Socio-economic conditions contributed to the entrenched nature of the problems. Aceh produces a third of Indonesia's gas exports and 10 per cent of its oil, making it an important region for Indonesia's mineral resource extraction. So bountiful were Aceh's resources, they provided GAM evidence that Aceh could in fact be a viable independent political and economic entity. Be that as it may, it is precisely this wealth of natural resources that has contributed to Jakarta's hardened position towards the province: Aceh was exploited for the Java-based central economy while the province remains one of the poorest in the archipelago. This state of affairs was further aggravated by the military's commercial activities in Aceh, where it established monopolies, or otherwise tight control, over commodities and taxed businesses and individuals as well (it should be noted that GAM too levied taxes on the Acehnese people, thereby aggravating their plight).

In addition to these political and economic factors, questions of ethnic and religious identity have also amplified differences between the central state and Aceh. That being said, their impact as fault lines has to be understood in the proper context. Although Aceh is immensely proud of its Islamic heritage, and religion lies at the heart of Acehnese identity, religion has often been misconstrued as a primary driving force of violence and conflict between the province and the central Indonesian government. Especially in recent years, the international media has tended to portray the separatist struggle in Aceh as one where rebels were fighting to establish an Islamic state. The reality, however, is far more complicated. In the first instance, GAM has never articulated an Islamic state as a goal. Moreover, its leaders are mostly secular in their orientation and have clearly articulated separatist rather than Islamic goals. This disjuncture between its nationalist ambitions and the religious credentials imputed to it was clearly demonstrated in its inability and reluctance to cooperate with militant Muslim groups such as Laskar Jihad or the Islamic Defenders Front (Front Pembela Islam, FPI) which have tried to establish themselves in Aceh as self-appointed custodians of Islam. Equally notable is the fact that while Aceh-based clerics have agitated for the implementation of sharia law in the province, these religious authorities are associated more with the government than with GAM or other constellations of separatist sympathisers.

Path to Autonomy

After the forced resignation of President Suharto in May 1998, Aceh's independence movement experienced a major resurgence as the door was open for the expression of long-standing grievances against Jakarta in a different political climate. In addition to this, revelations of past human rights abuses further fuelled demands for independence on the part of GAM, which was gradually regaining popularity in rural Aceh after being decimated by iron-fisted counter-insurgency operations during the Suharto era. On the other hand this new political climate and context also facilitated the emergence of a new peaceful referendum movement, which mobilised huge crowds throughout Aceh in November 1999. More importantly, the climate also allowed for the emergence of dialogue processes between GAM and representatives of the Indonesian government. As a whole, these conditions posed significant challenges to Jakarta, and they were subsequently met with a combination of concessions, which were then followed by repression when dialogue collapsed and both parties returned to arms.

In May 2003 martial law was implemented again in Aceh, stalling back-channel talks that had at the time begun to take place between the Indonesian government and GAM. This effectively killed off any prospects for the peace-building efforts. GAM negotiators were arrested on their way to Tokyo for negotiations and more than 30,000 troops were sent to suppress the separatists within the span of a few days in May 2003. However, martial law was rescinded a year later and replaced by a 'civil emergency', but without any major improvement on the ground. In turn, this emergency status was removed in May 2005, but again with no improvement in the situation in Aceh.

The tsunami of 26 December 2004 resulted in the deaths of more than 150,000 Acehnese, with tens of thousands more missing. While it proved a catastrophic humanitarian disaster, the tsunami also played an indirect role in forcing warring parties back to the negotiation table. Specifically, the tsunami brought international attention to Aceh and the Indonesian government could no longer curtail reporting on the province. Humanitarian concerns impressed upon warring parties that differences had to be put aside in order for the devastated region to be rebuilt. Both armed parties quickly called for a ceasefire in the area. Subsequent positive feelers from both sides led to meetings in Helsinki, Finland, facilitated by the Crisis Management Initiative (CMI) foundation. After a stuttering start, talks progressed steadily over several rounds.[4] Setting the tone, Jakarta offered special autonomy status and amnesty for GAM separatists from the outset, but made clear that it would reject any demand for Aceh's sovereignty. On the back of this conciliatory position, negotiators from both sides managed to keep hardliners in check as they explored possibilities. The process culminated in the signing of a Memorandum of Understanding (MoU) on 15 August 2005.

The signing of the watershed MoU was made possible by several factors – the first being the realisation that both sides need to put aside their differences to rebuild, reconstruct and rehabilitate Aceh after the devastating tsunami. This was the premise of the whole peace process. It also helped the sides overcome any major hurdles and barriers in reaching an agreement.

Provisions were made for the decommissioning of the troops – the withdrawal of about 23,000 soldiers, amnesty for GAM soldiers who could now go back to their old lives, and the surrender and destruction of GAM weapons. What was more difficult was the question of GAM's role in the post-conflict situation. At the outset, GAM agreed not to continue pushing for independence, albeit with the condition that it and any other Acehnese groups wishing to do so would be permitted to establish local political parties as legitimate vehicles that would contest local elections. The breakthrough came when the Indonesian government side agreed to this request, although it did have to deal with initial opposition from its own parliamentarians and other political parties in the country. A further issue that needed to be surmounted was the fact that Indonesian law had hitherto stipulated that only Jakarta-based parties were allowed to contest nationwide elections, thereby making it difficult for 'local' parties from Aceh to participate in purely 'local' politics, something which GAM had intended to focus on. Demonstrating political will, the government of Susilo Bambang Yudhoyono rectified this by pushing through the agreement with an understanding that a solution for this would be found later, possibly through the amendment of the special autonomy law for Aceh, allowing local political parties to be created only in Aceh. Provisions were also made for the monitoring of the peace process, involving monitors from the EU (European Union) and ASEAN (Association of Southeast Asian Nations) countries.

Triggering Conflict: Timor-Leste

Despite the fact that the emergent pre-war discourse of Indonesian nation-alism was fixated in large part on notions of ethno-linguistic identity, when Indonesian nationalists eventually declared independence in August 1945 they created the modern Indonesian territorial state by means of purely geopolitical points of reference: post-colonial Indonesia was to encompass the entire physical territory of the Netherlands East Indies. This under-standing of the territorial expanse of the post-colonial Indonesian state was heavily contested by the Netherlands (who, it should be added, had contested the very notion of Indonesian independence as well, from 1945 to 1949, before reluctantly granting the archipelago independent status), and this was borne out in the conflict over West Irian (Irian Jaya), which lasted until 1962. Notwithstanding the diplomatic drama surrounding the incorporation of West Irian into Indonesia, it was the later annexation of East Timor that created one of the most complex diplomatic, political and strategic challenges for Indonesia.

A colony of Portugal since the sixteenth century, East Timor was even-tually allowed to declare independence on 28 November 1975 after a brief period of civil war. The fact that the most popular party in East Timor at the time was the pro-independence and socialist FRETILIN sparked concern in many quarters in Indonesia, which by then was staunchly anti-communist. Concerns that an independent pro-communist country might soon be established at its doorstep forced Jakarta to act. Through infiltration, propaganda and finally annexation by force, East Timor was incorporated into the Republic of Indonesia in July 1976 as Timor Timur, the twenty-seventh province of Indonesia. While this move was in direct violation of international law, which prohibited the acquisition of terri-tory through aggressive action, the move was tacitly supported by Australia and other Western powers, who shared Jakarta's apprehensions regarding the tide of communism in the region and the creation of a pro-communist regime in East Timor.[5]

Jakarta anticipated a quick and decisive victory in their East Timor operation, followed by its routine incorporation into Indonesia. Instead, its actions precipitated widespread armed resistance that took place under the banner of FALINTIL, the revolutionary army, whose activities until that point had been confined to its role as FRETILIN's militia during the civil war prior to Indonesian annexation. This resistance was met by a brutal, yet ultimately unsuccessful, campaign against FRETILIN and

FALINTIL over the following twenty-four years, during which time the Indonesian state was widely believed to have committed grave atrocities in the province.[6] Even after the end of the Cold War, when communism in South-East Asia ceased to be a threat, the Indonesian military continued its repressive methods in dealing with unrest in troubled spots throughout Indonesia. As Ian Robinson argues, this 'illustrates the trepidation with which Jakarta views the potential implications of internal unrest'.[7]

If security factors catalysed Indonesian intervention in East Timor, it was economic factors that made Indonesia stay and press its policy of integration. In terms of economic benefits, the military was given access to largesse and commercial monopolies in exchange for running the integration campaign in East Timor. Concomitantly, continued investment in the island (particularly in the Timor Gap oil and gas fields) further entrenched the Indonesian government's interest to the detriment of the local community, which saw little of the wealth that Jakarta extracted returned to the province.

Notwithstanding the fact that low-key violence had continued in East Timor since Indonesian annexation, it was the Dili massacre of November 1991, when Indonesian security forces fired into civilian demonstrations, that ultimately turned international attention towards the situation in East Timor and increased pressure on the Indonesian government. Pressure on Jakarta from Portugal, Australia, the US and elsewhere in the Western world mounted, leading ultimately to the referendum of 1999 that paved the way for independence.[8]

Fault Lines

What was striking about the East Timor conflict, as suggested earlier, was that until 1975 the territory never featured in the nationalist imagination of 'Indonesia'. Unlike the rest of the archipelago, which was controlled by the Dutch, East Timor was a Portuguese colony and remained so several decades after Indonesian independence. As a matter of fact, the point can be made that in so far as the Indonesian nation was defined in ethnolinguistic terms (which is in itself a controversial claim not entirely borne out by historical evidence), then that was all the more reason for East Timor to be left out of the conceptualisation of the Indonesian nation.

Indeed, unlike the case elsewhere in South-East Asia, in East Timor the fault lines that fomented two and a half decades of violence between the centre and periphery stemmed not from notions of ethno-cultural identity but from the strategic decision Indonesia took – driven by geopolitical calculations – to annex the territory and the problems of integration that followed.

In this manner, it can be argued that the primary fault line is political, where the root cause of violence in East Timor can be attributed to the process of integration into the Indonesian state these groups were subjected to, and the subsequent policies introduced to maintain those boundaries. As Jacques Bertrand points out, 'the territories were integrated by force and the people were never consulted democratically. The local populations were victims of military campaigns aimed at eradicating small groups of armed rebels.'[9] This being the case, if a Timorese sense of identity was weak or ambiguous, it was reinforced and made coherent in the face of Indonesian occupation and repression. As Bertrand describes, for East Timorese 'being part of the Indonesian state meant a loss of their own identity and freedom, instead of the liberating, modernist conception with which other groups [in the archipelago] identified'.[10] Far from fostering loyalty to the state, the democratisation of the late 1990s in fact provided the conditions for a deepening of nationalist demands.

Path to Independence

As the Suharto regime faded away in the late 1990s and Indonesia found itself accelerating towards democracy, exiled East Timorese separatist leaders increased their diplomatic efforts internationally. Confronted with difficulties in consolidating his legitimacy and power, B. J. Habibie, Suharto's successor, came to rely on the military's ability and willingness to quell dissent as it arose across the country. Nevertheless, because the military was overstretched and the government was reeling from the effects of the 1997–8 economic crisis, using the military to quell dissent proved increasingly untenable, not to mention unpopular. To make matters worse for Jakarta, in its time of need in the face of economic crisis and rapid political change, East Timor proved a major obstacle in Indonesia's relationship with foreign donors. In other words, the cost of retaining the restive province was beginning to outweigh any benefit accrued. The decision was then taken in January 1999 to propose extensive autonomy for East Timor. Following talks between Indonesia, Portugal and the United Nations, Habibie proposed a referendum on autonomy or independence. The polls on 30 August 1999 attracted 98.5 per cent of East Timor's registered voters, of whom 78.5 per cent rejected autonomy and voted for independence.

The offer of a referendum caught everyone by surprise, and considering the lack of support from within the Indonesian establishment for Habibie's unilateral offer, it was hardly surprising that the verdict in favour of independence was met with a wave of violence and brutality on the part of pro-Indonesian militia, assisted by elements in the Indonesian military, and sparked intervention from the international community.

The UN Mission in East Timor (UNAMET), established on 11 June 1999, was tasked with organising and conducting the 1999 referendum. Unable to cope with the violence that followed the announcement of the results, the Australian-led International Force for East Timor (INTER-FET) was established on 20 September 1999 to restore order. After relatively successful operations, INTERFET subsequently handed control of the territory to the UN Transitional Administration of East Timor (UNTAET), which had been organised after the Cambodian model in November 1999. On 15 July 2000 UNTAET and the National Council of the Timorese Resistance (CNRT) agreed to form a coalition government with cabinet positions shared equally among UN officials and East Timorese to facilitate the transfer of power. The arrangement continued under the overall control of a UN-appointed administrator until 20 May 2002, when East Timor declared independence. With independence came a name change and East Timor became Timor-Leste.

International support did not end with independence. Indeed, on the day of the independence declaration, the UN Mission of Support in East Timor (UNMISET) was established to carry out the task of nation building, as well as to provide security for the new nation-state. On 19 May 2005 the new UN Office in Timor-Leste (UNOTIL), a one-year follow-on special political office, took over from UNMISET. On 25 August 2006 the UN Integrated Mission in Timor-Leste (UNMIT) was established with a six-month mandate that was later extended to 26 February 2008. UNMIT was tasked with maintaining law and order and also preparing the country for the 2007 presidential and parliamentary elections.

Notwithstanding the investment of the international community and the gradual improvement of relations with Indonesia over the past few years, East Timor continues to be mired in conflict and instability. In March 2006, a third of the country's fledgling military was sacked by President Xanana Gusmao. Meanwhile, a power struggle emerged between the president and Prime Minister Mari Alkatiri, resulting in the latter's deposition. Among the underlying issues was the alleged discrimination in the defence force by officers from the eastern part of the country (*lorosae*) against those from the west (*loromanu*), although, unsurprisingly, these differences were subsequently manipulated by political opportunists, plunging the country into further crisis. At the time of writing, this crisis continues to persist in Timor-Leste, aggravated by endemic corruption and weak state institutions.

Managing the Fault Lines

It is clear from the above discussion that the central Indonesian state has played a critical role in both conflict and reconciliation in Aceh and Timor-Leste. Since Indonesian independence, the question of the sanctity of the unitary Indonesian state has weighed heavily on the minds of the country's leadership. It was against this backdrop that resistance movements in Aceh and East Timor were long regarded and described in national discourse as illegitimate separatist movements that sought to undermine the territorial integrity of Indonesia.

In this respect, the sudden about-turn of Indonesian policy was nothing short of groundbreaking, as it opened the way for hitherto unimaginable policy directions. In the case of Aceh, the election of President Susilo Bambang Yudhoyono and Vice-President Yusuf Kalla provided an Indonesian leadership that was committed to and unified on the matter of resolution of the long-standing conflict, and was prepared to surmount the internal political obstacles and factionalism in order to achieve that end. This effectively set the stage for a substantive MoU that enumerated the key tenets of Aceh's autonomy.[11]

Closely linked to the role of leadership was the dramatic change in the political context in Indonesia. Simply put, autonomy for Aceh would not have been possible under the authoritarian administration of President Suharto. While the democratisation process precipitated by Indonesia's economic meltdown claimed Suharto as a victim, it also vastly expanded the political space in Indonesia and in so doing created the conditions that allowed the expression of aspirations of the Acehnese.

At the other side of the spectrum, years of counter-insurgency had weakened GAM and dismantled its shadow government to the extent that the separatist organisation was unable to assume a position of strength at the negotiation table. Instead, exhausted from decades of fighting, the GAM leadership itself had shifted from its two-pronged strategy of internationalisation and armed struggle towards independence, and was prepared to negotiate autonomy within the rubric of Indonesian territorial integrity. Likewise, the successful integration of GAM leaders into local mainstream politics via the electoral process further cemented the reconciliation process in Aceh.

While East Timor faced similar contextual conditions as Aceh, developments were markedly different on a number of counts. First, unlike Aceh, where dialogue and negotiation between Jakarta and GAM had been ongoing for a number of years prior to autonomy, President Habibie's announcement of the referendum in East Timor was entirely unexpected. To be sure, Habibie's move to put Indonesian control over East Timor on the line probably stemmed from his personal belief that the referendum results would point away from independence. In hindsight, his confidence was misplaced and the referendum result revealed the depth of sentiment in favour of self-determination. Even as Habibie was compelled to see through his offer of a referendum and, subsequently, independence, elements in the Indonesian military were complicit in the training and arming of pro-Indonesia paramilitary forces that mounted violent resistance against the move towards independence. Despite repeated assurances that Indonesia would restore order, Habibie and the powerful head of the military, General Wiranto, were either unwilling or unable to stop the bloodbath. Unlike the case of Aceh, the manner in which the move towards independence played out in East Timor was instructive of the lack of political will on the part of Jakarta, and the lack of preparation on the part of the East Timorese, to enable a smooth transition. The consequence of this is the ongoing strife and internal conflict in post-independence Timor-Leste, borne out of the weakness of institutions, the continued reliance on the international community and the actions of political opportunists who have taken advantage of ethno-cultural differences among the population.

This analysis of the management and resolution of internal fault lines in Indonesia is not complete without some mention of the international context and factors that invariably came into play. For Timor-Leste, the role of the international community has long been a tale of disillusion and hope. Indonesia's forceful annexation of the province in 1976 was endorsed not only by ASEAN, but also by the US, Japan and Australia. For Washington and Canberra, their respective positions on the Indonesian annexation and occupation of East Timor rested on a shared concern for the possible emergence of a pro-communist regime in an independent East Timor, as well as the strategic imperative to maintain good relations with Indonesia, which under the pro-West Suharto administration had become a key Cold War partner. Consequently, in spite of regular criticisms of the Suharto administration's human rights record in the province, neither Washington nor Canberra wavered from its position of tacit support for the Indonesian occupation.

Given the structural imperatives sketched above, it follows that the international community's position on East Timor could only shift in response to changes in either the geopolitical or the domestic political equation. To that end, it is notable that it was the events that ensued after the fall of the Suharto administration (i.e., domestic factors) that paved the way for a shift in the position of regional major powers on East Timor, rather than any sort of international pressure that was brought to bear on the Indonesian government for a change in its policy towards its easternmost province. Even then, there was initial hesitation to intervene because of concern for the sensitivities of Indonesia. Eventually, it was a combination of a brewing humanitarian crisis, victimisation of INGOs (International Non-Governmental Organisations) and Jakarta's acquiescence that paved the way for intervention on the part of the international community.[12] Led by Australia, for whom intervention was informed by its own domestic and geostrategic interests, the international community moved to build the newly independent but inherently fragile state of Timor-Leste through a number of UN missions.

In the case of Aceh, international intervention came in the form of various attempts at mediation from foreign governments and NGOs seeking to bring an end to the internal conflict in the region. Nevertheless, the extent to which the international community was permitted to play an active role in conflict transformation was very much defined by the Indonesian government's deep-seated aversion to and mistrust of external interventions for reasons highlighted earlier. In this regard, rather than ameliorating conflict, the intervention and activities of international humanitarian NGOs in Aceh at times in fact served to further polarise core-periphery relations and provoke reprisals on the part of the Indonesian military:

> The brief ceasefire, called the Humanitarian Pause (2000–2001), did not offer a political solution to the conflict or even create conditions for a process of mediated negotiation. The agreement had only two parties, and in consolidating the 'dark force' of provokator that it excluded from negotiations it legitimated a unitary command structure – GAM – to correspond with the state; thus contributing to the rebel group's actual consolidation under the leadership of armed forces, and abolishing the possibility of a neutral position.[13]

Indeed, it was only after the devastation caused by the tsunami that the Indonesian government openly called for the international aid community to enter a conflict zone that had hitherto been deliberately carefully kept from international scrutiny by Jakarta.

What is instructive about both cases is that while the international community possesses the resources, and some would argue the 'moral authority' – as proponents of the concept of the Responsibility to Protect will maintain – its role is likely to be limited, for ultimately it remains the domestic context and equation that will be paramount.

Conclusion

It is clear from the analysis that Aceh and East Timor (now Timor-Leste), hitherto two of the most bloody and intractable internal conflicts in post-colonial Indonesia, have taken different trajectories. On balance, the process of reconciliation in Aceh appears to be more stable as a result of a combination of political will on the part of Jakarta and waning insurgent resolve on the part of the separatist GAM movement, which was prepared to jettison aspirations for independence and accept the autonomy arrangements offered by Jakarta. Testifying to the success of reconciliation in Aceh, former GAM leaders have contested and won local elections, and now serve as members of the local government.

The picture in Timor-Leste is considerably bleaker. While Timor-Leste finally achieved its independence, it was not without bloodshed, nor was it the end of a long struggle. The manner in which independence was 'won' without strong political investment on the part of the Indonesian leadership, the weakness of state institutions, the continued reliance on foreign assistance in terms of both development and state building, and the persistence of conflict and violence perpetrated by local political leaders mean that rather than signalling the resolution of conflict and restoration of order, independence for Timor-Leste has ushered in new fault lines and social-political crevices that the state and its leadership may well be ill-equipped to resolve.

7

MANAGING THE TWO SOLITUDES: LESSONS FROM CANADA

Terence McNamee

THE CONFLICT which has defined Canada's political history from before independence to the present day has cost the life of just one person since the Second World War. Pierre Laporte, a Labour Minister in the provincial government of Quebec, was kidnapped and later murdered by members of an extremist nationalist group, the Front de libération du Québec (FLQ), in October 1970. Their goal was the secession[1] of the majority French-speaking province of Quebec from Canada, a majority English-speaking state.

Laporte's death did not trigger a violent eruption along the fault line which divides Canada.[2] The absence of violent conflict is not the only factor which marks out the Canadian example from the other case studies examined in this volume. Canada routinely ranks first on United Nations Human Development indicators, its immense land mass teems with natural resources and its people are often contrasted with those of their 'less caring, civilised and tolerant' southern neighbour, the United States. On the face of it Canada should be among the world's most stable polities. Yet the country came within a hair's breadth of splitting apart in the mid-1990s and its independence movement is the strongest in the developed world. The 'shock' outcome of the 2011 national election fuelled another round of intense speculation on whether Canada is the most likely democratic state to break up in the foreseeable future.

Indeed, for more than half a century, the fault line dividing French and English Canada has been the subject of countless books, articles and speeches. It is the backcloth on which some of Canada's most admired thinkers and politicians, from Pierre Trudeau to Charles Taylor, have painted the country's past and its possible futures.[3] The last two leaders of the Liberal Party, which has dominated federal politics for much of Canada's history, have been former academics who wrote extensively on French–English relations.[4] Navigating through the vast corpus of writing and theory on Canada's fault line reveals a tremendously rich scholarship, though, not surprisingly, much navel gazing too.[5] This chapter introduces its main themes but skirts the more elaborate conceptual ideas and pre-scriptions for managing Canada's historic cleavage. The aim is to set the broad contours in a way that invites international comparisons with the Canadian case, for all its particularities and paradoxes.

History

By the end of the seventeenth century France had established a thriv-ing French settlement in the north-eastern part of North America along the banks of the St Lawrence River, in what would become the Cana-dian province of Quebec. In 1759 a British expeditionary force defeated a French army within the confines of the capital, Quebec City. Determined to co-opt rather than subjugate a potentially restive population in their midst, the Protestant British permitted the French to keep their language and Roman Catholic Christianity.[6]

More than a century later, in 1867, the British North America (BNA) Act brought the French in 'lower Canada' into political union with the English in 'upper Canada'. Most French Canadians lived in the province of Quebec, which had a majority French-speaking population. The BNA Act accorded them certain important cultural rights, but the English were clearly the dominant economic group in the newly independent federal Dominion of Canada.

Over the next hundred years two different societies or 'solitudes'[7] evolved. The inhabitants of French Canada were generally poorer and less urban than their English counterparts. The main locus of authority in Quebec was the Roman Catholic Church. Business and commerce within the province were largely controlled by English Canadians and the English language was dominant among the wealthy elite. By the mid-twentieth century the renowned poet and essayist Felix Leclerc would bemoan the plight of his fellow French Canadians in Quebec, writing, 'Our people are the waterboys of their own country.'

The Quiet Revolution which began in Quebec in 1960 ushered in dramatic social and economic changes. No longer at ease with the anti-modernising identity promulgated by the Church, French Canadians shifted their principal source of allegiance to the Quebec government and set about redressing the historic inequalities which effectively made them second-class citizens within Canada. The term 'French Canadian' gave way to the more nationalist 'Quebecois', key industries were nationalised and the provincial government agitated for a greater share of federal powers. The perhaps inevitable outcome was the rise of Quebec nationalism – and the most serious internal security crisis Canada has ever faced: the October Crisis of 1970.

Between 1963 and 1970 the Marxist-inspired FLQ detonated nearly a hundred bombs in Quebec. Their targets were mainly federal institutions, such as army installations and Royal Canadian Mounted Police offices, and notably mailboxes – at homes in the affluent and predominantly anglophone Montreal suburb of Westmount. Yet no one had been killed until mid-October 1970, when FLQ cells kidnapped Laporte and a British diplomat, James Cross, who was eventually freed two months later. The kidnappings led to the only peacetime usage of the War Measures Act in Canada's history. The invocation of the act resulted in the widespread deployment of troops and tanks throughout Quebec and in Canada's capital, Ottawa. Although the armed forces remained under the authority of the civil power, for a few weeks the streets of some of Canada's biggest cities appeared to be under martial law.

The events of October 1970 served to first marginalise and then eradicate violent elements within Quebec's sovereignty movement. Yet the arrest and temporary detainment of hundreds of innocent political activists in Quebec left a bitter legacy of resentment towards the federal government and helped invigorate the nationalists' political struggle under the newly formed separatist Parti Quebecois (PQ), which came to power in 1976 on an avowedly separatist agenda, promising to make Quebecois *maîtres chez nous* (masters in their own house). The PQ enacted the province's most contentious legislation: the Charter of the French Language, Bill 101, whose goal is to protect the French language by making it the language of business in Quebec, as well as restricting the use of English on signs and as a language of instruction. That, and the party's promise to hold a referendum on Quebec's relationship with Canada during its mandate, triggered the swift exodus of more than 100,000 English-speakers from the province.[8]

In 1980 voters in Quebec were asked in a province-wide referendum to decide if Quebec should seek a new arrangement with Canada called 'sovereignty-association'. That referendum failed by a three to two margin. Fifteen years later, and after the failure of two separate attempts by the federal government to accommodate Quebec's grievances through major constitutional reform, another referendum on sovereignty was held. Although purposefully ambiguous, the question made full independence more likely in the event of a majority 'yes' vote. The 'no' vote carried the day – by 50.58 per cent to 49.42 per cent, or about 54,000 votes out of total of 4.67 million. There have been no referenda or significant constitutional reforms since.[9]

In his concession speech immediately after the 1995 referendum result was announced, the leader of the PQ, Jacques Parizeau, infamously blamed 'money and the *ethnic vote*'[10] for the sovereigntists' narrow defeat. He was correct, in so far as 60 per cent of francophones (who represent 80 per cent of all Quebecers) voted yes, whereas more than 95 per cent of anglophones and 80 per cent of 'allophones' – Quebec residents whose mother tongue is neither English nor French, glibly referred to as 'ethnic' by Parizeau – voted no. But his remarks gave some credence to federal government portrayals of the Quebec nationalist movement as ethnically driven, primordial, exclusive and intolerant. At the same time, Ottawa promoted a vision of pan-Canadian nationalism as progressive and virtuous, based on shared citizenship within Canada irrespective of race, ancestry or religion.

Separatists may not be entirely freed of their ethnic preoccupations, but there is less and less evidence for this sharp dichotomy. In the two centuries which followed the British conquest of 1759, Quebec's omnipresent Roman Catholic Church articulated a defensive vision of French Canadian society based on the principle of cultural and ethnic survival. The Church promoted large families and a traditional, agrarian identity.[11] Their mission was to preserve a French and Catholic homeland on the St Lawrence River, distinct from the Anglo-Saxon, Protestant entity which it bordered. Above all else, they feared assimilation into the larger and more powerful English community.[12]

Their fears were not unfounded, despite the generally enlightened position taken by the British colonists vis-à-vis Canada's French minority. The discourse of the incipient Canadian nationalism of the nineteenth century was 'imperially oriented and British'. The evolving English vision of a one-nation Canada, fortified by the experience of world wars and its innately 'superior' British-inspired (except federalism) institutions, was increasingly at odds with French-Canadian perceptions of themselves as constituting a distinct ethnic and religious community within Canada.[13]

It was only during the post-war era, with Britain's empire in swift decline, that Canada finally emerged out of the imperial shadow and conveyed a sense of independent nationhood, complete with its own founding myths and symbols, the most salient of which was the national flag, the 'Maple Leaf', adopted in 1965 (nearly a century after independence). Central to the idea of Canada was that of one nation 'from sea to sea to sea'. Its constituent minorities would have unparalleled scope to lead fulfilling national lives within an overarching framework of Canadianness. Canada's apparent success in this regard would lead the famed sociologist Anthony Giddens to assert that by transcending nationalism, Canada had become the world's first postmodern state.[14]

This portrayal clashed sharply with the vision of secessionists in Quebec. Their history spoke of defeats and disillusionments. As is often the case with minority communities, there was a pervasive sense of being dominated by centralised state institutions with which the majority identified. The Quebecois founding myth of Canada was of confederation as a compact between two equal nations rather than the birth of a single, unified nation. That compact had, in their minds, been irretrievably broken.[15] It was during the Quiet Revolution of the 1960s, as the power of the Church began to wane, that the ethnic-religious character of French Canadian identity was largely supplanted by language as the key reference and most important collective symbol. Indeed, it was the fight to protect the French language that brought the idea of independence out of the fringes of Quebec society. Language became the most reliable and potent sign of the community's vitality and uniqueness.[16]

Through the 1980s and 1990s linguistic insecurity would continue to nourish support for independence, especially after Quebec's birth rate, once the highest in the developed world, plummeted and greater numbers of English-leaning immigrants arrived in the province.

Nearly all significant figures in the sovereignty camp distanced themselves from the PQ leader's controversial remarks on the night of the referendum. By then the fight for an independent Quebec was primarily framed by nationalists not on race or religion but on territory and language. Parizeau was a dinosaur, even in his home province. Events over two decades had demonstrated that a broad coalition was required to carry any democratically conducted vote in an ethnically and linguistically diverse society like Quebec. As Philip Resnick writes, 'whatever the ethnic foundations of both sides of the Canada–Quebec divide may once have been, what is ultimately in contention today is a *civic versus civic* version of what the overarching state structure ought to be'. Ethnicity more broadly, he adds, 'is a good deal less attractive as a construct – even if language, culture and sense of shared history have ongoing importance'. Today there is not much to choose between Canadian and Quebecois nationalism, at least in its openness to new immigrants, democratic methods and respect for human rights. Ethnicity is all but absent in contemporary nationalist discourse in Quebec.[17]

The question for Canada, then, may not be the historic challenge of accommodating diverse ethnic identities within a single state, but rather, as Resnick asks: can you have more than one civic identity within a single state?[18] If the answer is no, then, as Kenneth McRoberts suggests, the inverse of Giddens's characterisation may be true: Canada is not the first postmodern state but is in fact one of the last states trying to become a nation state.[19]

Even if it were accepted that Canada is still in the throes of nation building – its destiny as a unified, contiguous state not yet assured – there is nevertheless much to learn from its experience of managing French–English divisions. Canada is perhaps the example par excellence for managing tensions along societal fault lines through non-violent means. Whether those same means have periodically brought the country to the brink of dissolution is, however, an open question.

Managing the Fault Line

Bilingualism

No single initiative or development has done more to retain the federal government's legitimacy in Quebec and undermine the secessionist cause than official bilingualism.

Prior to the late 1960s Canada was a country where anglophone prime ministers spoke no French and public servants could not serve one-quarter of the country's population in their own language. For most of the past four decades Canada has been led by prime ministers from Quebec. During that time the increased presence of francophones in the federal executive and civil service has been complemented by nationwide root-and-branch reform that has institutionalised bilingualism in all national bodies. In official discourse, French has formal equality with English in government and across all provinces and territories. Within Quebec, allophones are not allowed to send their children to English-speaking schools. Quebecers can ask for and receive federal government services in French whenever they travel in Canada, as the national carrier, Air Canada, discovered to its cost as recently as 2011, when a court awarded 12,000 dollars to a couple who sued after they were not served in French aboard Air Canada flights on two trips to the US; or if they relocate from Quebec to another province, their children can be educated in the French language. All products produced in Canada carry French and English labelling. In this way Canada has recast itself as a nation which celebrates the minority language. Therefore, as McRoberts argues, a central basis of Quebecois separatists' claim to nationhood, French language, is instead attached to the Canadian polity as a whole.[20]

Multiculturalism and First Nations

Canada is rare among multinational states in not portraying itself in terms of the majority population. It is rarer still, if not unique, in merging bilingualism with multiculturalism.

The seminal 1982 Constitution Act, which through several amendments to the BNA Act 'patriated' and renamed Canada's constitution, and the 1985 Official Multicultural Act expressed Canada as a multicultural mosaic under the direction of a decentralised federal state. Since then the federal government has argued that in an ethnically diverse country heavily influenced by and dependent on immigration from all parts of the world, an official policy of multiculturalism promotes the national interest by breaking down social and cultural barriers. Its key objectives include recognition of multiculturalism as a 'fundamental characteristic of the Canadian heritage and identity' and active promotion 'of the diverse cultures of Canadian society'. In recent decades the original categorisations of French, English and Aboriginal on Canadian census forms have given way to ever-greater specificity in identifying ethnic and racial origin. Ottawa has introduced affirmative action and employment equity legislation to highlight the role of 'visible minorities' in addition to the disabled and aboriginals in national life.[21] And more recently, the federal government has adopted in its official discourse the catch-all term 'First Nations' to describe Canada's disparate aboriginal peoples.

To some this increasing federal representation of Canada as a multinational *and* multicultural state was primarily designed to manage Canada's fault line: a policy 'to short-circuit Quebec nationalism by making the French Canadian nation but one component of the multi-ethnic dimension that is Canada'.[22] To others, however, multiculturalism has had a pernicious, self-reinforcing effect on Canadian identity, eroding its core tenets to such an extent that Canadian unity might one day be threatened.[23]

Economic and Political Power

The Constitution Act includes an amending formula which theoretically imposed the principle of equality among the provinces, but in practice the federal government has continued to provide special political and economic powers to Quebec. The province has enhanced autonomy in matters of taxation and, notably, immigration. Quebec can select its own immigrants from French-speaking states, such as Lebanon or Haiti. It has a greater international role and intervenes in more sectors than any of the other nine provinces; so much so that it is arguably the most powerful second level of government in all the OECD countries.[24]

Financially, Quebec has received more than 200 billion dollars from Ottawa, again more than any other province, in so-called equalisation payments since they were introduced in the late 1950s. In general terms the economic fortunes of French-speakers in Quebec have improved since the 1960s, measured by the shrinking income gap between anglophones and francophones and the latter's increasing ownership of Quebec businesses. That French economic advancement has occurred *within* the federation has negated the original claims of secessionists that Quebec's independence was an economic necessity. One of Ottawa's main pro-federalist arguments is that federalism offers Quebec businesses guaranteed access to Canadian markets, which is not an assurance secessionists can provide to Quebecers. Perhaps even more important, Ottawa routinely emphasises that much-cherished Canadian social programmes like universal health care might be imperilled in an independent Quebec due to economic pressures imposed by the United States.

Cyclical Constitutional Crises

Since the 1960s technocratic practitioners of federalism in Canada have largely held that the country's fault line could effectively 'disappear' – that is, Quebec's secessionist movement be rendered obsolete – if the right functional division of power between Ottawa and Quebec were found. The first major opportunity arrived with the repatriation of Canada's constitution from Britain in 1982. Even though its formal consent was never necessary, Quebec refused to sign the Constitution Act without significant concessions, in accordance with its 'special status' within Canada, from the federal government. In 1987 a further attempt, the Meech Lake Accord, was made to recognise Quebec as a 'distinct society', without really defining what this meant. After that effort failed to win the necessary unanimous support from Canada's ten provinces, another major constitutional reform was put forward five years later. The 1992 Charlottetown Accord would have given Quebec one-quarter of seats in the federal parliament in perpetuity. It too collapsed after provincial disagreements over how much special status could be accorded Quebec within the federation. To the present day, the government of Quebec has never formally ratified the 1982 Constitution Act.

The essential irony of the federal government's efforts to accommodate Quebec and make its independence movement irrelevant is that each attempt has resulted in a spike in support for secession within the province. In the wake of the most recent failure, the Charlottetown Accord, a pro-independence political party, the Bloc Québécois (BQ), was created at the federal level. Closely affiliated to the provincial Parti Quebecois, the BQ was for nearly two decades the third-biggest federal party (according to members of parliament) and held more than half the federal seats in Quebec. Whether their dismal performance in the 2011 national election represents a watershed in the secessionist movement is considered at the end of this chapter.

The constitutional failures of 1987 and 1992 largely sprang from a sense in other provinces that further special powers for Quebec would fatally undermine the 'one-nation' idea of Canada which has proved, perhaps surprisingly, very resilient. It is this concept of Canada from 'sea to sea to sea' which helps militate against all but the most extreme 'anti-Quebec' voices in English Canada advocating Quebec's removal from the federation. Regular carping about Quebec's perceived role as Canada's 'petulant prima donna' is a national pastime in parts of Canada.[25] Complaints are frequently heard about the refusal of many in Quebec to champion federal symbols and institutions, and much anger has been expressed over the alleged manipulation by Quebec governments of referenda, in which purposefully ambiguous questions are devised without input from the federal government. Yet across the country, even in the most independent-minded

English-speaking province, Alberta, there is very little support for what Resnick has described as the 'Pakistanisation of Canada', with a foreign state dividing Canada's Atlantic region from the rest of the country, something analogous in most Canadians' eyes to the excision of 'a vital limb or body organ'.[26] For better or worse, a Quebec in and part of Canada is a core element of their national identity.

Given the elemental nature of the separatist issue in Canada, the avoidance of violence is a considerable achievement. Most explanations for this start with history: Canada was not born in the crucible of war or revolution but rather evolved through conciliation and peaceful transition over a protracted period. Since independence its immensely powerful and dominant neighbour has never interfered politically in any significant way in its internal affairs, even though America's strategic interest in seeing Canada remain stable and unified is clear. Nor, despite French president Charles de Gaulle's infamous *Vive le Québec libre!* speech in Montreal in 1967, which enraged the Canadian government of the day because it seemed to be an endorsement of the secession of a province (i.e., for a 'free Quebec') – on a state visit no less – have any French-speaking states. The lack of outside meddling has doubtless contributed to the absence of violence, as has Canada's own geography. In the decades when French Canadians did not enjoy a fair share of power and prosperity within the federation, the state nevertheless sat comparatively lightly on them because of the virtually unlimited availability of land. It was this boundless space which, Saul Newman has suggested, made the kind of repressive policies employed in other divided societies, such as land-scarce Ireland, unnecessary.[27] More recently, even the most ardent separatists reject violent methods in part because of the demonstrated willingness of the federal government to afford Quebecers considerable scope, both within the province and at the national level – as evidenced by the BQ's establishment – to promote Quebec's independence. For all the controversy the 1980 and 1995 referenda evoked in the rest of Canada, they doubtless served as something of a 'release valve' for mounting Quebecois discontent.

Successive federal governments have accepted in principle that armed force would not be used to prevent Quebec's secession from Canada if there were strong popular support for independence. This principle was enshrined in the 2000 Clarity Act, prompted by the 'near miss' of 1995, which had brutally exposed Ottawa's lack of preparedness on key legal and constitutional questions related to secession. The act, which effectively acknowledges that Quebec has a moral right to secede provided that certain conditions are met, stipulates that the federal government would not enter into separation negotiations with a province unless a referendum question were 'clearly' framed (according to the judgement of the federal parliament) and the result of the referendum was a 'clear majority' in favour of independence, rather than merely, for instance, a 50 per cent +1 majority. Quebec's provincial government responded by passing a mirror act that 50 per cent +1 *would* represent a clear expression of Quebecers with regard to their right to determine their own future. The validity of both laws and compliance of their provisions will most likely remain uncertain for some time. Crucially, however, the Quebec law claims the right to territorial integrity of the province of Quebec.

In a moment of hyperbole someone once quipped that the difference between Americans and Canadians is that while Americans look back to their Civil War, Canadians look forward to theirs.[28] Although nothing in Canada's modern history would suggest that that is conceivable, the issue of land and borders would surely be the sternest test yet of Canada's commitment to peaceful accommodation, should secession ever become a reality.

The Future

It is difficult to predict whether or not Quebec nationalists will ever exceed the support for independence achieved in the 1995 referendum. Their campaign looked dead and buried until it was revitalised by the charismatic BQ leader Lucien Bouchard, who unofficially replaced the dowdy Parizeau as head of the 'yes' side only a few weeks before the vote. No nationalist politician of similar popular appeal has emerged since Bouchard left politics a decade ago, but there is always the possibility that one will. The PQ has not been in power in Quebec since 2003, therefore no referendum is in prospect.

At the national level, the BQ was decimated in the 2011 election, slumping from forty-four to just four seats in the federal parliament. Out of power in the province of Quebec and barely represented in Ottawa, secessionists appeared less potent and more adrift than perhaps at any time since the Quiet Revolution. At the very least, the election signalled that currently issues *other than* independence or sovereignty are paramount in most Quebecers' minds.

Yet the history of Quebecois nationalism has never been straightforward. New parties have risen and tumbled, sovereigntists have become federalists, federalists have become sovereigntists and so on. Indeed, the 2011 election result has been interpreted by some as a dangerous weakening of Quebec's voice within Canada. 'If the federalist answer to Quebec separatism is to enmesh Quebec within the federal fabric,' John Ibbitson warns, 'that answer is failing.'[29]

Even if very different conclusions are drawn from the election, no one is writing Quebecois nationalism's obituary yet. Consequently, the intractable issues that might one day arise in the event of a narrow victory for secessionists still merit detailed consideration. None of the issues below are likely to be addressed by either side until a referendum result forces their hand:

• Federalists frequently argue that if Canadian territory can be divided, so can Quebec's territory. Significant elements, such as the English and other linguistic minorities, within the seceding territory of Quebec would certainly call for its partition and for their own continued attachment to Canada. Perhaps most problematically for any aspiring independent Quebec state would be the province's aboriginal peoples, who are bound under a whole series of separate agreements with the federal state and have overwhelmingly refused (via their own referendum) to be part of any sovereign Quebec.

• Key outstanding economic questions are the status of Quebec's provincial debt, the highest per capita of any province; Quebec's access to Canadian markets and continued use of Canadian currency; and the management of transport, communication and energy infrastructure that would be necessary to link the Atlantic region of Canada to the remainder of the country west of Quebec.

• Survey data strongly suggests that while a Quebecois identity may be their strongest attachment, the majority also feel a significant connection to Canada and wish to retain their Canadian citizenship. To date the federal government has not articulated a firm policy on the citizenship question and therefore we might safely assume that it will remain ambiguous, believing that a Canadian passport might prove a powerful bargaining chip in any future separation negotiations.

Lessons

The oft-heard jibe that Canada is boring induces pique among most Canadians, but it's at least partly a backhanded compliment. A clause found in several British colonial acts, 'Peace, Order and Good Government', has resonated so enduringly in Canada that it is now upheld as something of a tripartite motto for the country. Hardly the stuff of Henry V at Agincourt. And that's the point. Canada has built an enviable international reputation for *avoiding* violent conflict. Its experience in managing the fault line separating French and English contains a number of lessons for other governments grappling with broadly similar challenges, especially multinational or multi-ethnic states.

The permanent solution to secessionism in multinational states is a chimera. The Canadian example compellingly demonstrates that in states with a powerful independence movement specific constitutional arrangements are never likely to be perceived as concrete, fixed for all time, because the minority will always reserve the right to challenge them if they believe their core interests are at stake. The fault lines that lay beneath the institutions of federalised multinational states like Canada 'can lead to convulsions at any time, to political crises requiring urgent attention. There can be no permanent solution to their problems.'[30] The secessionist threat is likely to ebb and flow, in response to the actions and character of federal and provincial governments, but never disappear entirely. The fact that Quebecois have secured key rights and concessions that are the envy of minorities in countless countries has not quenched their appetite for independence.

To some extent all constitutional reform efforts in Canada since independence have been underpinned by an assumption that there exists an elixir, an ideal set of institutional arrangements that would permanently end the secessionist threat in Quebec. Yet Resnick and others argue that Canada's constitutional wrangles strongly suggest that some kind of modus vivendi, a second-best solution, is probably the only viable aim to which governments seeking to manage deep cultural divides should aspire. Thus far Canada has been successful in managing its fault line through democratic means without giving the state away – but it may do just that if it clings to the belief that it can devise a definitive policy which resolves its inherent contradictions once and for all.[31]

Living with difference. Avoiding the break-up of multinational states like Canada requires a sober acceptance of the fact that differences are sometimes too stark and meaningful to those involved to be papered over by a single act or law and thus must find institutional expression within the state. Canada and other multinational states face an ongoing challenge in trying to devise innovative ways to bind multiple national identities together within key state structures like defence, foreign relations and economic affairs, while accepting often sharp differences in their level of attachment to the wider state. This challenge is central to Charles Taylor's work on 'deep diversity', which seeks to accommodate multiple forms of belonging to a federated state via various decentralised and asymmetric structures.[32] Whether Taylor's more radical prescriptions would prove viable or not in the case of Canada, it is doubtful that there will ever be full concordance between French and English on the country's founding myths or a single reading of its history. Perhaps the lesson for other states divided along a similar fault line is that comity, stability and prosperity are not necessarily dependent on it.

But don't underestimate the importance of symbolic politics. The federal–provincial negotiations of the 1980s and 1990s designed to accommodate Quebec and render its independence movement obsolete achieved the reverse: support for secession ballooned. In part this can be explained by the power of symbolic politics. Instead of technocratic questions about the division of legislative or economic powers, the debate focused largely on symbolic notions like 'recognition', 'distinctiveness' and 'collective identity'.[33] Consequently, there was an intense re-evaluation of 'what it meant to be a Canadian, or a Quebecer', which inflated the importance of abstract notions and symbols and led to invidious comparisons between Canada's two solitudes.[34] When most of the rest of Canada balked at any constitutional recognition of Quebec as a 'distinct society', secessionist leaders seized on the feelings of rejection that appeared suddenly and powerfully. They nearly won the 1995 referendum, not by technocratic arguments but because secessionist leaders were infinitely more adept at harnessing the power of symbols and articulating a clear national identity than their federal counterparts.

Federalism swings both ways. In perhaps no other country have debates on federalism, the sharing of powers between provincial and national governments, been as highly charged and contentious as in Canada. Federalism has provided Quebec with considerable institutional capacity, which over time has given it significant power to mobilise the population and reinforced a sense of collective identity within the province. And the increasing decentralisation of the federation – Ottawa has not disallowed or held in reserve any bill passed by a province since 1943[35] – has doubtless induced confidence in the feasibility of secession within Quebec. At the same time, decentralisation has demonstrated the federal government's willingness to accommodate Quebec's particular needs and allayed fears in Quebec that the central government represents an 'iron collar'.[36] So it may have also fostered a sense that the union is in Quebec's interests, at least economically and politically, and that secession is unnecessary.[37]

Participation and good governance are the best antidote to violence. To tinker just slightly with the country's motto, in Canada peace and order have been maintained *through* good government.[38] Although surely anathema to many states faced with deep divisions along societal fault lines, the willingness of the federal government to afford maximum political participation, both provincially and nationally, to its separatist adversaries has helped keep the genie of violence firmly sealed in the bottle. No separatist can legitimately accuse the government of repressive tactics or that a democratic path to Quebec's independence does not exist, even if disagreements persist on the criteria for secession. Both federalists and secessionists have conducted the perilous process of referenda and constitutional negotiations with exemplary calm and civility, even as Canada's very existence has been put at risk.

Will the future trajectory of Canada's fault line differ much from the course it has followed over the past thirty years? No one can be sure. The secessionist movement could still reinvent itself or give birth to a talismanic leader who delivers their long-cherished dream. Nevertheless, it is clear that the principal stresses – religion, ethnicity, language – on Canada's fault line have lost much of their potency in recent decades. The two solitudes may never become one, but the divide between them has never been thinner.

PART THREE:
A FINE BALANCE

8

ETHIOPIA: THE PERILS OF REFORM

Christopher Clapham

The Basic Structures of Division

Ethiopia is a divided country within a deeply fissured region. It is riven by conflicts along almost every fault line – ethnic, religious, ecological, class, ideological, political – many of which are broadly aligned, though not totally commensurate, with one another. Conflicts within Ethiopia itself spread across state frontiers – especially those with its three most important neighbours, Eritrea, Somalia and Sudan – to form a greater Horn of Africa conflict cluster, whose elements are inextricably linked. An Ethiopia, or a Horn of Africa, without major conflicts is simply inconceivable, and every attempt to resolve or even just contain those conflicts, however promising it at first appeared to be, has within a short time exacerbated other divisions within the conflict cluster as a whole and in turn fomented further conflicts. Ultimately, the fault lines within this region are irreconcilable and the goal of policymakers seeking to manage them can only plausibly be to do so in a way that renders them less rather than more violent.

The most basic fault lines in the region are geographical and are created – literally – by the great East African rift. This is responsible for the region's spectacular topography, and for climatic and hence social divisions that are most obviously defined by altitude. The highland zones of the great Ethiopian massif, which rises in places to over 4,000 metres and includes substantial areas over 2,000 metres, attract heavy though seasonal rainfall (with occasional droughts, which are the immediate cause of Ethiopia's notorious famines) and sustain relatively dense populations dependent (uniquely in Sub-Saharan Africa) on plough agriculture. Agriculture in turn lays the basis for hierarchical social structures (often, though in some respects misleadingly, described as 'feudal') and ultimately for the formation of states. For well over a thousand years the northern part of the Ethiopian massif has been dominated by societies deeply committed to Orthodox Christianity, though divided between the Amhara peoples to the south and the Tigrayans to the north.

In some places, notably along the great eastern escarpment that runs southward from near Massawa in modern Eritrea, the division between highland and lowland is precipitous. In others, especially to the south and west of the great massif, the descent is more gradual. But broadly, as altitude declines, so do rainfall and soil fertility, and agriculture is replaced by pastoralism, and Christianity by Islam. Populations become correspondingly less dense – parts of the Danakil depression east of the great escarpment are among the most inhospitable zones with human populations anywhere on earth – and complex social and political arrangements become increasingly difficult to sustain. States, defined by their control of territory, are displaced by shifting patterns of allegiance defined largely by descent. Here and there, 'islands' of greater fertility permit the emergence of localised structures of territorial control.

This ecological underpinning not only drives home the depth and intractability of fault lines in the region, but also defines the principal ways in which these have been defined, imposed, managed and exacerbated. Here, uniquely in Sub-Saharan Africa, modern state systems derive from indigenous social structures, rather than from external colonial conquest. The core fact of regional politics is the Ethiopian state, lineally descended from the empires that have controlled the northern highlands over some two thousand years, and in the process extended their dominion, to the extent that they were able to do so, over their less densely populated peripheries. Superimposed on the divisions created by ecology, ethnicity and religion have thus been those created by the often extremely uneven application of state power. Both the Ethiopian empire's internal unity and its control of the peripheries have fluctuated markedly over time, and occasionally the Muslim peripheries have even been able to launch assaults on the highlands, but the potential for domination has always been there. By a mixture of good fortune and astute political management, moreover, the imposition of European colonialism in the late nineteenth century coincided with a high point in the capacities of the Ethiopian state, which as a result was able both to defeat attempts at colonial conquest and to extend its own dominions over a massive swathe of territory, especially to the south and west of its original core. 'I have no intention of being an indifferent spectator,' as the emperor Menilek warned his European colonial competitors, 'if the distant powers hold the idea of dividing up Africa.'[1]

This had two major effects. First, European colonialism in the region was restricted to the coastal, lowland, and hence for the most part Muslim and pastoralist peripheries of the Ethiopian empire: the Italian Red Sea colony of Eritrea (which also included the northern tip of the Christian highlands); the French port city of Djibouti; British Somaliland facing the Gulf of Aden; and Italian Somalia facing the Indian Ocean. Second, the greatly expanded territory of the Ethiopian empire was governed by an increasingly centralised autocracy, based in the Shoa region at the extreme south of the historic core, in which the new capital of Addis Ababa is located. Though not explicitly discriminatory – individuals from conquered groups could gain powerful positions – it had a culture of rule in which Orthodox Christianity, the Amharic language and culture, and obeisance to the emperor were essential requirements for high office, and those who did not share these attributes were implicitly second-class citizens. It was likewise highly discriminatory in the imposition of an alien administration on the conquered regions, together with allocation of huge tracts of land both to leading members of the regime and to small-scale settlers, who were often retired soldiers in the imperial armies. It is not difficult to appreciate what problems this laid up for the future.

Ethiopia's internal problems then had their counterparts in the state's relations with its neighbours, always problematic but now formalised by the boundaries created by colonial rule. Two were especially difficult. In the north, the Italian colony of Eritrea cut Ethiopia off from the Red Sea coast, incorporated Christian areas that had formed part of 'historic' Ethiopia and provided a launch pad for Mussolini's 1935/6 invasion which for five years subjected the country to fascist occupation; it was an obvious target for Ethiopian irredentism. In the south-east, Ethiopian conquest had subjugated a large though sparsely inhabited Somali territory, generically known as the Ogaden, which drove a deep wedge between British Somaliland and Italian Somalia; this in turn was an obvious target for Somali irredentism. To the west, in addition, a Christian-governed Ethiopia with a potentially fractious Muslim population had perennially uneasy relations with a Muslim-governed Sudan with a potentially fractious

Christian one. The African norm of non-interference in the internal affairs of neighbouring states was never likely to apply.

Structures of Management

Over a period of seventy years, since the restoration of Ethiopian independence from Italian occupation in 1941, Ethiopia has had three regimes, each of which has approached the problems of conflict management in distinctly different ways. That there have been only three regimes in this period, the shortest-lived of which lasted for seventeen years, indicates that there are also powerful sources of stability in the system – albeit often highly repressive stability – to set against the fault lines already identified. Despite continuities imposed by the deeply entrenched social and political structures of the region, the approaches taken by each regime to the interlinked issues of domestic governance, regional relations and global alliance illustrate the possibilities and limitations of conflict management. The following three sections provide a brief synopsis of each.

Haile-Selassie, 1941–74: The Imperial Regime

Though loaded with the symbolic paraphernalia of 'tradition', Haile-Selassie's Ethiopia was in effect a modernising autocracy which sought to entrench and maintain the highly uneven distribution of power and resources that it inherited from the late-nineteenth-century imposition of centralised imperial rule and its extension to the newly conquered territories. Haile-Selassie himself, while lacking any broader vision of modern statehood, had an extremely acute grasp of political management and recognised the importance of state institutions – notably an army, an administrative and financial structure, and the cadre of educated officials needed to run it – in extending central power over a territory in which the effective reach of national government had hitherto been extremely weak. Under his rule, Ethiopia for the first time gained a government whose writ ran broadly across the whole of the national territory.

At the same time, the imperial regime was inherently incapable of developing any means of overcoming the fault lines implicit in the creation of the Ethiopian state, given that it rested on the very divisions that any genuine 'nation-building' strategy would have needed to remove. In religious terms, it was necessarily Orthodox Christian, drawing on an ancient source of identity which had for some fifteen hundred years upheld the role of the emperor, in the process relegating Muslims to the status of conquered peoples. In ethnic terms, it drew not only on the Amhara and Tigrayan peoples, who were the historic inhabitants of the northern plateau heartland of the Ethiopian state, but much more specifically on the region of Shoa, which until the late-nineteenth-century expansion had been on the southern frontier of the imperial domains. 'Representation' in government of the 'historic' northern regions of Tigray, Bagemder, Gojjam and Welo, as well as of the newly conquered territories, was achieved only to a minimal extent by such mechanisms as dynastic marriage with members of regional ruling families, or the recruitment of small numbers of educated individuals to a central bureaucracy dominated by the imperial court. The elected House of Representatives, introduced from 1957, had no political parties and no effective powers. The focus for loyalty remained the emperor himself, and in so far as there was any guiding set of assumptions about the development of the state, it was that all Ethiopians would eventually assume the culture of the highland core: they would become Christian, speak Amharic and acquire the habits of obedience associated with subjection to a long-established state. Perhaps most important of all, the structure of exploitation created by land alienation could never be rectified, because its beneficiaries were so closely associated with the regime.

That this system lasted so long – and it was easily the longest-lived, as well as generally most peaceful, Ethiopian regime of the past two and a half centuries – was due to a combination of factors. First, demands for popular participation of the kind that precipitated the end of colonial rule elsewhere in Africa were very slow to percolate down to the common people of a non-colonial state. Second, Haile-Selassie himself was generally extremely astute in manipulating political factions, which were reduced to dependence on the palace and played off against one another. Third, the regime was able to construct global and regional alliances, which bolstered its control over the domestic political arena.

The most important of these, established in the final years of the Second World War, was an alliance with the United States, which freed Ethiopia from dependence on European colonial powers, provided training and weapons for its new professional army and gave it invaluable diplomatic backing. From the American point of view, it established a recurring pattern in the external relations of the Horn: that the best way for any outside power to maintain both its own influence and the stability of the region as a whole was to support the current government of its most important state. One major success that this brought Ethiopia, however flawed it appeared in the light of later events, was the annexation of formerly Italian Eritrea, under a UN decision to which US support was critical, which gave Ethiopia access (for the first time since the mid-sixteenth century) to its own ports on the Red Sea and also removed a long-standing security threat. Swift diplomatic footwork likewise enabled Haile-Selassie to assume the leadership of the newly established grouping of independent African states, the Organisation of African Unity (OAU), which was founded and headquartered in Addis Ababa. The OAU's insistence on the inviolability of existing frontiers then helped to contain the threat from both Somali irredentists and Eritrean separatists.

The lesson of Haile-Selassie's long reign is nonetheless that political manipulation, no matter how astute, cannot resolve Ethiopia's deeply entrenched fault lines, and may indeed ultimately exacerbate them, by allowing them to fester, unattended to, behind a façade of apparent stability. It is symptomatic of its failure that the regime crumbled amidst the most deeply seated social revolution yet experienced by an African state. The clearest indicator of failure was the intense alienation of the very cadre of younger educated Ethiopians, in the university, the bureaucracy and most of all the army, on which the regime depended. To this were added the problems of rural revolts, by far the most important of which was in Eritrea, where the regime was completely unable to provide any political outlet for the resentments unleashed by annexation; and economic failure, indicated by a famine which the imperial government was equally incapable of dealing with. The immediate source of Haile-Selassie's overthrow in 1974 was a deep fissure within the urban elite, but its wider ramifications went much further.

Mengistu Haile-Mariam, 1974–91: The Derg

The successor regime, which overthrew (and later murdered) Haile-Selassie in 1974, and established itself in power after violent upheavals by 1977, had a very clear conception of Ethiopia's fault lines and the measures that needed to be taken to rectify them. Formed by junior army officers and backed, initially at least, by much of the urban intelligentsia, it was driven most explicitly by the Marxist-Leninist ideologies that were the common currency among this group in the later years of the imperial regime, and still more deeply by a loathing of what it saw as the corrupt and arrogant ruling clique that had prospered under the emperor. It readily resorted to extreme forms of violence as an automatic mode of dealing with opposition: some fifty leading members of the old regime were summarily executed, and similar measures were taken against members of revolutionary factions that came out on the losing side in the vicious internecine struggles that marked the early years of the revolution. It was hard to keep sight of the regime's direction amidst the bloodshed. There was a direction, however, which most explicitly derived from the example of the Soviet Union (which in the late 1970s, it is easy to forget, was at the apogee of its global influence), though in some ways it more closely resembled the Jacobins of revolutionary France. It was a vision in which, once the trappings of privilege, and the interests and individuals who profited from it, had been swept away, a new revolutionary nation could be created in which all were equal and the fault lines that had undermined the previous regime would no longer exist.

Nor was this a matter of mere rhetoric, as 'revolutionary' projects in Africa have so often been. At its base was the association between the deep social and economic inequalities created by the late-nineteenth- and twentieth-century imposition of the imperial state and the alienation of land. Not only were the formal markers of imperial rule – the imperial office itself and the privileged status of the Orthodox Church – abolished, but all land became the property of the state, destroying at a stroke the relations of production that were identified, in true Marxist fashion, as sustaining the 'feudal' class. The effects of this measure were indeed revolutionary, especially in the countryside. Landlords and settlers were driven out (and often killed), and in their place peasants' associations were established, charged with dividing the land in each community as evenly as possible between its indigenous inhabitants. For the first time, initially at least, those who farmed the land were able to profit fully from the fruits of their own labour, and both agricultural production and loyalty to the regime boomed as a result.

The advent of the revolutionary regime – commonly known as the Derg, in which a clique led by Lieutenant-Colonel Mengistu Haile-Mariam fought its way to dominance – also had global and regional consequences. The United States alliance was summarily discarded in favour of one with the Soviet Union, with which the regime had a strong ideological affinity and which readily provided the limitless quantities of weapons needed to keep at bay its opponents, both regional and domestic. Though full collectivisation was never undertaken, the Derg also looked to the USSR for its model of centrally planned development. Regional relations rapidly deteriorated. Though remnants of the imperial regime which sought to invade Ethiopia from Sudan were fairly easily disposed of, a symbiotic enmity remained, in which the government in Khartoum provided tacit aid to rebels in northern Ethiopia, while that in Addis Ababa did the same for rebels in southern Sudan. A Somali invasion in 1977, seeking to take over Somali-inhabited areas of Ethiopia while its government was beset by domestic upheavals, was eventually repulsed, setting in train the process that culminated in the complete collapse of the Somali state. Most important of all, the Jacobin project of Ethiopian nationalism was total anathema to the rebels in Eritrea, who – with the aid of heroic feats of discipline and organisation, and the maintenance of an external lifeline through Sudan – were able to sustain their struggle against everything that the Derg could throw at it.

The Derg's progressive decline, from its apogee in the later 1970s and early 1980s, testifies to the failure of its frontal assault on one major fault line to resolve the deeper problems of Ethiopia as a whole. In many ways, indeed, divisions were intensified. The key problem was that the highly centralised revolutionary state did not engage the loyalties of its population in the way that the model demanded. Far more efficiently organised than before, and making much greater demands on its people – notably in the form of taxation and military service – the state came to embody the inequities of imposed central government more intensively, and in the process induced greater alienation, than the ramshackle imperial regime that it had displaced. The inevitable deficiencies of socialist economic management added to its problems. In the end, the previously unthinkable happened: the Derg with its massive armies, backed by a now failing Soviet Union, fell to guerrilla forces that were able to march from the northern regions of Tigray and Eritrea and capture Addis Ababa.

Meles Zenawi, 1991–Present: The EPRDF

The new regime that took over in May 1991 likewise came equipped with its own analysis of Ethiopia's problems and its own programme for dealing with them. Cumbersomely entitled the Ethiopian Peoples' Revolutionary Democratic Front (EPRDF), it had at its core the Tigray People's Liberation Front (TPLF), led by the awesomely intelligent and articulate Meles Zenawi. One of its first acts was to acknowledge Eritrea's right to independent statehood, which in practice occurred immediately, though formal separation had to await the foregone conclusion of a referendum in 1993. This immediately removed a major fault line that had heavily contributed to the failure of both previous regimes – though as all too often happens in this part of Africa, this apparently straightforward settlement came to have adverse consequences of its own. Inevitably too, in the global context of the time, the Derg's socialist policies were abandoned, though the EPRDF, whose leaders were drawn from the same revolutionary Marxist generation as its predecessors, retained the state ownership of land. In principle at least, Ethiopia became a democratic multiparty state with a free-market economy.

By far the most important element in the new regime's programme was, however, the reconstitution of Ethiopia as a federal state, the constituent units of which were defined by ethnicity (or 'nationality', the term of Soviet origin invariably used in this context). Each group was guaranteed not only extensive powers over its own internal government, but much more remarkably a right of 'self-determination, up to and including secession'. The new government very plausibly argued that the model of imposed central statehood had comprehensively failed, whether in its imperial or in its revolutionary form, and that Ethiopia's survival depended on reconstituting the country as a voluntary union of equal peoples. The national territory was correspondingly divided into ethnic sections, the largest of which – Oromo, Amhara, Tigray, Somali – had separate regions of their own, while the smaller ones – notably the Southern Nations, Nationalities and Peoples' Regional State – were grouped together as federations within the federation.

This recognition of ethnicity as the fault line transcending all others had the immediate benefit of enabling the regime to put together a coalition of ethnically based parties, which was all the more important in that its core constituency, Tigray in the far north, was too small and too distant to provide a viable base from which to govern as large and diverse state as Ethiopia. It also meant that, for the first time under Ethiopian rule, peoples from the previously conquered areas of the country were governed by rulers at the local level who were visibly drawn from their own community. The problems created by ethnic federalism were nonetheless potentially crippling. The most basic was that identifying ethnicity as the key fault line, and establishing structures that reflected it, necessarily intensified the very divisions that had to be managed. Whereas previously ethnicity had largely been suppressed in Ethiopia, by associating nationhood with the language and culture of the highland core, now it became virtually the sole basis for political organisation. In the process, issues that had not mattered before came to be of critical importance. Individuals of mixed ethnicity had to decide where their own true identity lay. Fixed boundaries between ethnic regional states allocated territory definitively to one group rather than another – an issue of particular sensitivity on the long and blurred borderline between agriculturalists and pastoralists. People from one group who found themselves living in the territory of another were turned into aliens within their own country and at times either murdered or expelled.

It soon became clear, moreover, that the autonomy promised to each of the constituent groups of the federation was fraudulent. Federalism as a political system can operate only when diverse political actors, and especially the government at federal level, are prepared to recognise and respect the rights of other actors to organise and operate in ways different from, and at times opposed to, themselves. The EPRDF government showed no such tolerance. In part, despite originating as a guerrilla group in a distant part of the country, it came in time to share the hierarchical and authoritarian approach to governance that had characterised the imperial state since time immemorial. In part, its own cadres were every bit as imbued with the student Marxism of the 1970s as the regime that it overthrew, and its ideas of 'democracy' always owed far more to Leninist democratic centralism than to Western liberalism: the very project of ethnic federalism was drawn directly from Stalin's writings on the 'national question'. In addition, every 'liberation movement' that has fought its way to power has a conception of its own legitimacy that derives far more from the legacy of the 'struggle' than from the mere votes of the population, and the TPLF – parent of the EPRDF coalition – was no exception. The only parties permitted to exercise power within the constituent units of the federation were those affiliated – and subordinated – to the EPRDF; and even these were ruthlessly purged whenever any of their leaders showed the slightest sign of exercising the autonomy to which they were nominally entitled. Ethnic federalism thus aroused expectations that it signally failed to honour.

In addition, there was a significant level of Ethiopian nationalism that was deeply offended by the 'Balkanisation' of Ethiopia into separate ethnic states and was by no means entirely restricted to the Amhara people, who lay at the core of 'historic' Ethiopia and who often resented the key role of Tigrayans in the EPRDF regime. This came to the fore in May 1998, when the government of newly independent Eritrea seized by force a small area on the uncertain frontier between the two states which the

Eritreans claimed as their own, but which had historically been administered by Ethiopia. The outrage from all parts of Ethiopia that greeted this démarche helped to sustain the subsequent two-year war, eventually won by the Ethiopians at a very heavy cost, probably in the region of some 100,000 dead on both sides. The war in turn cast into question one of the EPRDF regime's undoubted accomplishments, the peaceful resolution of the Eritrean problem, and left the two countries locked in hostility. Since Eritrean ports were now closed to Ethiopia, it also raised anew the issue of the country's access to the sea. The regime's frailty was then revealed by the 2005 elections, in which the EPRDF was challenged by two opposition coalitions, one of which rested on a base of Ethiopian nationalism and economic liberalisation, and regarded the project of ethnic federalism with deep misgivings, while the other sought the implementation of the measures for regional autonomy that the regime had promised but not delivered. The nationalist coalition – the Coalition for Unity and Democracy (CUD), commonly known by the Amharic name of Andinet or Unity – swept the towns (including every single seat in Addis Ababa) and made major inroads into the countryside, whereas the federalist one – the Union of Ethiopian Democratic Forces (UEDF) – gained significant support especially in parts of Oromia and the Southern Region. All the indications were that the CUD was on the way to victory, when the regime took over control of the electoral commission, announced results to its own benefit and forcibly repressed the resulting protests. The federalist formula for managing Ethiopia's fault lines was thus most obviously aborted by the regime's refusal to adhere to the democratic process needed to make it work. Given the country's deep divisions and lack of any tradition of democratic governance, there can be no assurance that a democratic process could have been sustained, or indeed that it would not in turn have exacerbated conflicts in a manner all too familiar in the past; at any event, however, one potential and indeed promising avenue was closed.

Since that time, it has been clear that the formula promoted by the EPRDF has failed and that the regime – despite its success in clinging to power by whatever level of coercion is required – has reached a political impasse. Its eventual demise will have to be followed by some new attempt to deal with those issues that it inherited but has failed to resolve.

Conclusion

It is abundantly clear that the fissures expressed in Ethiopia's manifold fault lines are deeply resistant to resolution or indeed management. Even a return to a number of the relatively more successful forms of management employed in the past has been rendered difficult by the intensification of some divisions in the course of attempts to resolve others. Once the genie of ethnicity, in particular, has been let out of the bottle, in the form of its explicit recognition through the system of ethnic federalism, it is extremely difficult to push it back in again – and the fate of the Soviet Union, as the model from which the system was derived, is in that respect extremely unencouraging. The solution ultimately followed in the USSR, of allowing its fragmentation into fifteen different states along the frontiers created by the Union Republics, is still more fraught with difficulties in Ethiopia. I am quite unable to come up with any solutions to Ethiopia's predicament and can at best offer only two aspirations – one for the peoples and especially the governing elites of Ethiopia itself, one for the international community – which will in my view need to underlie any reasonably effective structure of management.

The domestic one is that there must be a change in cultures of governance in Ethiopia, which have been deeply resistant to concepts of compromise and negotiation. Any disagreement with the current holders of power has been regarded by the regime as a sign of treason, any willingness to listen to opponents has been regarded as a sign of weakness. Yet Ethiopia is now far too complex and diverse to be governed in the ways that have served it (often badly) in the past and are still entrenched in its current government. Ethiopia is not – like Somalia, to take the most obvious comparison – an ungovernable state, and indeed a deep respect for power has enabled it to maintain an extraordinary level of stability in the face of the divisions from which it suffers. It just needs to be governed differently; but that will require cultural no less than directly political shifts, which will in turn have to be consciously thought out and implemented.

The international one is that while the automatic response of both the continental and the global diplomatic communities – to support the current central government, as the most effective way to maintain stability, both within Ethiopia and in the broader setting of the Horn – is basically correct, it nonetheless has to be modified, and may in critical circumstances need to be temporarily reversed. The fomentation of internal divisions by international actors is potentially very hazardous indeed, risking extremely high levels of conflict and corresponding human misery, in a part of the world that has suffered from more than its share of both. I believe that Ethiopia in its present form is a broadly viable state, with an underlying sense of nationhood and identity that may be expected to override the divisions resulting especially from ethnicity. Some territorial adjustments might in the long term be regarded as beneficial: in particular, Ethiopia's generally futile attempts to control its Somali population are counterproductive, and these people would be better off as part of Somalia, however chaotic; and there is a strong case for Ethiopian territory to be expanded to include the sparsely inhabited Red Sea coast of south-eastern Eritrea, in a way that would both assure access to the sea and bring most of the Afar people under a common government. Given the intense significance attached to state frontiers in the region, however, these are not aspirations that the international community can openly support, without arousing intense hostility from regional states.

But there comes a time when outside support for the Ethiopian government itself becomes counterproductive. Such occasions occurred prior to the changes of regime in both 1974 and 1991, and the tipping point is clearly approaching now. A government that has run out of options, to the extent that it is reduced, like its predecessors, to concealing evidence of famine and obstructing attempts at relief, will need replacement sooner rather than later; and the diplomatic community should be on the alert to help ensure a smooth transition once the moment for it comes.

9

ETHNIC FRACTIONALISATION AND THE PROPENSITY FOR CONFLICT IN UGANDA, KENYA AND TANZANIA

Joel D. Barkan

Determinants of Fault Lines in Africa

Not all countries have fault lines that result in conflict. Some do. Others do not. Moreover, like faults in the earth's surface, some countries' fault lines run deeper than others. This paper seeks to explain the presence or absence of fault lines and their varying 'depth' in three African countries with reference to two others in terms of the following proposition: that in the context of agrarian and plural societies where most people live below the poverty line, the potential for conflict is a function of the interplay between three variables. First, the extent of ethnic fractionalisation and the relative size of competing ethnic groups. Second, whether the geographic space of the country in question is marked by uneven levels of development and incorporation into the world economy that has privileged some groups over others. Third, the extent to which political leaders seek to mobilise the electorate on the basis of appeals to ethnic identification and especially to a sense of ethnic grievance. The argument behind this proposition is straightforward: namely, that in agrarian, poor and plural societies, citizens usually define themselves and their respective political interests on the basis of where they reside, rather on the basis of what they do. Put differently, one's place of residence and one's neighbours are more salient determinants of political interest than occupation, income or class.

Where ethnic fractionalisation is low (i.e., where there is a small number of large and populous ethnic groups), where development is highly uneven so that some groups become favoured (and are perceived as being favoured) at the expense of others and where political leaders seek to mobilise the electorate on the basis of their ethnic identities, then politics are fundamentally distributive and redistributive in orientation with respect to competing ethno-regional claims. Conversely, where ethnic fractionalisation is high (i.e., where there is a large number of small groups), where the pattern of uneven development is less pronounced and where politicians do not stress identity politics, then the probability that the fault lines of conflict mimic the boundaries between ethno-regional communities is low. Instead, political conflict occurs between potential 'winners' and 'losers' of policy decisions that are framed in terms of class and occupational interests (e.g., farmers versus urban dwellers; unions versus management; physicians and retirees versus insurers and drug manufacturers; environmental activists and regulators versus business; etc.), rather than in terms of competing ethno-regional claims. This is why the politics of ethno-regional identities are found most frequently in Africa, a continent of agrarian and plural societies,[1] while the politics of class and occupation are most common in advanced industrial societies.

Notwithstanding these two polar types of politics and the association of Africa[2] with the politics of ethnicity, there is considerable variation between the two types across the continent as a result of the different permutations of the three variables cited above. For example, in Uganda and Kenya, where the politics of ethno-regional claims are paramount, and in Tanzania, where they are not. Or in South Africa, where the level of ethnic fractionalisation is low, but where the combination of industrialisation, urbanisation and especially occupational differentiation has broken up the largest ethnic blocs to the point that politicians rarely seek to mobilise supporters on the basis of their sense of ethnic identities, which is low.

Ethnic Fractionalisation, Uneven Development and Political Mobilisation Before Independence and After

At the end of the nineteenth century, when the imposition of colonial rule established the basis of Africa's current state system, Africa was the most agrarian continent. Populated by more than 3,000 groups of unequal size and varying structures of authority – from small acephalous societies to large hierarchical states – the peoples south of the Sahara were forced into forty-two entities plus Ethiopia and Liberia, which later became the basis of today's state system. The establishment of the colonial state

often respected the boundaries between indigenous ethnic groups, especially across anglophone Africa, where the United Kingdom's approach
to colonial governance was that of indirect rule. Under this approach, the
boundaries of administrative units below the national level were usually
drawn to follow the 'natural' boundaries between indigenous groups and
colonial officials posted to these units ruled via the leaders of the dominant group within each unit. In the former French territories, where the
boundaries of administrative units often cut across indigenous boundaries, the French eventually learned that to govern effectively they had to
respect and co-opt indigenous authority into the colonial order.[3] To a
considerable albeit varying extent, government shadowed, either formally
or informally, the indigenous systems. In the case of the British, indirect
rule reinforced the 'natural boundaries' between groups and reinforced
indigenous authority – provided, of course, that local leaders did not challenge colonial rule. This often resulted in the establishment of administrative units of unequal size and with varying formal powers. Colonial
resources allocated to administrative units also varied in respect to the
number and quality of personnel, the construction of infrastructure and
the provision of social services, especially education. Investment, to the
extent that there was any, was often concentrated in a handful of areas
where it would produce the greatest return – in the capital city of the
colony, or in selected areas of the hinterland where commodities could
be grown or extracted for export. By the beginning of the Second World
War, and in many colonies earlier, the pattern of uneven development, a
pattern that interacted with the geographic location of individual ethnic
groups, was well entrenched.

During the run-up to independence after the war, the nationalist
movements that demanded an end to colonial rule usually took one of
two forms: either a single pan-territorial movement organised to confront
the colonial regime, or two or more regionally based political parties that
were united in their common demand for independence but represented
different ethno-regional constituencies and worried about the distribution of power after independence. In an attempt to transfer power gradually and smoothly to an emerging African political elite, the British sought
to phase in a Westminster form of parliamentary government via a series
of elections held in single-member electoral districts (SMDs). With each
successive election, the number of constituencies was increased and the
constituencies became smaller in size. This put a primacy on the ability
of nationalist leaders to mobilise the rural population one constituency

and locality at a time.[4] But it also required these leaders to appeal to a series of local electorates that were frequently ethnically homogeneous in composition. Candidates nominated by their parties for these elections were invariably selected on their ability to campaign in the local language or lingua franca of the area. Exacerbating this practice in some colonies, including Kenya, was the policy that parties were not allowed to campaign on a nationwide basis during the initial stages of the process. The result was the emergence of different parties to represent different groups or different coalitions of groups that were ethnically distinct from each other and resided in different regions of the colony.

Whether the nationalist movement mobilised the electorate as a single party or split among several parties, the structure of political competition was in large part determined during this transitional yet formative stage of most countries' history. Unless purposely restructured by the national leadership at a later date (e.g., in post-civil war Nigeria), that structure of competition, including its fault lines for conflict, is carried over to the present era. Thus, although all but a handful of African states fell under one-party dictatorships or military rule by the end of the 1960s, and remained governed by these regimes for more than twenty years, the restoration of multiparty politics during the early 1990s reproduced the structure of politics established three decades earlier. This is because, in most African countries, two of the three critical variables – the extent of ethnic fractionalisation and uneven development – remained unchanged throughout the period of authoritarian rule. *It is thus the approach taken by a country's political elites and their interaction with the two structural variables that accentuate or mitigate the fault lines that divide society.*[5] Do such elites attempt to mobilise ethnic constituencies to maximise their vote in an election or for other purposes? That is the question.[6]

The variations in the extent of ethnic fractionalisation and uneven development as found in five countries that have experienced varying degrees of ethno-regional conflict are summarised in Table 1. The five countries range from Rwanda and Nigeria, which experienced genocide and civil war respectively, to Tanzania, which has been at peace since independence. Uganda and Kenya, which have experienced ethnic violence at more moderate levels (i.e., life-threatening, but not state-threatening), fall somewhere in between.

As indicted by the table, the number of groups across the five countries varies greatly, from a low of three (some would say only two) in Rwanda to a high of over 100 in the cases of Nigeria and Tanzania. The

Table 1: Ethnic Fractionalisation and Uneven Development in Five African Countries

	Rwanda	Nigeria	Kenya	Uganda	Tanzania
History of ethnic conflict					
Intensity:	high	high	moderate	moderate	very low
Type:	genocide	civil war	ethnic clashes	ethnic clashes	peace
Number of ethnic groups:	3	200+	43	35+	126
% of population in largest group	90	32	28	17	12
% of population in 3 largest groups	100	70	56	32	23
% of population in 5 largest groups	n.a.	91	78	47	31
% of population in 10 largest groups	n.a.	99	92	73	41
Ethnic fractionalisation index score (EFI)*	1.22	4.96	5.98	12.3	38.3
Extent of uneven development?	medium	high	high	high	low
Largest group privileged by uneven development?	no	no	yes	yes	no

*The EFI for each country is calculated using the Laakso-Taagepera formula for the effective number of political parties in a country: $1/\Sigma g^2$ where g is the percentage of a country's population belonging to each ethnic group

Source: Shaheen Mozaffar, Bridgewater State College and CIA Fact Book

most critical variable, however, is the extent to which a small number of moderate to very large and populous groups account for a third or more of a country's population. Rwanda exhibits the extreme in this regard. It is a country divided between a single ethnic minority that asserts political hegemony and a huge ethnic majority which has periodically sought to annihilate the minority. In Nigeria, Kenya and Uganda, the largest three groups account for between one-third and two-thirds of the population, while the largest five groups account for between nearly one half and nine-tenths of the population. This raises the prospect for conflict because, depending on its size, the largest group needs only form an effective coalition with two to four partners to control the state. This reality in turn prompts other large groups to form counter-coalitions to match their rivals. Politics, as demonstrated most clearly in Kenya and Uganda, become a never-ending game of ethnic 'musical chairs'. In the run-up to each election, coalitions form and re-form among the largest groups, but in the process divide their countries, often deeply, into what becomes a zero-sum game between rival ethnic coalitions.[7] However, in countries like Tanzania, where the extent of ethnic fractionalisation is very high, no one group or coalition of two or three large groups can become a political force, because there are no large groups.

A summary measure of the extent of ethnic fractionalisation is provided in the table in the form of the Ethnic Fractionalisation Index score or EFI for each of the five countries. The score simultaneously considers the size of all ethnic groups in relation to each other to provide a single measure of the 'effective number' of groups in each country. The scores range from the extremely low 1.22 for Rwanda to the very high 38.3 for Tanzania, meaning that, based on their relative size, Rwanda has slightly more than one group while Tanzania has nearly forty. The correlation between a country's EFI and its propensity towards (and past history of) violent conflict or peace is clear. Yet as noted above, *it is the mobilisation of ethnicity, not the configuration of ethnicity alone* that results in deep fault lines along ethnic boundaries and conflict across these boundaries. That said, countries with low EFIs are certainly more susceptible to ethnic mobilisation than those with high scores for the reasons discussed.

Piling It On: The Exacerbation of Ethnic Fractionalisation – Uneven Development (and More!) in Uganda and Kenya

Whether or not political leaders seek to mobilise the electorate or segments of it on the basis of ethnicity is also a function of the extent of uneven economic development and whether some groups, particularly the large ones, are privileged by the geographic distribution of development. Put differently, although a low EFI may not by itself lead to ethnic conflict, a low EFI exacerbated by uneven development is more likely to create a situation where rival political elites will mobilise their respective ethnic constituencies on the claim that some are 'haves' that must protect their advantage, while others are 'have nots' and must secure a measure of compensation or equity. The histories of Kenya and especially Uganda since independence and since the restoration of multiparty politics in the early 1990s support this observation. In both countries the largest ethnic group – the Kikuyu in Kenya[8] and the Baganda[9] in Uganda – benefited greatly from the pattern of uneven development that was established during the colonial era. In both cases, the largest group benefited from its proximity to the capital city and in both cases the largest ethnic group became the main producer of the country's leading export crop, coffee.

Uganda

Other factors, unique to each country, contributed to and exacerbated the pattern of uneven development and privilege for the largest group. In Uganda, the Kingdom of Buganda was an indigenous political entity with its own imperial history vis-à-vis its neighbours before it became a British Protectorate in 1900.[10] Early British administrators at the turn of the twentieth century were impressed by the kingdom and viewed it as a useful tool for extending British control and implementing indirect rule across the country. They established the colonial capital at Entebbe in the heart of Buganda, forty kilometres south of Kampala, the present capital, and Mengo, the capital of the kingdom. Buganda was eventually accorded a special political status that carried over to the post-independence period as a semi-autonomous state within Uganda as a whole. In addition to preserving the monarchy, Buganda had its own executive arm of government with the authority to raise revenue, its own elected legislature and prime minister, its own school system and its own police force. Together with four smaller kingdoms of Ankole, Bunyoro, Busoga and Toro, Buganda was given formal recognition in the constitution promulgated just before independence in 1962. However, apart from the recognition of their monarchs and their realms, the other kingdoms were given no special powers and were administered directly from Entebbe, like the other districts in Uganda, by a district commissioner and his staff. Although Uganda attained independence under a parliamentary form of government headed by Prime Minister Milton Obote, negotiations over the country's constitution ended with the appointment of the Kabaka, the king of Buganda, to the ceremonial post of president of Uganda.

British efforts to develop Uganda also favoured the kingdom. Infrastructure established during the colonial period, including roads, electricity and telecommunications, was substantially more extensive in Buganda than in the rest of Uganda, particularly the north. Elite secondary schools, including King's College Buddo and St Mary's College, were also established in Buganda, as was Makerere University College during the colonial period. The British also introduced the cultivation of coffee in the kingdom. Not surprisingly, the emerging African elite nurtured by the British in the run-up to independence was likewise largely Baganda in composition. When colonial administrators departed after independence in 1962, nearly 90 per cent of their replacements were initially Baganda. Last but not least, the saliency of the monarchy among the Baganda generally and among the educated elite in particular created a 'royalist' element which, when combined with their Western educations, produced a hubris that grated upon the peoples and leaders of Uganda's other ethnic groups.

From the run-up to independence to the present, the question of how to incorporate Buganda, its people and its king (the Kabaka) has arguably been the biggest issue confronting each successive national government of Uganda. The British concluded that it was impossible to govern Uganda without the Baganda and sought to accommodate the kingdom within the framework of indirect rule. By contrast, their immediate successors, Milton Obote and Idi Amin, who ruled the country from 1962 to 1979, tried to isolate and suppress the kingdom. In 1966, following the breakdown of a political alliance between the Baganda and Prime Minister Obote, the Kabaka and the kingdom government demanded that the Uganda national government leave Buganda. The Kabaka, acting in his capacity as the president of Uganda, also asked the United Nations to send in troops to protect his kingdom. Obote's response was swift. The Uganda army, then headed by Amin, stormed the Kabaka's palace at Mengo, from which he escaped to exile in Britain, where he remained for the rest of his life. By the end of 1966, Obote – an Acholi from northern Uganda – forced parliament to pass a new constitution that abolished all the kingdoms and stripped Buganda of its special powers. Uganda was henceforth a unitary state with Obote as its president, and dominated by his party, the Uganda Peoples Congress (UPC).[11] Amin overthrew the Obote regime in 1971, but did not restore any of the kingdoms. Nor did a series of successors (including Obote) who served as president between 1980 and 1985, when Yoweri Museveni and the National Resistance Movement (NRM) seized power. Since that time, Museveni has taken a different approach, by attempting to both co-opt and divide the kingdom.

From the early 1990s until mid-2009 Museveni largely succeeded in co-opting the Baganda by aggressively courting their leaders to become prominent members of the NRM and by including the Baganda in an informal coalition of Bantu-speaking peoples, who comprise two-thirds of

Uganda's population and who live across the southern half of the country. By contrast, the peoples who inhabit northern Uganda are mainly speakers of Nilotic languagues. The division of the country was exacerbated by the fact that while the British concentrated economic development and the provision of social services in the south, they recruited the army from the north.

By the end of Obote's second presidency, which lasted from 1981 to 1985, southerners and the Baganda in particular were easily mobilised against the north, as the country had been ruled despotically by two northerners, Obote and Amin, for most of its existence as an independent state. More than 200,000 Ugandans, mainly southerners, are estimated to have perished under northern rule.[12] The rise of the Lord's Resistance Army (LRA) in the early 1990s, a brutal insurgency composed of remnants of Obote's army, reinforced the sense of grievance and fear among southerners towards the north. Perhaps most important, Museveni co-opted the Baganda by recognising the existence of their kingdom and restoring the office of the Kabaka. The body of the Kabaka who had fled to Britain was brought back to Uganda for reburial, while one of his sons was elevated to the throne. Buganda, however, remained divided into a series of districts, each of which is governed by a directly elected leader and elected council, as is the practice across the country. The kingdom's government was not restored, albeit a provision in Uganda's present constitution allows adjacent districts to join together 'for common purposes'.

While Museveni's strategy of accommodation was successful until 2009, it may no longer be a viable approach, as Baganda royalists are flexing their muscles and demand greater autonomy and authority from the central government. But Museveni's principal problem is that after nearly a quarter-century in power and four elected terms as Uganda's president, Ugandans are becoming tired of living under a government that increasingly resembles Africa's corrupt authoritarian states of the 1980s. Having forced the repeal of term limits to run for a third presidential term in 2006, Museveni ran and was re-elected to a fourth in 2011. Neither of these elections could be described as 'free and fair', as Museveni's principal opponent in both elections, Kizza Besigye, was constantly harassed. The question now is whether he will run for a fifth in 2016, when he will be seventy-three years old. In the meantime, tensions are rising. Uganda's capital city of Kampala was rocked by mass demonstrations in September 2009, in March 2010 and again in April 2011. The paramilitary police were brought out to quell each of these demonstrations. More than twenty people were killed in the first and many, including Kizza Besigye, were severely injured in the most recent round of violence.

After nearly two decades of peace and political reform, including the strengthening of parliament and a genuine devolution of power to the district level, Uganda has slipped back into a mode of neo-patrimonial governance that cannot manage the politics of a country populated by a small number of large ethnic groups and in which one group has occupied a unique and relatively privileged position vis-à-vis the rest. Uganda's once promising parliament has been largely emasculated since 2005, while the move towards federalism has been reversed. Museveni's tolerance for political opposition and pluralism has diminished as he seeks to perpetuate his rule. A recent law to register NGOs keeps civil society on a short leash, while regulation and harassment of the media are rising. It is not a recipe for stable governance, let alone democratic rule.

Kenya

Conditions peculiar to Kenya also amplified the already dominant position of the Kikuyu that resulted from the group's size and Kenya's pattern of uneven development. The Kikuyu constitute 22 per cent of Kenya's population and are the largest ethnic group in East Africa. Because of its soils and climate, Kenya became a destination for European settlers during colonial rule. Although whites accounted for only 60,000 of the country's 9 million inhabitants at the end of the colonial period in 1963, their influence over the British colonial government resulted in a system of racial segregation similar to Rhodesia and South Africa that shaped the country's post-independence politics in two ways. First, although all of Kenya's major groups suffered punitive measures by the British, the Kikuyu bore the brunt of such treatment, because they were the most populous group and because significant portions of their lands were taken by the colonial regime for reallocation to the settlers. Land alienation politicised the Kikuyu as early as the 1920s and ultimately led to the so-called 'Mau Mau' insurgency (1952–8) that required more than 15,000 British troops to suppress. Forty years before independence, the Kikuyu became a political force as the spearhead of the nationalist movement, although members of other tribes later joined its ranks.

Second, because of their proximity to Nairobi, and because parts of their homeland were occupied by European settlers, Central Province, the area with the highest concentrations of Kikuyu, was endowed with a greater level of infrastructure than anywhere else in the country except Nakuru district (another area of European settlement and a large Kikuyu presence in the western Rift Valley). Like Buganda, Central Province became the site of several elite secondary schools, including Alliance High School, the Duke of York School and the Prince of Wales School.[13] Their graduates went on to university, at Makerere University in Uganda, in the United Kingdom and, beginning in the late 1950s, in the United States. Disproportionately represented among the educated elite, the Kikuyu dominated both the nationalist movement and the civil service in the years immediately before and after independence. Fifty years later, the Kikuyu continue to be over-represented in the latter despite efforts to recruit from other tribes, especially during the twenty-four-year presidency of Daniel arap Moi (1978–2002). For the same reasons, the Kikuyu dominate the business and professional upper middle class. As in Uganda, the largest ethnic group has been favoured by the geographic pattern of uneven development. As in Uganda, the politics of Kenya since independence, and especially since 1978, have revolved around the question of how to best accommodate, contain or isolate the country's largest and best-endowed ethnic group.

Kenya's political history can be divided into roughly three periods that correspond to the tenures of the country's three presidents. During the first, from 1963 to 1978, Kenya was ruled by its first president, Jomo Kenyatta. Kenyatta was succeeded by Daniel arap Moi, who headed the country from 1978 to 2002. He was in turn succeeded by Mwai Kibaki, whose tenure is limited to two elected five-year terms and who will thus retire in 2012.

Kenyatta and Kibaki are both Kikuyu and examples of how Kikuyu benefited from the disproportionate investments made in schools in Central Province during the colonial period. Both went to university and both earned master's degrees (Kenyatta in anthropology and Kibaki in economics). Both used their education to become leaders of their ethnic group and members of its landed establishment. And both shared a patrician's view of how Kenya should be governed: via a centralised political system, but one that would maintain law and order and develop the country via a highly trained, competent and accountable civil service. They also sought to perpetuate Kikuyu hegemony, both political and economic. Put simply, what was good for the Kikuyu would benefit the rest of Kenya. And given their commitment to competent government, they were largely right. During the first ten years of Kenyatta's presidency,

Kenya's rate of economic growth was among the highest in Africa, averaging 7 to 8 per cent annually. Kibaki's tenure was likewise marked by rising rates of economic growth to 7 per cent in 2007. Under both, Kenya's rate of economic growth rose, but did so at the expense of rising inequality in the distribution of incomes – between rich and poor, and between rich tribes and poor.

Kenya's second president, Daniel arap Moi, was very different in both background and approach. Trained as a schoolteacher, Moi is a Tugen, a small sub-group of the Kalenjin peoples, a loose amalgam of groups in the western Rift Valley who speak languages that are mutually intelligible but distinct in structure from Bantu and Nilotic languages. Together the Kalenjin account for 13 per cent of Kenya's population. In marked contrast to the Kikuyu, who were favoured during the colonial period, the Kalenjins were, for the most part, ignored, though many also lost their lands to the white settlers. In the grand scheme of Kenyan politics, the Kikuyu are best described as being one of 'the bigs and the haves', while the Kalenjins are among the 'smalls and the have nots'.

In the run-up to Kenya's independence in 1963, the British held a series of four elections (in 1957, 1958, 1961 and 1963) for an ever larger Legislative Council, which was transformed into a bicameral legislature consisting of a House of Representatives and Senate six months before independence. In the last two elections, two parties emerged as the principal contestants: the Kenya African National Union (KANU), which was an alliance of the largest and best-educated tribes, most importantly the Kikuyu and the Luo; and the Kenya African Democratic Union (KADU), which was a loose alliance of 'the smalls and have nots'. KANU was headed by Kenyatta, while KADU was headed by Moi. KANU beat KADU by roughly 2 to 1 in both elections, which were followed by negotiations over a new constitution.

The positions of the two parties during the negotiations were markedly different. Kenyatta and KANU wanted a centralised state to maintain Kenyan unity yet assert Kikuyu hegemony, while Moi and KADU wanted a federal system of government to block Kikuyu dominance. They compromised by agreeing to a weak version of federalism consisting of eight provinces which were to have their own elected legislatures and a measure of devolved power. Within them would be forty-three districts which had been the basis of colonial administration and which would continue after independence. However, within one year the deal fell apart. With a large majority in parliament, Kenyatta and KANU simply froze KADU out of the game, while suggesting that if the latter joined KANU the benefits would flow. At the same time, Kenyatta's government refused to implement devolution to the provinces. Elections for the provincial assemblies were never held and the provinces were reduced to administrative structures, albeit powerful ones, within a centralised state.[14] Moi and the other leaders of KADU had no choice. In 1964 they dissolved their party and joined KANU. Moi became Kenya's vice-president and obtained large landholdings as part of the deal, but the centre of power was with the Kikuyu establishment. Indeed, the Luo, then headed by Jaramogi Oginga Odinga, the father of Kenya's current prime minister, went into opposition in 1966 – and were powerless for four decades thereafter.

As Kenyatta grew older and his health declined, some prominent Kikuyu leaders sought to replace Moi as vice-president because the constitution specified that the VP would succeed the president for a period of ninety days should the president die. Kenyatta, however, stood by Moi, who had become his loyal lieutenant and his eyes and ears across Kenya. Though relatively uneducated compared to the Kikuyu establishment, Moi knew Kenya's grassroots politics like the back of his hand. Kenyatta needed him to maintain a regime that became progressively corrupt during his final years. When Kenyatta died in 1978, Moi thus ascended to the presidency.

The fears of the Kikuyu establishment were realised within two years. Now the head of KANU, Moi cleaned house. While all of Kenya's ethnic principal groups were represented in the cabinet, most of the major posts, as well as key positions in the civil service and the army, were put in the hands of Kalenjins or other non-Kikuyu. Moi also changed the constitution in 1981 to mandate that Kenya would henceforth be a one-party state. In addition he moved to assert tight control over all other institutions, including the press, civil society and the country's universities. Only the churches remained uncaptured. Whereas Kenyatta ran a Kikuyu-dominant government that stressed performance and allowed a modest level of disagreement and public debate, Moi demanded absolute loyalty. By the mid-1980s he had transformed Kenya into a classic neo-patrimonial regime. He also reallocated the country's resources to the Rift Valley, his political base, and away from Central Province, the home region of the Kikuyu and related groups. The results are well known. By the end of the decade Kenya was corrupt and broke. Per capita income growth declined, while the treasury was repeatedly looted by senior members of the government or state-owned corporations. As in Mobutu's Zaire, the appointment to office meant the licence to loot.

In this context, it is not surprising that the demand for democracy and the return to multiparty politics in Kenya was led mainly (though not exclusively) by Kikuyu, particularly its prominent clergy and members of its professional establishment. Their demand was echoed to varying degrees by the leading members of the donor community, which provided Kenya with roughly 250 million dollars annually in budget support. With the end of the Cold War, they could demand democracy and the end of corruption in return for their assistance. Moi resisted, but bowed to the inevitable in November 1991, when he requested parliament to repeal the clause in the constitution that had been enacted to define Kenya as a one-party state. A provision to limit the number of presidential terms to two was also enacted, but with a loophole that allowed Moi to run again in 1992 and 1997.

With the return of multiparty politics, the ethnic fault lines were clear – as Moi predicted – for all to see. In the campaign for the 1992 elections, KANU was more or less reduced to a party of the original KADU – namely, a party of the Kalenjins in alliance with the other small tribes of the Rift Valley, Northeast Province and the Coast. The opposition, however, became divided into three and then four parties, all of which were organised along ethnic lines. Mwai Kibaki, Kenya's former Minister of Finance and later vice-president under Moi, formed the Democratic Party but could not generate much support beyond its Kikuyu base in Central Province and Kikuyu-inhabited regions of the Rift Valley. Oginga Odinga, the acknowledged leader of the Luo, and later his son Raila Odinga could not generate support outside of Nyanza Province, the Luo heartland. A third party, Ford-Kenya, drew support mainly from the Luhya people in Western Kenya. Held together by patronage, Moi and KANU (read 'old KADU') retained power with only 40 per cent of the vote as the opposition split three ways. The same pattern was repeated, five years hence, in 1997. Both elections, especially the elections held in 1992, were accompanied by inter-ethnic violence. Approximately 1,500 people were killed and 350,000 were forced from their homes as Kalenjins attacked Kikyu migrants in Molo and in the area around Eldoret in the western Rift Valley. The level of violence was only slightly less than what followed the elections of 2007.

Moi abided by the constitution and made no attempt to run again in 2002. He did, however, attempt to retain influence by anointing Uhuru Kenyatta, the son of Jomo Kenyatta, to be the presidential candidate of KANU in a bid for the Kikuyu vote. The opposition, however, did not repeat their mistake of 1992 and 1997 and united behind Mwai Kibaki, who won a lopsided victory with nearly 60 per cent of the vote, as well as a large majority of seats in the National Assembly. But in reality nothing changed, as the parties remained ethnic coalitions of convenience.

With Moi gone and Kibaki president, the Kikuyu were once again the dominant force in Kenyan politics. Rather than maintain his broad-based coalition, which had brought him victory and which included the Luo under Raila Odinga, Kibaki returned the country to Kenyatta's style of governance. Power was concentrated among Kikuyu loyalists who became known as the Mount Kenya Mafia,[15] but power was also delegated to the civil service, which was expected to perform. Indeed, Kibaki entered into performance contracts with senior members of the civil service. The result was the return of Kenya's once vaunted civil service. The press and civil society were no longer harassed. Kenya also returned to sound fiscal and monetary policy for the first time since Kenyatta's rule. The results soon became apparent. When Kibaki came into office Kenya's economy was stalled. By the end of his first term in 2007, the rate of economic growth had risen to 7 per cent, the highest in years, investment was flowing back into the country and competent government had been re-established. Why then, did the president fail to gain a majority of the popular vote, and, in the eyes of many, lose the election?

In the run-up to the 2007 national elections, Kenya became deeply polarised as non-Kikuyu political elites mobilised the rest of the country on an anti-Kikuyu message. The polarisation of Kenya's politics was largely the result of Kibaki's style of governance and his failure to maintain his alliance with the Luo leader, Raila Odinga. Although it was widely recognised that Kibaki owed his election to Odinga, who campaigned tirelessly across Kenya on Kibaki's behalf, the president and the Kikuyu side of the winning alliance short-changed Odinga and the Luo with respect to key posts in the cabinet. From the outset, the government was split, a split that became exacerbated over disagreements on provisions for a new constitution. By 2005 Odinga had quit the coalition and formed a rival party, the Orange Democratic Movement (ODM). Kibaki then formed the Party of National Unity (PNU) as the vehicle for his re-election. In what should have been an easy win, he could not muster a majority, but was hastily sworn in after a protracted delay in the counting of the votes resulted in the Electoral Commission of Kenya declaring him the winner with 46 per cent of the vote.

In the wake of the announcement, which many Kenyans regarded as fraudulent, more than 1,500 Kenyans died, while between 350,000 and 600,000 were displaced from their homes. There was a complete breakdown of the political process and the country tottered on the abyss of civil war. Peace was ultimately restored after more than a month of negotiations brokered by former UN Secretary-General Kofi Annan and pressure for a power-sharing government exerted by the international community, including the United States. Although Kibaki retained the presidency, Raila Odinga became prime minister and positions in the cabinet were divided equally between the ODM and PNU. Kenya's fault lines, however, were deepened as never before as ethnic leaders played upon long-standing grievances arising out of the low level of ethnic fractionalisation and the legacies of uneven development. Kenya's politics has always been a competition between rival and shifting coalitions of ethnic groups. What was different this time is that the country split into two large coalitions of equal size. And with parity, the propensity for violence dramatically increased.

Peace and Nationhood in Tanzania

With 126 ethnic groups no one of which accounts for more than 10 per cent of the population, the contrast between the distribution of ethnicity in that country compared to Rwanda, Uganda and Kenya could not be greater. Equally important, the country's geographic pattern of economic development does not coincide with or reinforce the position of the country's largest ethnic groups. The largest group, the Sukuma, who constitute 12 per cent of the population, reside more than 550 kilometres from the capital and port city of Dar es Salaam[16] in one of the poorest and least developed regions of the country. While two groups, the Haya and the Chagga, are the principal producers of coffee, and have historically supported the greatest concentration of primary and secondary schools in their areas, the first constitutes only 4 per cent of the population, while the latter accounts for 3 per cent. Moreover, the Haya reside along the western shores of Lake Victoria, just south of the Uganda border and around 1,000 kilometres from Dar es Salaam, while the Chagga inhabit the area around the slopes of Mount Kilimanjaro, which is 400 kilometres from the capital. Put simply, their small size and location pale in comparison with the Baganda and Kikuyu in Uganda and Kenya. Conversely, the residents of Dar es Salaam are a diverse mixture of migrants from across the country and from the small groups that populate the region along the Indian Ocean coast. Rather than reinforcing and entrenching the size and power of the country's largest groups, as in Kenya and Uganda, the pattern of uneven development across Tanzania does just the opposite: it undermines the importance of size. As a country that was poorer and less developed than Uganda and Kenya at the time of independence, the degree of uneven development – that is to say, the extent of the variations in the level of economic development and the provision of social services from one district to the next – was and remains arguably much less. Put differently and notwithstanding the uneven pattern of development existing across the country, its impact on ethnic fault lines is low to negligible.

The situation just described makes Tanzania relatively unattractive for politicians seeking to mobilise the electorate on the basis of ethnic constituencies even where elections to the national legislature are held on the basis of 'first past the post' in single-member constituencies. *In the Tanzanian context, voters seek representation for their locality, but rarely for their tribe.* Notwithstanding this set of 'natural' conditions, the critical variable is how political elites interact with these realities. In the case of Tanzania, then Tanganyika during its run-up to independence, the country had the good fortune of the presence of Julius K. Nyerere.

Like many nationalist leaders of his generation, Nyerere was a socialist who viewed the state as the engine of economic development for achieving equity and who preached 'unity' to overcome the divisions spawned by ethnicity. Like Ghanaian leader Kwame Nkrumah and others of this era, he was determined to forge a strong sense of national identity and was an advocate of one-party governance to achieve this goal.[17] As the leader of the Tanganyika African National Union (TANU), Nyerere and his party won every seat but one in the final election before independence in 1961.

In 1965 Nyerere orchestrated a change in Tanzania's constitution to legitimise the one-party state. However, he reversed his position in 1991 to pave the way for the resumption of multiparty politics. What he initially viewed as 'a luxury' that compromised the prospects for national unity, he later viewed as essential for maintaining both accountability and the ideological purity of CCM,[18] the successor party to TANU. The first multiparty elections since independence were held in 1995. Since then the mainland part of the country has remained a one-party dominant system governed by CCM. Nyerere himself retired from the presidency in 1985 and died in 1999. Since his retirement, Tanzania has elected three successors, each of whom has served two five-year terms. While the ruling party continues to obtain between 75 and 85 per cent of the vote, power has been transferred peacefully on three occasions since Nyerere stepped down.

Although Nyerere failed badly as an architect of socialist develop-ment,[19] he succeeded brilliantly as the father of his nation and remains revered for this accomplishment more than a decade after his death. Unlike most of his counterparts of his era, he had four advantages that made the forging of a Tanzanian nation relatively easy to attain. First, a high level of ethnic fractionalisation. Second, an uneven pattern of economic develop-ment that did not privilege any one large ethnic group. Third, the fact that all but one of Tanzania's 126 ethnic groups speak a Bantu language – that is to say, their own local language, but one that shares a common syntax with all the others in a manner similar to that shared by Romance languages and other language groups. In marked contrast to both Uganda and Kenya, the country is not divided deeply by ethnicity, nor by the pres-ence of groups that speak languages which are structurally different from each other. Fourth, the presence of Swahili, a Bantu language spoken on the Indian Ocean coast, but which spread inland to become the lingua franca of Tanzania, southern Kenya and parts of Rwanda and eastern Congo because it was the language of trade and also shared a syntax with the vernacular languages of other Bantu-speaking groups. Eloquent in both Swahili and English, Nyerere realised that he could use the former to promote Tanzania's national identity, given the country's high level of ethnic fractionalisation. Just as no one group or small coalition could dominate the others, so none could communicate and trade with each other without resorting to Swahili – or English, which few spoke. Nyerere actively promoted the former at the expense of the latter throughout his career, both in his own writings and through state policy.[20] Whereas in Kenya and Uganda citizens often speak their tribal language or English, in Tanzania they speak Swahili. The widespread use of Swahili elevated it to a true national language with its own idioms. Political discourse in Tanzania, including all speeches by political leaders and nearly all debate in the country's parliament, is in the language. A vibrant Swahili press and broadcast media, both radio and TV, both state and private, entrench the language and bridge the boundaries between ethnic groups. Last but not least, Nyerere's socialist perspective resulted in a series of policies to reduce the levels of uneven development, particularly the policies of recruitment by the nation's secondary schools. Although coffee-producing areas such as those around Mount Kilimanjaro and Bukoba favoured the Chagga and Haya, and provided more social services including education for these groups, the pattern was mitigated by requiring secondary schools in these regions to recruit on a nationwide basis.

The result of this demography and the legacy of Nyerere's leadership – a leadership perpetuated by his successors – has all but eradicated all potential fault lines based on ethnicity in mainland Tanzania. Only on the islands of Zanzibar and Pemba does the more familiar pattern found elsewhere in Africa replicate itself in the country. But on the mainland, political factions do not form on ethnic lines. Rather, they do so on the basis of policy preferences and cliques of cohorts within the CCM leadership. This makes for a more 'civil' and indeed 'gentle' politics compared to the African norm, as well as one much less prone to violence.

Accommodating Ethnic Fractionalisation: What is a Country to Do?

Space does not permit, nor do we need to review the political histories of the three East African countries in greater detail. Suffice to say, two have been marked by periods of intense ethnic conflict while one has not. Similarly, political parties and electoral politics in Kenya and Uganda have formed along ethnic lines while in Tanzania they have not.

No leader can change the configuration of ethnicity in his or her country. Nor can leaders change the prior pattern of uneven development in the short term. Some leaders and regimes must therefore deal with ethnic fault lines that run deep, while others do not. During the first thirty years of African independence, most leaders perpetuated the myth of national unity while containing the fissiparous tendencies of ethnic politics through a combination of patronage and repression. This approach, however, did not forestall ethnic conflict in countries with low levels of ethnic fractionalisation exacerbated by moderate to high levels of uneven development. More recently – in Nigeria, in Uganda and now in Kenya – leaders have sought to deal with the 'fractionalisation problem' by establishing some form of 'compensatory regime' that simultaneously considers the level of ethnic fractionalisation and the geographic pattern of uneven development. The result is various forms of federalism tailored to the particular permutation of ethnicity and development, an idea that was universally rejected in the 1960s through to the early 1990s across Africa, but which today is an idea whose 'time has come' in several countries.

Federalism in combination with breaking up the largest ethnic blocs appears to be the most effective way to both accommodate and navigate the existence of ethnic fault lines. However, to be financially viable and mitigate the impact of uneven development, federalism requires a system of equalisation grants managed by the central government. This is because the residents of poor areas are rarely able to raise sufficient revenue to finance their local or state governments, including the provision of adequate social services, on their own. *Put simply, the leaders of large and rich groups must recognise that their long-term interests lie in financing a sub-national tier of government for the 'smalls' and the 'have nots'.* President Mwai Kibaki's biggest mistake in Kenya is that he didn't listen to younger Kikuyu professionals and business people to do just that upon assuming power in 2002. However, in the wake of the violence that followed Kenya's ill-fated election of December 2007, the president and his chief opponent, Raila Odinga, agreed to the establishment of a commission to draft a new constitution that would address Kenya's needs. The outcome produced by the Constitution of Kenya Review Commission in April 2010 and ratified by the electorate in August provides for a system of devolved governance that breaks with the past.[21] Beginning in 2012, Kenya will establish and elect forty-seven county-level governments that will accommodate the small groups while breaking up the large. The new tier of government will be financed mainly through block equalisation grants according to formulae that consider population size and the extent of poverty in the unit, and which will amount to no less than 15 per cent of all government revenue per year. It is a plan that appears to have broad-based support.

By contrast, other African leaders, such as Museveni in Uganda and Meles in Ethiopia, have recognised the need for federalism, but drawn back from supporting genuine federal structures because they fear that this will entail a loss of central control over some areas of their countries. Though Kenya and Uganda have been racked by a history of ethnic conflict, the contrasts between them could not be greater. Their experience, together with that of Nigeria, where a viable formula for federalism appears to have been found, suggests the future of dealing with ethnic fault lines across Africa and elsewhere. One would now expect a long-term process of trial and error by states with low levels of ethnic fractionalisation to the point that, after several iterations, a negotiated equilibrium will ultimately be reached between those who wish to assert the power of one or more of the largest ethnic groups from the centre and those who are willing to subsidise peace at the cost of ethnic hegemony. For Tanzania, and other countries with very high levels of ethnic fractionalisation, the calculus and challenges for these countries' leaders are very different for the reasons discussed.

10

FROM DISTRICTS SIX TO NINE: MANAGING SOUTH AFRICA'S MANY FAULT LINES

Greg Mills

'I have one great fear in my heart, that one day when they [the whites of South Africa] have turned to loving, they will find we [the blacks] are turned to hating.'

Alan Paton, Cry the Beloved Country

DISTRICT SIX, on the outskirts of Cape Town's central business district, is the name of the former predominantly 'coloured' residential area situated at the foot of Table Mountain. In February 1966, under the Group Areas Act, the then white-run South African government declared District Six a 'whites-only' area. Thereafter, between 1968 and 1982, more than 60,000 people were relocated to the Cape Flats twenty-five kilometres away, a significantly underdeveloped region, while their former homes were bulldozed to make way for new development. The area became a rallying call for the anti-apartheid movement and emblematic of the forced removal policy of the National Party (NP) government, of its callousness and its racist underpinnings that held the belief that interracial interaction bred conflict.

Some four decades on, *District Nine*, an acclaimed South African film, was released. This allegorical film presents viewers with a disturbing vision of disintegration, or perhaps failed integration, of South African society. The violent bigotry of the film – which depicts the forced removal of a ghoulish-looking but highly intelligent extraterrestrial race (referred to as 'the prawns') from a slum to which they had been consigned since arriving on earth – evokes the South Africa of the District Six era, a period the country had supposedly left behind. It is a jarring and timely reminder of the xenophobia that still haunts contemporary South Africa. The film, shot on location in Soweto in May 2008, coincided with an upsurge in violence in South African townships between locals and African foreigners which resulted in the deployment of the South African army into the townships for the first time since the end of apartheid in 1994. The unrest resulted in more than sixty deaths and the creation of UNHCR-supervised tented camps across the country, coupled with extensive repatriation programmes to deal with the 100,000 displaced people.

Given its 350-year history of racial division, repression, violence and legislated separation during apartheid, there is perhaps no country with such a seemingly obvious fault line as South Africa. It is the country that has it all in this regard, from religion to race, ethnicity to xenophobia towards foreigners. It is a country with ongoing violence nearly twenty years after apartheid. With a murder rate eight times higher than that of the US and twenty times higher than Western Europe's, it has been described as a 'country at war with itself'.[1] There is no doubt that for all the progress made by the 'rainbow nation', race is still a defining feature. A 2008 trade union report found that whites enjoyed incomes that were on average 450 per cent higher than those earned by blacks. This was despite the growth of a black middle class and an annual social welfare budget of over R70 billion. The 'patience' of blacks towards whites should not, some leaders warned, be assumed to be infinite.[2]

Leading South African politicians have continued to see the country in terms of the historical legacies of apartheid. As President Thabo Mbeki spoke in 2005 in terms of the existence of two societies – one white and one black: 'Part of the society, very rich, where we are here [in Sandton]. It looks very nice, very developed and so on. And like in Switzerland, the Swiss said, you are quite unlikely to see beggars on the street. But not very far from here you would find this dire poverty that characterises the majority of the people of this country.'[3]

Yet, since the advent of democracy in 1994, race[4] is no longer the only – and perhaps not the most important – social divide; nor is it necessarily the one fault line along which the country could possibly fracture. Similarly, although ethnicity was viewed as a major potential fault line in the run-up to the first democratic election in 1994, and around which a great deal of violence occurred at the time, this has not been the case. Instead, ethnicity has been diluted by both the focus on nation building and the waning fortunes of its principal political protagonists. But despite a modern constitution that institutionalises rights and all manner of checks and balances, including apportioning powers to the regions and supposedly empowering parliament and the people at the cost of the executive, new fault lines have emerged around class and policy.

Avoiding Catastrophe

By the end of the 1980s it was increasingly evident to the leadership of the NP, which had ruled South Africa since 1948, that the status quo was becoming unmanageable. The situation had reverted to that of the mid-1970s, with increasing regional military pressure, the ratcheting up of international sanctions and widespread internal unrest.

Although secret talks with the ANC-in-exile had already commenced, it was the ousting of the irascible yet weakening P. W. Botha from power by the unlikely reformer F. W. de Klerk in 1989 that enabled serious negotiations on a transition from white minority rule to democracy to begin. This coincided with a shift in the regional status quo, with the end of the Namibia 'border war', which gave many whites confidence about change, and the simultaneous crumbling of the Cold War and the Soviet Union. In the months after Nelson Mandela was released and the ANC unbanned, some predicted that South Africa would not resolve its deep racial fault line but instead swiftly plunge into conflict far worse than anything that had occurred during the apartheid era. With the country poised at five minutes to midnight, time was running out.

For negotiations to succeed, sacrifices were required on all sides. The talks took in an array of opposition parties, churches, business and community leaders, although the two main protagonists were the NP and the ANC. The NP, which then represented a majority of white South Africans, wanted to secure assurances on the protection of rights, civil service jobs and property, in exchange for which they would relinquish political power. Of chief concern was that South Africa could go down the route of violent retribution, land seizures, nationalisation and the like. This was allayed when Mandela's ANC, once an avowedly Marxist movement, dropped many of its socialist ideas and embraced free-market principles, and by the initiation of a power-sharing Government of National Unity. All-important was the adroit leadership exhibited, first and foremost, by Mandela and de Klerk, who navigated through a number of serious setbacks during the talks and frequent outbreaks of violent ethno-political clashes. At one critical juncture in the transition, Nobel Prize-winning South African Archbishop Desmond Tutu remarked, 'Once we have got it right, South Africa will be the paradigm for the rest of the world.'[5] It certainly appeared so after South Africa's first free and fair election in April 1994, won convincingly by the ANC.

The NP withdrew from the Government of National Unity two years later. Regardless, the spirit of reconciliation pervaded. A Truth and Reconciliation Commission was established to uncover and heal some of the gravest wounds perpetrated across the racial fault line, mostly at the hands of the former white regime, though both the NP and the ANC failed to declare fully their own crimes. In 1999 Deputy President Thabo Mbeki, who had effectively run South Africa from that office since 1994, replaced Mandela as president. Under Mbeki a system of Black Economic Empowerment (BEE), the government's major vehicle for addressing the inequalities of apartheid by affording previously disadvantaged groups a range of economic opportunities, was expanded. One consequence was the emergence of a super-rich black elite. As the gap between rich and poor widened, South Africa's fault line shifted. Race was by no means irrelevant, but the most pronounced divide was now between the haves and have-nots.

South Africa's Post-Apartheid Make-up

Despite the increasing dominance of economic questions – alongside crime and HIV – in South Africa's national discourse, the historical legacy of apartheid still featured prominently, and potently, in the country's politics. Few put it more succinctly, or famously, than Mbeki did in 1998: 'One of these nations is white, relatively prosperous, regardless of gender or geographic dispersal. It has ready access to a developed economic, physical, educational, communication and other infrastructure. This enables it to argue that, except for the persistence of gender discrimination against women, all members of this nation have the possibility to exercise their right to equal opportunity … The second and larger nation of South Africa is black and poor, with the worst affected being women in the rural areas, the black rural population in general and the disabled.'[6] Certainly the country has an extreme poverty problem. According to the UNDP's 2009 Human Development Report,[7] South Africa ranks 129 out of 182 countries (between Namibia and Morocco) for 'Human and Income Poverty', with nearly 43 per cent of the South African population living

Table 1: Global per capita income (PPP) and income inequality[9]

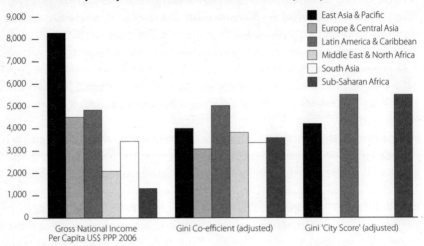

on less than two dollars a day between 2000 and 2007 (Norway is ranked first, while Mali, Central African Republic, Sierra Leone, Afghanistan and Niger are in the last five places).[8]

With a Gini coefficient of 57.8, South Africa is also one of the most unequal societies in the world in a region that is not only very poor, but also very unequal. As Table 1 illustrates, African states are among the most unequal. (Sub-Saharan Africa is the third most unequal region behind Latin America and East Asia, but this is skewed by the absence of data from nearly one-quarter of African countries.) Africa has the bottom five most unequal states measured globally: in descending order, Botswana (60.5), Central African Republic (61.3), Sierra Leone (62.9), Lesotho (63.2) and Namibia (74.2).[10] Gini figures are also higher in cities than in rural areas. Africa's 'city score' is 0.55 (as opposed to the overall continental average of under 0.4), compared to the same for Latin America and 0.42 for Asia. Johannesburg is the highest of those measured in Africa at 0.75 (with Abidjan and Maputo next up at 0.53 and 0.52), compared to 0.6 in São Paulo, 0.61 in Bogota, 0.56 in Mexico City and 0.6 in Rio de Janeiro.[11] Poverty might be a reason for a sense of hopelessness and despair, but it is more likely to produce political and social instability in a context of extreme inequality.

Thus in contemporary South Africa there remain huge wealth divides congregated mainly, but decreasingly, along racial lines. While the leadership has explicitly spelt out the distribution of wealth in racial terms – of 'two nations', one rich white and one poor black – the reality is that these two nations are increasingly multiracial, and the divides between income groups are widening. As such the proportion of black South Africans in the highest income bracket in South Africa rose from 2 per cent in 1975 to 22 per cent in 1996, an increase of 1,000 per cent. Over the same period, the proportion of whites in the top income bracket dropped by one-third, while the proportion in the seven lowest income brackets that was white increased.[12]

The wealth gap is increasingly notable between urban and rural areas. South Africa's urban population comprises 61 per cent of the total population, increasing by 1.4 per cent per annum during the late 2000s – significantly above the average African urbanisation figure of 40 per cent.[13]

The means to wealth highlight the wealth fault line. Moeletsi Mbeki, a respected South African commentator and the former president's brother, has taken aim at the policy of Black Economic Empowerment as a driver of new divisions between the elite and the rest:

> BEE and its subsidiaries – affirmative action and affirmative procurement – which started off as defensive instruments created by the economic oligarchs to protect their assets, have metamorphosed. They have become both the core ideology of the black political elite and, simultaneously, the driving material and enrichment agenda which is to be achieved by maximising the proceeds of reparations that accrue to the political elite. This has proved to be disastrous for the country.[14]

Moeletsi indirectly points to the paradox inherent in an environment beset by high levels of inequality, where politics and the solutions that it derives are driven by the very elites that profit first from such policies.

Indeed, polls appear to downplay the contemporary relevance of race as a social divide. They show that almost half of South Africans feel that race relations have improved since 1994 – even though the same proportion never socialises with people of other races. They also point out, however, that race is not the most important social division in South Africa. It dropped from 22 per cent to 18 per cent between 2007 and 2009. The divide between rich and poor is viewed as more important (around 27 per cent), and the percentage of people believing that political parties are divisive has doubled from 12 per cent to 24 per cent over the same period. Opinion polls also show that confidence in public institutions, political leadership and government performance has declined. Confidence in the presidency has declined by 25 percentage points since 2006 and by around 20 points in both national and provincial government. Parliament had dropped by 16 points and political parties by 14. In one poll conducted around the 2009 election, two-thirds of people agreed with the statement 'Leaders are not concerned with people like me'. Only 38 per cent of those polled reckoned that their personal economic situation would improve in the next two years, while around one-third thought that their personal safety would improve in the same period. These figures are 21 and 19 percentage points lower than their equivalents in 2004.[15]

These changes are interpreted by commentators in a variety of ways, according to their political colours. For example, in the August 2009 edition of the journal of the South African Communist Party (SACP), *Umsebenzi*, party leader Blade Nzimande argued that the struggle in South Africa was about neither race nor class primarily, but about both:

> At the same time, much as the SACP has understood the deep interrelationship between these two contradictions in South African society, the two are not identical. The racial contradiction has been (and still is) the primary (most immediate) contradiction in South Africa, whilst the class contradiction represents the fundamental (determinant) contradiction. It is on the terrain of class analysis that the racial contradiction in South Africa is best understood.

This, for the SACP, provides the tools to tackle gender discrimination in South Africa, another fault line compounded by the racial and class legacy of apartheid and inadequate social reform:

> In other words, whilst the struggle for gender equality seeks to liberate all women from the yoke of patriarchal oppression, we must not lose sight of the racial and class stratification amongst women themselves. This means that we need to constantly build the capacity of African working class women as part of the leading motive forces in the struggle for the emancipation of women as a whole.[16]

On paper, however, and certainly by comparison to societies elsewhere in Africa, South Africa's women fare little worse than their male counterparts: South Africa ranked 26 out of 109 on the UNDP's 'Gender Empowerment Measure' (measuring gender inequality in three basic dimensions of empowerment: economic participation and decision-making; political participation and decision-making; and power over economic resources) for 2009, just behind Italy, Ireland and Israel, but ahead of Costa Rica, Greece and Cuba.[17] But on the 'Gender Development Index' (measuring achievement in three dimensions: a long and healthy life; knowledge; and a decent standard of living) South Africa fell to 109 out of 155, behind Namibia and just ahead of Sao Tome and Principe. All bar thirteen of the bottom fifty-five in the Gender Development Index were African and all bar one (Afghanistan) of the bottom thirty.[18]

Race in South Africa is criss-crossed by a range of other identities. As might be expected of an immigrant society with a wide range of ethnic origins (and eleven official languages[19]), South Africa offers a kaleidoscope of religions. In the 2001 national census, Christians accounted for 79.7 per cent of the population, the largest sub-group being Zion Christian (11 per cent). Islam, the fastest-growing religion, accounted for around 1.5 per cent of the population, with Hinduism at 1.3 per cent and Judaism at just 0.2 per cent. The number of black Muslims had, in 2011, grown sixfold. In addition, it is estimated that there are around 250,000 each of Pakistanis and Chinese in South Africa, 50,000 Vietnamese, perhaps as many as 3 million Zimbabweans, between 250,000 and 350,000 Mozambicans and (among others) numerous Nigerians, Somalis, Senegalese, Ivoirians and Congolese. Some estimates put the number of illegal immigrants as high as the whole of South Africa's white population (5 million) and others at even twice as many.[20] However, as has been pointed out, such figures are 'potentially inflammatory' and a more balanced assessment gives the number of foreign-born people in South Africa as around 1.3 million.[21]

Gender and religious concerns cross-cut with the tension between South Africa as a 'traditional' versus a 'modern' society. Such issues are prominent, for example, surrounding polygamy and the tension between customary and other legal systems. In a country where the president has five wives and reportedly more than twenty children, this is not surprising. But while these concerns are the most visible, they are not necessarily the most salient divisions in a country finding its national feet which has, until now, managed them largely under the liberation banner of a 'non-sexist, non-racial' South Africa.

The Heart of the Matter?: South Africa's Political Divisions and Policy Conundrums

In October 2009 the ruling ANC Secretary-General and chairman of the SACP, Gwede Mantashe, said, 'We need the party today more than ever before. Class contradictions within our movement are going to be more intensive as we move ahead. We must strengthen our leadership structures and make the party more effective.' He also felt that the party should 'confront the reality' that racists were becoming more confident in South Africa: 'Both affirmative action and the BEE are under siege and progressive forces are not as forthcoming as they should. This is one area that needs our urgent attention as the movement.'[22]

Such commentary is strikingly unusual for a party (the ANC) that enjoyed such an overwhelming majority (66 per cent of the vote – 264 out of 400 seats) at the polls in the April 2009 general election, and against which no serious contender appears likely for the foreseeable future, despite the electoral increases in support for the opposition Democratic Alliance (16.75 per cent or sixty-seven seats).

Mantashe is not alone. In December 2009 President Jacob Zuma contended that the South African economy had failed to help poor citizens despite steady growth since 1994: 'The gap between the rich and the poor has been widening as the economy grows. Any economy must talk to the problems of its people.'[23]

South Africa's problems relate in part to the structural 'nature' of the economy (where exports are still mostly – just under 60 per cent – made up of minerals or mineral products) and in part to policy choices made by politicians reluctant to undercut their liberation support base. Even so, South Africa has not enjoyed enough growth from the commodity boom, falling 'stubbornly short' of the desired 6 per cent figure. And though 1.6 million jobs were created between 2002 and 2007, unemployment remained very high. Zuma's toughest task – or, put differently, South Africa's most intractable division – is balancing the interests of the unions who helped to put him in power with those of the investors the country sorely requires. Here foreign direct investment (FDI) flows to South Africa in 2010 declined by more than 70 per cent from 2009 to just 1.6 billion from 5.4 billion dollars, according to the United Nations Conference on Trade and Development. This pushed South Africa, the continent's largest economy, into tenth position as a recipient of FDI across the continent, from a ranking of fourth in 2009. Africa received a total of 55 billion dollars in FDI flows in 2010.[24]

But the ensuing political and policy disquiet cannot be wished away. At its roots is a combination of inequality, unemployment (around one-quarter of the economically active population), high personal expectations and political differences on policy.

For while there has overall been positive economic change since 1994, the South African economy is beset with problems of slow export growth and little export diversification away from minerals, even though there has been solid growth in the domestic-orientated services sector. Poverty and joblessness remain persistent and entrenched problems. While a small sector of the population is formally employed, and this is still today congregated around the mining sector,[25] the remainder is dependent on government redistributive welfare efforts for their survival. Numerous studies have pointed to the need to improve the quality and cost of infrastructure; skills and productivity; the lack of competitiveness of the private sector and of the exchange rate; and the poor quality of government services.[26] On paper this requires, in the short term, liberalising trade further, ensuring greater competitiveness in the exchange rate and improving flexibility in the labour market, and, over the long term, improving skills and infrastructure.

Most politicians, however, would prefer to focus on skills, technology, education and infrastructure in addressing these constraints, adding greater value to commodities. The point where the technocrats and politicians meet is in the need for a 'developmental state' – for greater government involvement in devising and implementing industrial policy, even though paradoxically that capacity is weak and difficult to create. In so doing, implicitly or explicitly both question the premise that the private sector is at the centre of economic growth and that even growth itself, if sufficient, is a necessary condition for development. Planning, in this context as a form of process, is used to justify and reinforce the centrality of the state over the private sector. Meeting infrastructure backlogs is seen as a key government responsibility, but more fundamentally, for growth to take off as in South-East Asia, the state has yet to recognise the limits of its role and accept the centrality of the private sector.

To take the contrary view, for some this situation points to the need for a more interventionist and fiscally expansive state, focused at the extreme by those who recommend nationalisation, widespread and far-reaching land reform, and a willingness to assume more debt.

Partly these preferences relate to the baggage of South Africa's transition. Politics and the related need to be sensitive to apartheid history of low wages and poor living conditions explain why, for example, South Africa apparently prefers to ignore the lessons of others in stimulating value addition through low-wage labour, even though this offers a means of what economists like to call 'convergence' – the narrowing of differences in income between rich and poor countries. It explains why many Africans glaze over when they hear that Singapore does not have a minimum wage based on the logic that 'it would soon become a maximum one', and why they prefer to find another high-wage-earning path (involving the state as the principal generator of development options and, inevitably, employer). This has the added advantage of ensuring political compliance and support.

In some ways this is down to a prevailing world view and a mythology about South Africa's own struggle – who led it, why it was won, who won it and the compromises that were (or were not) made in the process. Patrick Bond, the doyen of socialist, anti-neoliberal writers in South Africa, asks, for example, in the wake of the global credit crisis, whether South Africa can 'again guide internationalist reactions to capitalist overreach? ... Beyond the miracle of a half-dozen leftist governments in Latin America, the world seems ripe for socialist renewal from below, forged from labour-community unity.'[27]

His picture of economic doom and gloom in South Africa, however, had little from his vantage to do with uncompetitive wages, policies and practices or currency, but 'neoliberal policies' which 'have made SA economically more vulnerable than at any time since 1929'. And 'thanks to the liberalisation of trade and finance, SA now has amongst the world's highest current account deficits and is the most risky emerging market ...'[28]

It is probably less about being capitalist or socialist, however, than it is down to the assessment of the benefits of closer global liberalisation and integration (or not). While there are those who see dramatic advantages in greater global trade and capital flows (gaining the slice of a much bigger pie than afforded by introversion), many in the ruling ANC apparently prefer to see the world in 'neo-mercantilist' terms – as a zero-sum game. Of course the history of trade shows that protectionism, while encouraging self-sufficiency, not only fails to develop sustainable industries but burdens citizens with high costs and often lower-quality goods, as well as encouraging rent-seeking by politicians and corruption. Perhaps most importantly, and even more costly, is that protectionism fosters a sense of international autarchy – a sense of 'them' and 'us' – which has considerable costs beyond trade flows and growth figures.

This has given rise to ongoing challenges to Western leadership, most recently in questioning the wisdom and efficacy of the prevailing economic orthodoxy in the aftermath of the global financial crisis and especially given the enormous bail-outs of banks by American and other taxpayers. A group of South African state economists on a study tour to Vietnam and Singapore in February 2009 could not help smirking as they repeatedly pointed out that it was the United States, led by the Republican Party, that had now had to 'nationalise' its banks. Aside from the obvious immaturity of such behaviour, they missed the point in their condemnation of the free-market economy: the United States was still the world's greatest economic power, and its travails affected us all, while they were in two countries that had grown vigorously as they provided an enabling environment for the private sector to operate.

It is partly also about a related failure to accept responsibility – and to set priorities accordingly. There is still a climate of suspicion between South Africans and about the rest of the world. To take another example, during the xenophobic attacks in May 2008, instead of admitting the high level of local frustration about unemployment and the government's record of service delivery, political parties blamed each other and pointed to so-called 'third-hand' influences as being behind the attacks. The then Minister of Intelligence, Ronnie Kasrils and his director-general of the National Intelligence Agency said that the violence was politically motivated and targeted at the ANC – even though there were instances of the rioters singing the theme tunes associated with ANC President Jacob Zuma. The buck stopped nowhere. This has led to a 'them-and-us' mentality between business, civil society and government. Whereas some in government tend to view business as opportunistic, myopic and distanced from dealing with national questions outside of their commercial silos, business now, relative to the apartheid period, prefers to view its relationship with government in contractual terms – as taxpayer and service provider respectively – rather than grappling with wider socio-economic and political questions. There is, too, a related schism between those (mainly in government and among its allies) that look inward to meeting socio-political demands and those (mainly in business) that are outwardly focused on global opportunities and threats.

If economic choices are likely to remain the most striking division, this links in as well with ongoing divisions between the centre and the provinces, between local and national authority, and the corruption and administrative dysfunction that currently pervades administration at each of these levels. Originally intended as a constitutional check and balance on over-centralised government and a means of reducing the potential for ethnic tension, South Africa's nine provinces[29] all have their own legislature, premier and executive council – and are all, bar the Western Cape, in the ANC's hands, though their relative power has diminished over the past fifteen years.[30] Such traits are likely to be exacerbated by ongoing tensions around a lack of service delivery. In 2009 protests spread countrywide as dissatisfaction increased over the lack of delivery by the ANC government. In the ten years since 1996, the tax base increased from 1.9 million people to about 5 million. But the government remained unable to spend the proceeds on worthwhile projects, with the result that in 2007 and 2008 the government ran a budget surplus. Here, too, there is a contradiction between the ANC's desire for a developmental state, focusing developmental decisions and actions in the hands of government, and the reality evident across many government ministries – of weak capacity, poor delivery and rampant corruption.

Why? Between Design and Denial

The answer as to why South Africa is vulnerable to eruptions along several fault lines hints at possible means to ameliorate and manage them – it is partly by design.

In apartheid South Africa, access to education and job opportunities was heavily skewed in favour of whites. As a consequence, it 'was therefore inevitable that political liberation was envisaged by black people as providing not only free and improved access to education and jobs previously denied to them, but also [as a way] to the redress of racial imbalances in both the state and private sectors'.[31]

In 1995 the government White Paper on the Transformation of the Public Service contended that within four years 50 per cent of management positions within the civil service should be staffed by blacks. From 1993 the racial composition of the civil service changed dramatically, partly by the inclusion of the former homeland bureaucrats (some 241,335 of them) and by affirmative action. Whites had decreased in national positions by 2003 from 38.5 per cent (of 767,521) to 23.6 per cent (of 310,907), and blacks increased from 41.3 per cent to 62.8 per cent. In addition, 78.6 per cent of the provincial civil service (totalling 716,742 people) were black as opposed to 9.3 per cent white. Overall the civil service, including the former homelands, stayed at roughly 1 million people.[32]

Another design, of former President Mbeki, was to contain the autonomy of provinces and to centralise state power, undoing the constitutional provisions for a federalist, three-tiered (local, provincial and national) structure. The centralising presidency under Mbeki was a related feature of this tendency. After taking over in 1999, he merged the separate offices of the presidency, deputy president and office of the president, under whom ministries were brought together in five overlapping clusters: international relations and trade; social affairs; governance and administration; investment and employment; and economic affairs. By 2004 the presidency had grown to 469 people with a budget of R170 million, up from R89 million in 2001.[33] One driver for this centralising trend was also the need to impose stricter discipline on the ANC itself, given its disparate character and diversity of political cultures, from the United Democratic Front, to homeland politicians and bureaucrats, to exiles.

This may be the cost of not having a revolution, but there has been a cost nonetheless in the balance between 'representation' with 'efficiency' and greater party discipline with delivery. Although South Africa has enjoyed tremendous achievements (including consistent economic growth, fiscal discipline and delivery of social benefits), there have been policy failures (HIV/Aids, Zimbabwe and government capacity in managing delivery). Capacity problems have been compounded by what the SACP Secretary-General Blade Nzimande has denigrated as 'tendercrats' (bureaucrats benefiting financially from the issuing of tenders) and others the 'systemisation of corruption' among government. As Roger Southall has noted in this regard, 'whether or not present-day corruption is "better" or "worse" than under apartheid is essentially a red herring, for under its newly democratic order, South Africa aspires to an unimpeachable level of civic virtue, and numerous institutions have been established and laws passed which require the accountability of politicians and public servants to the citizenry, and indeed, of corporate executives to their shareholders'.[34]

Corruption has been allowed to gain ground, he argues, partly because of the 'mixed messages' sent out by the ANC's national leadership (such as over the highly controversial $5 billion 1999 arms deal,[35] which was since mired in corruption allegations), the reluctance to investigate allegations over the misuse of state positions and resources, notably where there have been close connections with the party and where politicians have not been pressed to declare their financial interests (as was heightened by the assassination in 2005 of the mining magnate Brett Kebble, given his business interests inter alia with the ANC Youth League).

Loyalty to poorly performing or corrupt officials was not just an Mbeki failing, but has been evident since the time of Mandela – a president who while in office fired only one cabinet minister, and that was for affairs of party politics rather than poor performance. As Mandela justified:

'One of the marks of a great chief is the ability to keep together all sections of his people, the traditionalists and reformers, conservatives and liberals.'[36] Hence the 'big tent' approach taken, keeping together the amalgam of races, classes, religions and politics, from the era of 'reconciliation' to Mbeki's of 'transformative government'.

Conclusion

In April 2011 the leader of the ANC Youth League, Julius Malema, entered court in Johannesburg, accused of hate speech for refusing to stop singing the lyrics 'Shoot the Boer', a liberation song widely used in the struggle against apartheid. The lobby group which brought the action claimed that it could incite harm or hatred against Afrikaners and white farmers. The case dominated the national media, in part because Malema had by then taken on the mantle of the country's leading spokesman for young disillusioned blacks and was arguably one its most influential political figures, but more worryingly because it bore all the hallmarks of the old South Africa, riven with racial divisions and seething with hatred. To emphasise the point, he was flanked by the controversial anti-apartheid leader Winnie Madikizela-Mandela, and seven assault-rifle-toting guards dressed in matching black suits, white shirts and red ties. It would have been a Mafia caricature if it were not so serious.

But the trial was more distraction than substance, a chimera obscuring a cancer gnawing away at the very substance of South Africa's civil and civilised society – investment, growth, jobs, wealth, prosperity, stability, development and reinvestment. What was of far more consequence was the apparent salience of the highly divisive economic prescriptions Malema and his supporters, and others in the trade unions, put forward – none more so than nationalisation, a policy which has historically proved disastrous across Africa and elsewhere.

Thus twenty-one years after de Klerk unbanned the ANC and released its leaders from jail, South Africa appeared once more to be at a tipping point. The country was no longer poised between racial upheaval and stability, but a new type of division seemed to have fractured the country's political landscape: between a radical state-led transformation of the economy and supporters of the negotiated settlement struck in the early 1990s and enshrined in the country's much-admired constitution. Fuelling the division is the widely experienced frustration that BEE and more generally democracy have not delivered anywhere near the level of economic and social upliftment that they promised for a vast swathe of previously disadvantaged black South Africans. The words of one prominent anti-apartheid leader, 'We did not struggle to be poor' reverberate in the rhetoric of popular figures like Malema and have deep resonances among the millions of unemployed youth.

Yet the new fault line is not nearly so clear-cut. Nepotism and patronage, exposed almost daily in media stories of preferential contracts for the party faithful (so-called 'tenderpreneurs'), are rife. Not the least of those accused are, ironically, some of the most ardent proponents of nationalisation. Zwelinzima Vavi, the general secretary of the ANC's government ally the Congress of South African Trade Unions (COSATU), warned in 2011: 'If we do not do something about corruption we will find ourselves in a predatory state, where the social order of feeding will be as it is alleged in Angola and Kenya.' He also remarked that South Africa might soon have a 'President Zille', referring to the leader of the opposition, Helen Zille, because the ANC was 'infested with *corruption* and greed'.[37] Evidence from Transparency International bears out Vavi's charges: South Africa's corruption score has steadily worsened between 2007 and 2011 across numerous indicators.[38]

Race today is, as in the apartheid past, the refuge of scoundrels and profiteers. In a country defined by apartheid and the hurt it still generates, racial tensions will always have to be managed. By raising the spectre of renewed conflict, many of the leading firebrands who champion failed economic ideas are only concealing their own malign activities. They seek personal gain in destroying the bridges that were so painstakingly constructed across South Africa's racial divide in the early 1990s.

PART FOUR:
TRANSITION AND DIVERGENCE IN THE MIDDLE EAST

11

OUT OF THE ASHES: PROGRESS IN IRAQ 2003–11

Chris Brown

DEBATE MAY CONTINUE on whether Iraq is fundamentally flawed as a state because of fault lines that can be held together only by despotism. Yet much was done between 2003 and 2011 to dispel that myth and also to create a model for similar healing – particularly in the wider Middle East.

Iraq's political achievements since the ousting of Saddam Hussein in 2003 are as remarkable as they are under-appreciated, at least outside the country. By the end of the decade improvements in the security situation had finally permitted the country's economic potential to be unleashed. However, many of the traditional fault lines remain and Iraq's political and economic advances are not free goods: they will deepen some of the existing fault lines and expose new ones. The key to continued progress lies with nationalist, coalition-building and compromise politics. The question is whether the Iraqis can sustain this once the 'stabilisation wheels' afforded by the US-led coalition's presence in Iraq come off. The last US soldiers are due to leave the country by the end of 2011.

Iraq's fault lines are not just internal; healing rifts must be seen as a regional challenge in which Iraq's neighbours have opportunities to help, or hinder, as coalition influence wanes.

In considering solutions to Iraq's fault lines it is important to differentiate between conflict prevention, which attempts to stop a fault line from erupting in the first place; conflict termination measures, which aim to stem an existing eruption while not necessarily addressing the underlying cause; and conflict resolution, which seeks reconvergence. These are not necessarily mutually reinforcing. Understanding when a fault line is genuinely healing as opposed to temporarily dormant is essential for internal and external actors alike.

History

As with many states forged on the anvil of imperial cartographic neatness, Iraq is riven with fault lines: economic, political, cultural and social. Iraq's constituent Ottoman provinces of Basra, Baghdad and Mosul enjoyed links with each other, not least through their mutual reliance on the Tigris for trade. However, they had maintained fierce independence throughout their history, both from Istanbul and from each other, particularly in their confessional and tribal leanings. Mosul, geographically closest to the centre of the Caliphate, straddled the Arab–Kurd fault line. Baghdad sits at the interface of the Sunni–Shia confessional divide. Basra's traditional orientation from a trading perspective was to the Gulf, with inevitable links to Persia and its Shiism, not least through the centres of pilgrimage and learning at Karbala and Najaf. Indeed, external regional influences, emanating from Iraq's neighbours, remain as much at the heart of Iraq's fault lines as its internal divides. Mesopotamia was and is seen, not least by Saudi Arabia, as the buffer between Sunni and Shia; a minority Sunni government in Iraq, even one as unpalatable as Saddam Hussein's Ba'ath regime, provided a degree of cushioning in the kingdom which changes since 2003 have removed, creating a new dynamic for the House of Saud to ponder. This illustrates another rubric to Iraq's fault lines: many of Iraq's neighbours, excluded from direct influence and frequently threatened by Saddam Hussein, have found themselves torn between revengeful and benign influence over these long-standing regional fault lines. This complex mosaic has not only led to multiple insurgencies following the fall of Saddam; it also defies simple categorisation, let alone resolution. But separating and understanding the contributing factors are crucial to their mitigation.

Religion

The Sunni–Shia divide emerged after 2003 as the dominant factor in Iraq's instability during the period 2004–7. The trigger from a Shia perspective was revenge for decades of oppression at the hands of a Sunni minority.[1]

It was fuelled by the decision by the Coalition Provisional Authority – the US-led transitional government established after the invasion of Iraq – to disband the Iraqi army, thereby providing a ready source of trained militants with access to secreted weaponry. Tens of thousands on both sides were killed in tit-for-tat insurgency,[2] particularly in Baghdad, where the eruption of this fault line led effectively to sectarian cleansing and coalesced into mono-sectarian districts. The effect of the oppression which had characterised pre-2003 Iraq was false security for the Sunni.[3] As the fault line erupted in late 2003, both sects developed their own means of providing security for their respective communities, the destabilising effect of which was magnified by media attention on the capital. The nature of this fault line lent itself to intervention by an impartial security force. Coalition forces provided the obvious and immediate conflict termination strategy. However, the focus of the coalition forces in 2004–6 was on destroying 'terrorists' rather than protecting the population. Coalition tactics in central and northern Iraq during this time revolved around 'clear and sweep' raids, which alienated the Sunni population. The more the situation deteriorated, the more coalition forces were perceived by both sides as lacking impartiality. In addition, if the coalition was not to be perceived as an occupier, responsibility had to transfer as rapidly as possible to an indigenous security force.[4] Coalition efforts to train a new Iraqi army were already under way, but there was a deepening divergence between the capability of the Iraqi military forces and the underdeveloped civil police force, particularly at community level. The coalition Multinational Security Transition Command in Iraq (MNSTC-I) increasingly focused its efforts on the Iraqi police.[5] Iraqi Security Forces gradually took responsibility for security in their respective provinces,[6] with relatively benign provinces first in order to demonstrate capability and engender confidence.[7]

Two initiatives conflated to bring about a vast reduction in interethnic violence after 2007. The first was a Sunni tribal initiative, initially centred on Anbar Province in western Iraq but spreading throughout the Sunni-dominated north, to turn against al-Qaeda, whose brutal leadership of the insurgency had destroyed whole communities, frequently regardless of confessional persuasion. The initiative, Sawat ('Awakening'), encouraged and funded initially by the US but latterly by the government of Iraq, turned thousands of insurgents into a civil defence force with the promise of government employment once security had been restored.[8]

The second was a change in US doctrine which put protection of

Iraqis at the heart of the counter-insurgency. In order to achieve that goal, there was a requirement for troops to be based in the communities they were responsible for protecting, rather than operating from large isolated bases outside those communities. This required reinforcement at a time when US (and UK) public and political disenchantment with engagement in Iraq was driving down troop numbers. US troop strength was substantially increased in order to dominate Baghdad. It was not a strategy without risk, but 'the main hope ... was that if Sunni attacks were blunted, Shias would rein in their own sectarian agenda'.[9]

Security in Iraq improved dramatically from a peak of 1,800 terrorist attacks per week in mid-2007 to fewer than 200 per week by mid-2009. At the time of writing, sporadic incidents continue, and will continue, but levels are now consistently below 10 per cent of their peak. The remaining terrorist threat is increasingly focused on attempts to undermine the government of Iraq rather than regenerate the ethnic violence which swept northern and central Iraq in the period 2004–7. Although the population increase in Mosul[10] from 650,000 in 1987 to 1.8 million in 2008 created unemployment and disenchantment which helped fuel the remaining hub of the insurgency, the relative stability in the rest of Iraq allowed security to be reinforced in Ninewa. At the same time, concerted efforts to cut al-Qaeda's supply of funds and weaponry forced the insurgents to harness their diminished resources for spectacular attacks, which, while attracting media attention, have thus far not reversed the underlying downward trend in violence.

But the relative anarchy after 2003 also catalysed a power struggle within the confessional division, particularly in the south, where Shia fought Shia along fault lines which ranged from strictly religious[11] to tribal to outright criminal. However, unlike the inter-confessional divide, the intra-Shia divisions were inflamed by external military action, exemplified by British efforts in Basra between 2004 and 2007. Coalition forces provided a unifying purpose for intra-Shia rivalry which was always going to resolve itself without annihilation when viewed against the greater Sunni threat.

In addition to the Sunni–Shia divide, Iraq has an 800,000-odd Christian minority, around one-third of which has fled since 2003. The wider Christian Church has naturally taken a keen interest in what it saw as persecution. The new Iraqi government has responded to this divide, if belatedly.[12]

Ethnic Divide[13]

The Sunni–Shia fault line described above is exacerbated by the ethnic fault line between Arabs and Kurds. The divide, reinforced in 1991 by Saddam's recognition of the Kurdish Regional Government, separates the four provinces of north-east Iraq from the remainder. It is therefore also a political fault line, but not a clean one in terms of either geography or ethnicity. Geographically, a series of disputed internal boundaries (DIBs) fall along the whole length of the fault line.

This problem has been exacerbated since 2003 by the Kurds' 'self-liberation' from Saddam's rule, in which their armed fighters – the Peshmerga – pushed south of the traditional divide, followed by considerable Kurdish civilian population movement, and by the subsequent peaceful prosperity which the Kurds have enjoyed. Article 140 of the Iraqi constitution was designed to resolve these disputes, with the UN Mission in Iraq (UNAMI) advising, supporting and assisting the government of Iraq.[14] It mandates the government of Iraq to complete Article 58 of the Transition Administration Law – a series of measures to remedy the Ba'athist regime's ethnic cleansing. However, a referendum should have taken place by 31 December 2007 and UNAMI's initial attempts in 2008 to resolve what it considered the easier DIBs backfired, resulting in a year's delay while a more comprehensive report was compiled. Initial engagement between the two sides in mid-2009 was promising but soon ran into sand. Because of their support for the coalition, the Kurds have enjoyed a degree of US political and economic support which will inevitably diminish with the US troop withdrawal. It remains to be seen whether the DIBs can be resolved – a top priority for the Kurds – before then; the Arabs have more to gain by playing long.

Moreover, the fault line between Kurds and the remainder of the population is not unique to Iraq: Turkey, Syria and Iran exhibit similar tensions. Indeed, it is impossible to describe the ethnic divide between Kurds and Arabs without reference to the wider Kurdish issue, particularly in Turkey. The internal Turkish Kurdish insurgency, fronted by the Kurdistan Workers' Party (PKK), inevitably spilled over into Iraq. The Kurdish region of Iraq was perceived by Ankara as a safe haven from which Kurdish insurgents could launch attacks into Turkey. Turkey maintains the right to conduct cross-border counter-attacks against PKK targets, which it has regularly exercised, with a thinly veiled threat of mounting attacks deeper into the Kurdish region of Iraq on suspicion of Iraqi Kurdish complicity.

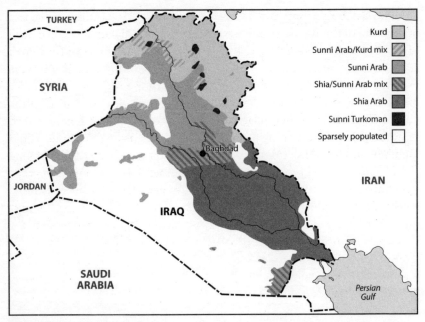

Ethnoreligious groups in Iraq

From 2009, however, Ankara's line, particularly from the Turkish General Staff, softened.[15] The Turkish Foreign Minister, Ahmet Davutoglu, became the first Turkish minister to set foot in the Kurdish region of Iraq, announcing alongside Iraqi Kurdish President Masud Barzani, who had previously promised to fight back against Turkish military incursion, that Turkey would open a consulate in Erbil.[16] Moreover, Turkish political, cultural and economic concessions to its own Kurdish population in recent years bode well, albeit not without political risk to Turkey's ruling Justice and Democracy (AK) Party.

All this changes the dynamic for Iraq's Kurds. On the one hand, the lessening of the threat from Turkey and the opportunity for cross-border economic links, particularly an outlet direct through Turkey for the Iraqi Kurds' hydrocarbons, could embolden Erbil against greater political and economic integration with Baghdad. On the other hand, it is in neither Ankara's nor Baghdad's interests to inflame calls for greater independence for the Iraqi Kurds, let alone a 'Greater Kurdistan'. Turkey's pressure in this respect could be helpful in resolution of the Arab–Kurd fault line in Iraq in return for economic benefits for Erbil: a win-win situation which merits further work.

The 850,000-strong city of Kirkuk plus its surrounding region is a microcosm of this divide, sitting astride the Arab–Kurd fault line and on top of vast hydrocarbon reserves, with an even higher-octane mix of Turkoman and Christian communities.[17] Under Saddam around 250,000 Kurds were expelled from Kirkuk in a twenty-year Arabisation programme[18] – under previous Provincial Elections' law, the Kurds had a minority share in the Provincial Council – but their relative percentage of the population increased significantly as a result of the post-2003 influx. The proposed census would highlight and formalise this tectonic shift. Under Article 23 of the Provincial Election Law a committee of seven members of the Council of Representatives was established to negotiate a power-sharing plan in Kirkuk, resolve demographic issues and settle property disputes prior to conducting the postponed provincial poll to determine the representation for Kirkuk. The Kurds have pressed for an early poll, something the Provincial Council can in theory call unilaterally, but the other ethnic groups and the Iraqi government will not agree to the inevitable outcome: integration of Kirkuk into the autonomous Kurdish region.[19] Proposals for a city council with 32 per cent of the seats each for Kurds, Arabs and Turkmen, with 4 per cent for the Christians, have been made, but at the time of writing the process had ground to a halt.[20] A breakthrough was achieved for the 2010 electoral law – the committee accepted the most recent voter registration as the basis of the electoral roll. The many Kurds who moved to Kirkuk after 2003 were able to vote there. The danger for 2012 and beyond is that this may embolden them in the face of a growing Arab realisation that the Kurds will soon be without their US backer, at which point the Arab–Kurd fault line becomes more susceptible to eruption.

In the meantime, UNAMI, supported by the US Embassy and MNF-I (Multi-National Force, Iraq), put forward a series of measures designed to heal the rift. Kirkuk is one of the few areas in Iraq that has police primacy. The ethnic mix of the police roughly matches that of its population, but the police leadership is skewed towards the Kurds. An attempt has been made to integrate the Asayish,[21] who provide most of the actionable intelligence to the police, into an intelligence fusion cell. This would enhance transparency and thus allow all security forces to establish a common operating picture and communications links so that they can work together, within their own boundaries, to keep the peace. Destabilising Kirkuk is in the interests of the Sunni insurgent groups, their aim to force the government to place Kirkuk under army control. Adopting a military solution to what is a political problem would inflame the Arab–Kurd fault line.[22]

To counter this, the first joint training exercise between the federal Iraqi and Kurdish police forces took place on 22 November 2009, leading to joint security structures mentored and supervised by MNF-I. In parliament the long-standing issues over oil revenues, integration of Kurdish military forces into the Iraqi army and the Kurdish constitution all played into the coalition forming after the 2010 elections. There is talk of a 'grand bargain' – a package of measures which addresses all the issues in Kirkuk, or the Arab–Kurd fault line more widely – where all sides would be seen to be treated fairly, gaining in some respects while losing in others, but benefiting overall, not least from the economic boost which resolution would generate.

Prior to 2011, Iraq's defence budget was consumed by the requirements for internal security, principally against the terrorist threat. However, political and military leaders are all products of a generation and a culture which associate weapons with *wasta*. If Iraq's economy continues to grow, the acquisition of modern weapon systems has the potential for offensive as well as a legitimate defensive use for external defence, even if the threat currently lacks credibility. The Arab–Kurd fault line, let alone regional sensitivities, would not be helped by Saddam-like zabernism.

Political Divisions

While Iraqi politics at the local level remain largely tribal, the Sunni–Shia divide emerged at the core of Iraqi politics at the national level after 2003. The majority Shia regained the ascendancy, but insufficiently so to guarantee an absolute majority as democracy was foisted on Iraq by the coalition. The Kurds became the king-makers through their ability to turn a Shia or Sunni vote into an unassailable victory. The Sunni felt increasingly disenfranchised. This peaked with the Sunni withdrawal from the 2005 elections, a decision which they subsequently came to regret and which was fortunately reversed in the 2009 provincial elections and the 2010 parliamentary elections.

There is also an underlying fault line between strong central government and federalism. In its most extreme guise it is characterised by the fundamental debate over whether Iraq should remain a single state or divide into its ethno-religious constituencies, but it is more subtle: between those extremes lies a spectrum of grey which could see power split between regions, particularly Baghdad and Erbil, and between central government and provincial/district/tribal administration.

The interesting phenomenon in the 2009 and 2010 elections was the emergence of electoral alliances, normally under a banner of 'national unity', as a means of securing a majority. From the 296 parties registered for the 2010 elections, six main alliances emerged: three along the traditional ethno-sectarian divides[23] and three non-ethno-sectarian blocks.[24] This divide between Islamist and secular coalitions is itself indicative of a widening fault line in Iraqi society. Despite a narrow majority for Iraqiya, alliance brokering continued for months.[25] A split in the Kurdish block[26] removed their role as king-makers and the increasing divide between Islamists and secularity added to the difficulty of coalition building. This is not the end of ethno-sectarianism in Iraqi politics. Both the Sunni and the Kurds know that a Shia prime minister is a certainty, but many assess they have more to gain from alliances with the Shia than digging in along ethno-sectarian lines – a tactic which proved disastrous for the Sunni in the 2009 provincial elections. Harmony will reign as long as the perceived gain is greater than the pain of having to bite one's lip and cosy up to old enemies. But herein lies the potential political resolution to the ethno-sectarian conflict: the longer the perception of well-being, both political and economic, is enhanced by coalition building, the greater the chance that pragmatism will dominate. It won't heal the confessional rift – Saudi Arabia and Iran both have too much at stake – but it could be a harmonious democratic accommodation that, importantly, provides an example to the rest of the region.

One political divide which is diminishing, although doubtless it will remain a factor for some time, lies between the Iraqis and the United States, which built the largest embassy in the world in Baghdad, a cuckoo in the nest of Iraqi politics. The coalition presence in all its guises permeated Iraq from 2003 to 2011 and added a dimension to the state's fault lines. The divide started to emerge as soon as it became clear that coalition presence would be measured in years rather than months,[27] but at that early stage the Iraqis had little choice but to defer to US advice and guidance. As the Iraqi political process matured, the US increasingly took a back seat. Iraqi deference evaporated. A significant milestone in this process was the ending of the UN Security Council mandate on 31 December 2008, replaced by bilateral Strategic Framework and Security Agreements, managed through a system of joint committees responsible for the continuing handover of security responsibility to the Iraqis in advance of the 31 December 2011 ending of the Security Agreement and for the regulation of the enduring partnership in areas of political, economic, cultural and legal cooperation. This model, unwieldy though its process may be and reluctant as some Iraqis are to engage with it, appears to be a worthy method of minimising the US–Iraqi fault lines as power ultimately shifts into Iraqi hands. However, it escapes no one in Iraq or its neighbours that the withdrawal of US forces and the normalisation of the political relationship between the US and Iraq leave a potential vacuum into which Iran, Saudi Arabia, Turkey and – to a lesser extent, owing to its internal unrest – Syria are manoeuvring. Saudi Arabia and Iran both back the sectarian alliances of their own confessional persuasion. Ali Larijani, the Iranian Foreign Minister, visited Baghdad to persuade Shias to stick together in the Iraqi National Alliance rather than support non-sectarian coalitions. This tactic did not pay off in the 2009 provincial elections, where the ability of Iraqi Shias, particularly Prime Minister Nouri al-Maliki, to stand independently from Iran was underscored by the heavy defeats suffered by ISCI and Sadrist politicians who avowed allegiance to Iran. But the Iranians appear undeterred. The Turks back the Turkomans and the Syrians have links to Al Hadthba, the Sunni nationalist front which won the 2009 provincial election in Ninewa. Over the long term, regional neighbours are likely to act in ways which could deepen the existing political divides. The US, on the other hand, will have less influence than previously to broker conflict resolution.

The Economic Divide

Dependence on oil is as much of a curse for Iraq as it is for many OPEC members.[28] Economic diversification remains largely a dream. Fluctuation of the oil price produces violent swings in a fledgling Iraqi economy which has little tradition of government borrowing to see itself through lean times, although World Bank and IMF initiatives could drag Iraq into twenty-first century banking in the medium term. And Iraq's history from the British mandate underpins a perception that the West is trying to swindle Iraq out of its resources. Iraq has therefore been slow to realise its economic potential, seeking internal solutions to exploitation of its oil and gas rather than invite Western oil companies to maximise production. However, Iraq's economic squeeze, precipitated by the fall in oil prices in late 2008 and early 2009, catalysed a change in approach which led to the letting of a series of significant contracts from 2009. This change will not resolve Iraq's short-term budgetary challenge, but should increasingly reap dividends: Iraq's long-term expansion plan sees production rising from 2.5 to 12 million barrels per day by 2017, which would exceed

Saudi Arabia's output. However, given the neglect of Iraq's oil infrastructure, such ambition will take considerable time, external investment and expertise to realise. Moreover, it would create imbalance between OPEC nations, deepening existing fault lines, not least with Iran. Indeed, Iraq's economic challenges are magnified by many of the fault lines described above. Much of its hydrocarbon reserves are in the Kurdish region or in the Shia-dominated south. Sharing of oil revenues is therefore overshadowed by ethnic and sectarian considerations. The Kurds receive revenue from Iraqi oil in a formula based on an out-of-date census which by mid-2011 had still not been updated, owing to an overheated political agenda. The Kurds' improving relations with Turkey also increase their scope for avoidance of the Iraqi pipeline system by exporting direct to Çeyhan on Turkey's Mediterranean coast. Oil is therefore a potential trigger for eruption of the Arab–Kurd fault line.

Water is a dominant factor in the diversification of most Middle Eastern states, none more so than Iraq, which is theoretically blessed with two of the greatest rivers in the region. However, the headwaters of the Euphrates and Tigris lie outside Iraq and the Euphrates also flows through Syria. The arrangements for sharing the bounties of these two rivers are established and have been shown to be flexible when necessary. On the other hand, Turkey's increasing damming of the headwaters of each river enables Ankara to hold both Syria and Iraq to aqua-ransom. Latif Rashid, the long-standing Iraqi Minister for Water, remains sanguine[29] about the situation, his relationship with his Turkish and Syrian counterparts, and has laudable plans for improving Iraq's efficiency in using its water resources, although limited budgetary headroom to fund capital-intensive projects[30] means that there will be few quick fixes.

Iraq's economy has been further stimulated through the embrace of technology denied, and in some cases banned, under Saddam. The number of mobile telephone subscribers rose from zero to 20 million (in a population of under 30 million) from 2005 to 2011. Particularly during the height of the insurgency, from 2004 to 2007, mobile phones enabled commerce to continue even when people could not travel to conduct business. In the absence of electronic banking, a gap now being addressed, telephone scratch card credit became a means of transferring money. The expansion has also netted the Iraqi government around 4 billion dollars in revenue for mobile-operating licences, with potential to generate substantially more.

Rule of Law: The State v. the People

Since its creation, Iraq has manifested constant tension between the state's demands on its diverse people and the people themselves as individuals and tribes. A monopoly on the use of force and the abuse of politics to ensure conformity of the population with the ruling power are fault lines which have kept hierarchies of status, patronage and privilege intact in Iraq, undermining the concept of national unity in whose name successive governments have claimed to act. Moreover, prior to 2003 justice was a feature of Iraqi society more for its absence than its inclusion. It is therefore unsurprising that by 2011 Iraqis viewed modest improvements in this area as miraculous, while accepting standards of human rights that would be unconscionable elsewhere. As an integral element of the rule of law, the fine line between patronage and state corruption has been moved slowly in the right direction, courtesy not least to the increasing transparency which Western influence and technology have enabled. While emphasis and support, particularly from the coalition, on improvements in the rule of law have had a disproportionately beneficial effect on the loyalty of Iraqis to the state, this initiative, and indeed good governance as a whole, were not helped by the CPA decision in 2003 to ban all members of the Ba'ath Party above a certain rank from holding public office.

External Destabilisers

In addition to the potentially destabilising political and ethnic regional influences described above, the considerable Iraqi diaspora, not least Ba'athists who fled after 2003, tend to inflame the fault-line agendas from positions of relative impunity. As with reconciliation inside Iraq, the government, encouraged by the international community, made greater efforts to reach out to these groups once the insurgency began to wane.

There will always be those who are beyond redemption, but reintegration of the majority into Iraqi society is a realistic goal which could also have a disproportionately beneficial economic effect, as many possess skills which are in short supply in Iraq.

Perhaps the greatest threat to resolution of many of Iraq's fault lines is also external: any precipitous action against Iran's nuclear capability is bound to spill over into Iraq. So long as there is a US military capability in Iraq, it is hard to envisage a situation in which the US would not be either directly involved or at least targeted by Iran in retribution. Even in the longer term, any Israeli attack, particularly if launched through Iraqi airspace, could well change the dynamic of Iranian influence in Iraq, certainly politically but also potentially militarily.

Conclusion: Prospects for Resolution of Iraq's Fault Lines

There has been considerable discussion of a 'grand bargain' in which many of the underlying causes of the fault lines described above would be addressed on the basis that one side may gain in respect of one fault line while another gains in respect of a different divide, the overall effect being balanced from all perspectives and at the same time greatly to the benefit of Iraq as a whole. Although not suggesting that this should be abandoned – the Iraqi government has a unique opportunity in this respect, not least in the support and leverage which could be brought to bear by the US – such broad vision has not been the typical output of Iraq's political process.

Political stability is the key to Iraqi long-term harmony. The advent of nationalist politicians such as Maliki, irrespective of their confessional or tribal roots, and political structures such as the parliament have demonstrated that there are alternatives to violence for the resolution of Iraq's wounds. But the Arab–Kurd divide is still the greatest threat to long-term stability. Scratch the surface and many politicians on all sides are too ready to revert to type. Politics is tied to the economy in the context of oil revenues and Iraq is not a poor country. The economy will be a roller coaster for the foreseeable future, courtesy of the price of oil, but Iraq is already learning how to deal with that in terms of instruments of finance, so long denied to the banking community. Diversification will be as elusive as it has been for most oil-rich states, but the economy per se is unlikely to derail progress in healing Iraq's fault lines. Security likewise is unlikely to break down to the extent that Iraq fails as a state. With the increasing, and importantly sustainable, capability of Iraqi security forces balancing a reducing dependence on external support, Iraq is both strong enough to deal with its internal security and insufficiently equipped, at least until around 2020, to seriously threaten its neighbours. There will continue to be attacks from an increasingly weakened and desperate terrorist legacy, but the majority of the population are increasingly seeing the benefits of eschewing a violent approach.

12

IRAN: FOUNDERING UNDER THE WEIGHT OF ITS OWN CONTRADICTIONS

Tom Porteous

I N THE FACE OF serious internal and external challenges, Iran has managed to maintain a remarkable degree of stability and national cohesion in the three decades since the Islamic revolution, while at the same time achieving significant advances in economic and social development. In recent years low-level internal violence has erupted in two principal spheres. Until now, in neither of these has the violence come close to threatening the government, let alone the state. Nonetheless the current political crisis following the June 2009 election represents an unprecedented challenge to the Islamic Republic.

The long-running conflict at the centre of Iranian politics between those seeking to maintain or strengthen the conservative nature of the 1979 Islamic revolution and those seeking greater political and social freedom has at times spilled over into anti-government protest. Such protest has consistently been met by violent repression, most recently after the June 2009 election. In 1997 the landslide election of the reformist President Mohammed Khatami sharpened the political struggle between reformers and conservatives that had been simmering within the political establishment since the revolution. Khatami introduced a programme of modest social and political reforms. But the conservative backlash started immediately, with violent attacks on student demonstrations in 1999, assassinations, arrests and show trials of prominent liberal intellectuals.[1] In the face of such resistance from conservatives, who maintained control of the security apparatus and other key ministries, and enjoyed the support of the Supreme Leader, Ayatollah Ali Khamenei, Khatami failed to push through any lasting liberal reform programme during his two-term presidency. Mahmoud Ahmadinejad, a former mayor of Tehran and a populist with close ties to the Revolutionary Guard Corps and support from conservative Muslim clerics within the Shia religious hierarchy, including Khamenei, emerged as the victor of the 2005 presidential elections after a second-round run-off between Ahmadinejad and the former president Akbar Hashemi Rafsanjani. Ahmadinejad and his conservative allies immediately set about purging hundreds of reformers from the bureaucracy and government and rolling back the limited liberal reforms undertaken by Khatami. The reformists hoped to reverse the conservative gains through the ballot box in the June 2009 election. They gave their support to the moderate reformist candidates in that election, Mir Hossein Mousavi and the cleric Mehdi Karroubi. But Ahmadinejad's disputed re-election dashed the reformists' hopes and brought tens of thousands of pro-reform protesters out on to the streets, prompting a violent crackdown by the security forces and judiciary, a string of show trials of those accused of organising the protests and further repression of political freedoms. Ever since June 2009 there have been sporadic street protests, some quite large, which have been met with violent repression by the security forces. The 'Arab Spring' has so far not led to a significant increase in anti-government protests in Iran. The Iranian leadership may be hoping that the fall of some of the repressive governments in the Arab world will increase Iran's regional influence because they are likely to be replaced by governments that are less subservient to US, European and Israeli interests.

Less momentous but nonetheless significant as arenas of political violence in Iran are the conflicts between the centre and the periphery related to the various demands (political, economic, sectarian, cultural) of some of Iran's ethnic minorities, especially Kurds, Baluchis and Arabs. There is nothing new in tensions between Iran's ethnic minorities and the central government, but there has been a spike in ethnic unrest in recent years – attributed by some to Ahmadinejad's religious and ethnic chauvinism and by others to covert US support for ethnic militancy.[2] The increase in ethnic instability over the past five years in the predominantly Baluchi province of Sistan-Baluchistan (in south-eastern Iran bordering Pakistan and Afghanistan), in the Kurdish areas of Iran (the north-western provinces bordering northern Iraq and Turkey) and in the mainly Arab and oil-rich Khuzestan province (in western Iran bordering southern Iraq) is partly related to domestic political and economic factors and partly to regional and international ones. Common domestic themes are economic and political marginalisation, as well as sectarian discrimination in the case of Baluchis and Kurds, the majority of whom are Sunni. It is significant that the largest ethnic minority in Iran, the Azeri Turks (who, like most Iranians, are Shia Muslims), have been well integrated into Iran's political, social, economic and cultural life and have remained largely loyal to the central government.[3] Even in the more troublesome areas it is important not to overestimate the level of ethnic violence or underestimate the extent to which over the past century Iranian nationalism and the country's economic development have created a relatively successful multi-ethnic state. In Baluchistan the only known militant group, the shadowy Jondallah, claims 2,000 militants under arms and has been able to attack Iranian security forces and state officials with increasing frequency since it first emerged in 2003. However, Jondallah's activities need to be seen in the context of Baluchi militancy in Pakistan and broader instability in both Afghanistan and Pakistan caused by the invasion of Afghanistan by the US and its allies in 2001. (Jondallah has been linked by the Iranian authorities to al-Qaeda.) The Baluchi unrest in Iran is also linked to the dramatic increase in drugs trafficking in the tri-border area between Pakistan, Afghanistan and Iran.[4] Recent Arab ethnic violence in Khuzestan, which was triggered in 2005 following the violent suppression of a demonstration (see below), is limited to sporadic bombings and so far has caused only a limited number of casualties.[5] Even in the Kurdish areas of Iran, where there is a long history of rebellion related to wider regional Kurdish ethno-nationalism, militancy is currently limited to sporadic attacks against government and military targets by the Party for Freedom and Life in Kurdistan (PJAK), which originated as a student movement and has close ties to the Kurdish rebel movement in Turkey, the PKK. PJAK is based in northern Iraq and claims to have about 3,000 armed militants.[6] None of the ethnic insurgencies in Iran poses a serious threat to the central government.

Divisions

Iran has a long history of strong, modernising, centralised government forged in the face of foreign occupations, revolutions, foreign-backed coups, international isolation and sanctions, and an intense eight-year-long war with neighbouring Iraq in which as many as half a million Iranians lost their lives.

Iran's relative stability is partly explained by its ethnic make-up. An accurate breakdown of Iran's ethnic groups probably does not exist, but according to Western sources[7] about 51 per cent of the country's population of around 75 million[8] are ethnic Persians. The next largest ethnic group are the Azeris (who perhaps represent around 24 per cent of the population) who, like the Gilakis and Mazandaranis (estimated 8 per cent), are well integrated and represented in Iranian political, economic and cultural life. The more marginalised and less well-represented ethnic groups are also relatively small: the Kurds (7 per cent), Arabs (3 per cent), Baluchis (2 per cent) and Turkmen (2 per cent).

Likewise Iran's religious character is a source of unity and cohesion rather than the opposite: around 98 per cent of Iranians are Muslim, with the remaining 2 per cent Zoroastrian, Jewish, Christian and Baha'i. Among Iran's Muslims the large majority (92 per cent) are Shia, while the rest are Sunni. Two of the most troublesome ethnic conflicts in Iran (i.e., among the Kurds and Baluchis) have been those where marginalisation along ethnic lines has been overlaid by sectarianism. On the other hand, Iran's largely Shia religious affiliation – in stark contrast to the Sunni affiliation of most of the Arab states and of its other Muslim neighbours – is a strong source of national identity and cohesion.

Much more serious, but nonetheless manageable (so far), are the political, ideological and economic fault lines in Iranian society. In the realm of politics and ideology there is a significant division within the political establishment between the alliance of broadly 'conservative' legal political parties and a coalition of broadly 'reformist' parties. There is also a political distinction between, on the one hand, those political parties (conservative and reformist) operating within the political establishment that are committed to the principles of the 1979 constitution and, on the other hand, the so-called 'third force', more or less underground political groups (dissident student associations etc.) which oppose the Islamic Republic outright and the principle of Velayat-e faqih (guardianship of the jurisprudent) on which it is based. This 'third force' seeks to change the whole system. In addition, there are a number of exiled political groups which also oppose the Islamic Republic. Both the internal dissident 'third force' and the exiled groups are somewhat weak and disunited and are composed of diverse political trends, including secular liberal and social democrats, communists, royalists and Islamist leftists (such as the cultish Mujahedin-Khalq Organisation).[9]

Since the election of June 2009 there has been a significant strengthening of the alliance of legal reformist groups and dissident underground associations in opposition to the perceived 'silent coup' by the hardliners and security elite around Ahmadinejad at that time. However, both groups have been severely targeted by the violent crackdown on the post-election protests by government forces led by the Revolutionary Guard Corps and the judiciary. In the face of the repression by the security forces, it is now clear that, for the time being at least, the coalition of opponents of the regime who took to the streets in the summer have not been able to form themselves into a coherent political organisation with specific goals and a clear strategy.[10] At the same time the prominent role played in the government crackdown by the Revolutionary Guard Corps and its junior sibling, the Basij youth militia, has revealed the extent to which under Ahmadinejad these highly politicised branches of the security forces have become a dominant and controlling force within the conservative camp.

The ideological and political fault lines that came to a head in the June 2009 election and its aftermath to some extent reflect economic and social trends. Iran's economic development in recent years has served to polarise Iranian society. On the one hand, there is a rapidly growing urban middle class with high expectations that are not capable of being met given the government's poor handling of the economy. On the other hand, there are Iran's poor, who, though shrinking in numbers, are still an important political force whose long-standing demands for a greater share of Iran's oil wealth, encouraged by the populist propaganda and redistributive ideals of the Islamic revolution, have grown more insistent thanks to the recent oil boom.

The rapid growth of the middle class has been spurred by impressive advances in access to health and education (Iran's health and education indicators are among the best in the region[11]), as well as a rapidly increasing urban population – 68 per cent of the total, with a growth rate of 2.1 per cent.[12] These factors have transformed the average Iranian family from traditional/rural to modern/urban and created a new generation of highly educated young people with strong ambitions for a middle-class life, including demands for jobs, housing, equal rights for women and greater social and political freedoms. The burgeoning Iranian middle class also wants to see a strengthening of the rule of law and greater equality of economic opportunity as a means of countering the corruption and patronage of the ruling elites that is exercised in part through the elites' control of the large public sector and government controlled *bonyads* (huge charitable trusts that serve as a key source of economic patronage for the government). But with high unemployment (some analysts estimate it as double the official rate of 13 per cent), high inflation rates and an acute housing crisis, the demands of the young middle class for greater economic opportunities are likely to remain unmet in the foreseeable future. Likewise, with arch-conservatives now consolidating their control of government, the demands for greater political and social freedom are also set to be frustrated. This is a political time bomb.

On the other side of the electoral divide are Iran's poor, whose demands for a fairer distribution of the country's oil wealth have been a constant in Iranian electoral politics since the Islamic revolution was ushered in on a promise of assistance to the *mostaz'afin* (the downtrodden). Although some progress has been made in reducing overall poverty in Iran since the revolution, inequality remains at a relatively high level, exacerbated by the oil boom (which disproportionately benefits those at the top of the hierarchical power structure) and high inflation (which disproportionately hurts the poor).[13] Ahmadinejad's electoral successes can be explained in part by his populist policies and measures aimed at delivering a fairer distribution of Iran's oil income, as well as by the enduring appeal of the Islamic revolutionary ideology among the poor.

Change in Context

Iran has maintained its relative internal political stability in spite of (and perhaps in part because of) international and regional hostility, isolation and deliberate efforts by external players to destabilise the country. From 1980 to 1988 Iran fought a devastating war with Iraq in which for the most part Iraq was supported by the US, Western Europe and much of the Arab world. However, since the end of that war Iran has seen its regional influence increase significantly – mainly because of the policy choices of its opponents. The first US Gulf War reduced the very real threat to Iran from Saddam Hussein's Iraq and the second one removed it altogether, installing a Shia-dominated government in Iraq that was closely aligned to the interests of Iran. Likewise, the 2001 US invasion of Afghanistan removed from power the Taliban, which had been hostile to Iran. Explicit threats of military action from the US and Israel, together with the presence of US and other Western military forces in both Iraq and Afghanistan, have lent credibility to the Iranian government's persistent claims that ethnic unrest among Iranian Kurds, Baluchis and Arabs is fomented from abroad. External threats have also been a convenient cover under which the hardliners have been able to justify consolidating their domestic economic and political control through violent repression.

Kurdish and Baluchi ethnic unrest in Iran cannot be isolated from Kurdish and Baluchi ethnic politics in the wider region. There are, for example, links between Kurdish militancy in Iran and the establishment of an autonomous Kurdish region in northern Iraq (where PJAK is based), as well as links with the PKK-led Kurdish insurgency in Turkey (with which PJAK is allied). In the case of the ethnic conflict in Iran's Baluchi areas, there are likely to be important links between the Jondallah insurgency and developments in Afghanistan and Pakistan since 2001.

Fluctuations in the price of oil have inevitably affected Iran's political fault lines, though it is by no means obvious what the precise impact is. While high oil revenues have helped to expand the middle class, cut poverty, modernise Iranian society and increase access to education, health and other basic services, dependence on oil has also contributed to macroeconomic instability, including high unemployment and high rates of inflation. Oil dependence has furthermore tended to increase levels of inequality, providing electoral opportunities for populist politicians such as Ahmadinejad.

There is little evidence that the US trade embargo has had much discernible effect on the Iranian economy. Nor is there much evidence that an extension of economic sanctions on Iran over the nuclear issue would have the desired effect of putting pressure on the government. Indeed, some economic commentators suggest that a tightening of sanctions could actually benefit the hardliners now consolidating their power around Ahmadinejad.[14]

The rapid penetration of the Internet and mobile telephones into the Iranian market (itself a signal of Iran's developmental achievements) has had a more profound impact on Iran's political fault lines, as was clearly demonstrated by the key role played by social-networking sites and mobile telephone video and photographic images during the post-election protests. Less commented on at the time but nonetheless significant has been the role of the Internet, combined with increasing access to education, in raising the political awareness of Iran's burgeoning middle-class youth on issues such as political and human rights, international affairs and Western/global popular culture. Nonetheless it should also be understood that these new technologies are just as useful to extremists and to pro-government bloggers and activists as they are to pro-democracy reformers.

It is too early to predict the impact of the turmoil in the Arab world on Iranian politics. The pro-democracy protest movement in Iran pre-dates that of the Arab countries that have witnessed such turmoil in 2011. But the protests in Iran that followed the election in June 2009, while probably larger than anything that has been seen in the Arab world during 2011, have so far been successfully dealt with by the authorities and have not yet seriously threatened the government. On the other hand, the gov-ernment in Iran appears to believe that it may benefit from the turmoil in the Arab world if, as seems likely, it leads to the establishment of new governments in the region that are more resistant to US and European influence and readier to enter into closer relations with Iran. The warming of relations between the transitional government in Egypt and Iran in the first half of 2011 suggests that this view has some basis in reality.

Triggers for Conflict

Political

The immediate trigger for the violence in Iran after the June 2009 election was the disputed result. According to some analysts, a comparison between the 2005 and 2009 elections points in the direction of outright fraud.[15] While there is little concrete evidence that the election was rigged, the anger seen on the streets afterwards was as much an expression of popular frustration at the whole political system in Iran – increasingly skewed as it is in favour of hardline conservatives – as it was at the actual result. Besides the election itself, therefore, another trigger for the post-election vio-lence was the increasingly authoritarian and socially repressive policies and measures adopted by the government since the election of Ahmadinejad as president in 2005 – characterised by some as a slow coup d'état by the hardliners, culminating in the post-election crackdown on protesters and prominent reformers.[16] In this respect the increasing economic and politi-cal influence of the Revolutionary Guard Corps since Ahmadinejad came to power has been an important factor in the crisis (see below).

The triggers of ethnic unrest in Iran are not always clear. In May 2006 a cartoon in a government-backed newspaper depicting Azeris as cockroaches sparked violent anti-government demonstrations in the hith-erto quiescent Azeri regions of Iran. The government quickly condemned the cartoon and order was restored. The integration of most Azeris into the Iranian elites makes it highly unlikely that this largest of Iran's ethnic minorities will rebel against the state. The 1979 Kurdish rebellion was triggered by the Islamic revolution as Iranian Kurds, who are mostly Sunni, feared, with some reason, that they would be even further marginalised in a Shia-dominated Islamic Republic. That rebellion was further fuelled by the war between Iran and Iraq, which Kurdish groups in both countries saw as an opportunity to intensify efforts to pursue their political goal of greater autonomy. More recent rounds of political violence in the Kurdish areas have been sparked by assassinations or executions of prominent Kurdish activists (see below). The trigger for the upsurge of unrest in Baluchistan in the past four years is very hard to identify, as information from the remote Iranian province of Sistan-Baluchistan is hard to come by. However, the timing of the emergence of the Baluchi militant group Jondallah in 2003 suggests a possible causal relationship with the invasion of Afghanistan and its allies, the fall of the Taliban and perhaps the steep increase in drugs trafficking. The surge in Arab militancy in Khuzestan after 2005 was caused by the brutal repression of a large peaceful demonstration by Arabs protesting against a letter by a presidential adviser which allegedly proposed reducing the Arab population of Khuzestan by transferring them to other regions of Iran.[17] Scores of Arabs are reported to have been killed by the security forces and others detained and tortured. This repression sparked a cycle of violence which continues today.

As discussed above, the uprisings in the Arab world in 2011 may well have emboldened protesters in Iran. But so far anti-government demonstrations in Iran since the start of the Arab Spring have not reached anything like the same level as those of 2009, in part due to the fact that the government appears to have found effective ways of stifling dissent through security deployments on the streets, arrests of activists and other forms of intimidation.

Economic

A sharp economic downturn in 2008 combined with high, unmet expectations among Iran's burgeoning young middle class for jobs may well have fuelled the anti-government sentiment that exploded in the June 2009 post-election protests. Estimates of unemployment range from 13 to 30 per cent. Inflation was a staggering 26 per cent in 2008, according to the Central Bank, though falling oil prices led to a drop in 2009. Housing prices in Tehran quadrupled between 2004 and 2008. At the same time the economic downturn may have sharpened polarisation between opponents of the government and its supporters (those among the rural and urban poor who have benefited from populist economic measures and other recipients of government patronage).

Economic marginalisation of the Kurdish, Baluchi and Arab regions has been an important cause of discontent and political unrest there. The Baluchi and Kurdish regions are among the most deprived in Iran, with higher levels of unemployment and poverty. Arab unrest in Khuzestan is further linked to the perception that the Arab majority in the province have not benefited from the province's vast oil wealth, even in a period of high oil prices.

Security

In Transparency International's 2009 corruption index, Iran fell into the bottom ten most corrupt countries for the first time.[18] All the candidates in the 2009 election campaign made corruption a major issue, reflecting widespread concern among the electorate at the high levels in Iran. President Ahmadinejad has sought to project himself as a champion of morality and probity, an outsider distant from the corrupt political elite, and has levelled charges of corruption at his political opponents within the elite, especially the wealthy former president Akbar Hashemi Rafsanjani.[19] At the same time the perception of extensive corruption (which Ahmadinejad has failed to tackle effectively) is another cause of the widespread anti-government sentiment that underlies the post-election unrest.

Furthermore, the spoils of corruption and patronage in Iran's oil-rich economy provide a strong incentive for those who control the levers of power to maintain and consolidate their position. In this respect increasing involvement of the Revolutionary Guard Corps in the *bonyads*, the energy sector, construction, heavy industry, trade and trafficking signals a remarkable shift of economic power from the private sector and the bazaar to the security elite. The behind the scenes struggle for control of the economy between these competing groups was almost certainly an important trigger for the post-election crisis and explains the important role that the Revolutionary Guard Corps and Basij have played in the subsequent repression. The security elites have important vested interests in maintaining the political and economic direction in which Ahmadinejad has been taking the country.[20]

Violent repression of protest and dissent has provided a trigger for violence in Kurdish, Arab and Baluchi regions. For example, in July 2005 students in the mainly Kurdish city of Mahabad held demonstrations to mark the sixth anniversary of the 1999 student protests in Tehran. Security forces arrived and tried to arrest a prominent Kurdish activist. When the activist ran away he was shot, tied to a car and dragged through the streets until he died. The event triggered eight days of violent protests in Mahabad and other Kurdish cities.[21] Likewise, as noted above, the recent increase in ethnic unrest among the Arabs of Khuzestan was triggered by violent suppression of legitimate political protest. Unrest in Baluchistan, Kurdistan and Khuzestan may be linked to changes in the regional security situation.

Social

As mentioned above, the expansion of the middle class, rapid urbanisation and modernisation, together with pressure for reform from an increasing population of well-educated youth with aspirations for jobs and other economic opportunities, as well as greater political and social freedoms, have all played a role in the developing political crisis in Iran.

Managing Iran's Fault Lines

Iran has a hybrid political system which combines elements of democracy (elected *majles*, or parliament, and president) with elements of a uniquely Iranian Shi'ite theocracy (Velayat-e faqih, Supreme Leader, Guardian Council, Expediency Council etc.). Both elements normally play a role in balancing and mediating between opposing political forces within the establishment, maintaining stability and averting serious crises. Increasingly, the system has shown itself to be not up to the job of resolving the mounting political conflicts within Iranian society, tackling neither the growing frustration within Iranian society at the political system nor the acute political and economic conflicts within the establishment. This failure is compounded by corruption, the increasing economic and political power of the security elite and the government's failure to tackle Iran's profound macro-economic problems, including high unemployment, inflation and inequality. The depth of the post-election political crisis and the resort to a massive security crackdown and a sharp increase in political repression to deal with it indicate the shortcomings of the political system in the face of Iran's political, social and economic realities. For the first time, the Supreme Leader has taken sides in a political conflict within the political establishment, departing from his traditional role as neutral arbiter – although in the course of 2011 there was a remarkable cooling in the relationship between Khamanei and Ahmadinejad, indicating new splits within the regime. None of Iran's political institutions, including the Guardian Council, which oversees elections, proved capable of responding with transparency and credibility to the charges of election fraud. Repression and abuses by the security forces and by the judiciary may have cowed the anti-government protest movement, but they have only deepened the crisis by further undermining the legitimacy of the political system in the eyes of many Iranians. The civil society groups and reformist media that had provided a political safety valve by offering some hope for peaceful reform of the system have been among the main targets of the crackdown. The 2009 election has truly left Iran in a political impasse from which it is hard to see how it can emerge.

Iran's constitution protects the rights of the country's minorities and minorities are represented in the Iranian *majles*. Some minorities, such as the Azeris, have been well integrated into Iranian society, indicating that Iran is capable of managing ethnic differences. However, the tendency of the central government to resort to violent repression in the face of ethnic unrest tends to trigger a cycle of violence which often proves difficult to resolve.

Iran's regional context serves to exacerbate its fault lines rather than to limit them. It is deeply suspicious of most of its neighbours and wary of the massive US military presence in Iraq, Afghanistan and the Persian Gulf. Four of Iran's neighbours, Afghanistan, Iraq, Pakistan and Bahrain, are in a state of serious political crisis and violent conflict. Its neighbours to the north, Azerbaijan and Turkmenistan, are hardly paragons of stability and good governance. Iran accuses the US and its allies of seeking to destabilise Iran by supporting both ethnic militancy and a 'velvet revolution' that would topple the Islamic government. In addition, Israel and the US have threatened Iran with military action over its alleged nuclear weapons programme, although President Obama has toned down US rhetoric against Iran since coming to power. There is no regional organisation that would be capable of intervening effectively in Iran's internal crises even if Iran sought such intervention, which it does not. Nor is there a regional body capable of managing cross-border issues such as smuggling, which serves to exacerbate some of Iran's ethnic unrest. Although the outcome of the Arab Spring remains uncertain, it is likely to lead to profound political changes in the Arab world that will also affect Iran. While there is a possibility that the success of reformers in the Arab world will in the longer term increase the momentum for reform in Iran, there is also the chance that continuing turmoil in the region will play into the hands of the

Iranian government and provide further opportunities for Iran to increase its regional influence.

International actors are more interested in preventing Iran from developing nuclear weapons and reducing its regional influence than in managing its internal fault lines. Indeed, it is reported that the Bush administration devoted considerable resources to covert operations aimed at destabilising Iran, including channelling support to ethnic militant groups in Iran.[22] The US and the EU, and to a lesser extent the IAEA and Russia, have sought to put pressure on Iran over the nuclear issue (Iran denies it is seeking to produce nuclear weapons and claims that its nuclear programme is for peaceful purposes). In truth, however, none of these actors has much leverage. A tightening of sanctions is on the cards and the US (along with Israel) has not ruled out military action. But it is not clear that either will be effective in the long term. Tightening sanctions could benefit the very hardliners they are supposed to hurt, while military action may put back Iran's alleged nuclear weapons programme but only at the cost of fanning the flames of anti-Western sentiment and strengthening the influence of religious radicals inside Iran and in the region more generally.

Conclusion

One lesson to be drawn from Iran is that managing fault lines is not always a priority for the West. Indeed, in Iran the policies of the US and its allies are aimed more at exacerbating the country's fault lines as a means of achieving the priority objectives of preventing Iran from acquiring nuclear weapons and limiting its regional influence.

Another lesson is that in a country like Iran, where the government is not interested in external assistance in managing fault lines, there is very little leverage external actors can bring to bear. The tools at their disposal, whether economic and diplomatic sanctions or military action, are blunt and could produce unintended consequences.

Iran's crisis is acute. For all its shortcomings, the hybrid Islamist/democratic system of the past thirty years has delivered a measure of economic development (including some remarkable achievements in health and education) and political stability. That system is now at risk of foundering under the weight of its own contradictions. The signs are that under Ahmadinejad a silent coup has taken place in which a coalition of hardline politicians, clerics and the Revolutionary Guard Corps has taken control. The post-June 2009 election violence and repression appear to have heralded the establishment of a corrupt and thuggish security state and the removal of any hope of peaceful liberal reform of Iran's political economy. Under such a system Iran's fault lines (ethnic, sectarian, economic and political) are likely to deepen, causing further violent conflict. Given the regional and international context, including concerns over Iran's nuclear programme, the implications of this are wide-ranging and serious.

13

ISRAEL, JORDAN AND PALESTINE: LINKED FATES, HARD REALITIES

Asher Susser

ISRAEL AND JORDAN are bound together by the Palestinian problem to the extent that it is virtually impossible to discuss Israeli-Jordanian relations in isolation from the Palestinian context. One cannot comprehend Israeli-Palestinian interaction if one ignores the Jordanian component, and likewise Jordanian-Palestinian relations are inexplicable if detached from Israeli input.

In the Israel–Jordan–Palestine triangle the fault lines are both ethnic and historical. While there are intrinsic tensions between Jordanians and Palestinians, they also have extensive cultural, ethnic and religious common ground. This is not true of Israelis and Palestinians, for an abyss separates the Zionist and Arab Palestinian historical narratives. While the Israelis seek to preserve what they believe they have justly achieved, the Palestinians yearn to turn back the clock of history and retrieve what they believe has been unjustly denied to them. The question is just how far back? Is it to Israel's conquests of 1967 or to Israel's creation in 1948?

Foreign powers would do well to come to terms with Middle Eastern realities rather than trying to engineer the peoples of the region to become what they are not. There is a tendency to overestimate the power of external players, while underestimating the power and resilience of local players, their traditions and cultures. The Israeli-Palestinian conflict has very specific causes and consequences. These should not be obscured by unfounded universalisms that lead to the making of false analogies, which in turn means that realistic solutions are that much harder to find.

The Historical Setting

The areas of today's Middle East that form Jordan, the West Bank and Israel have shared geography, demography, history and politics since time immemorial. Their destinies as modern political entities are therefore inextricably linked.

Jordan is home to a Palestinian population that possibly constitutes over half the kingdom's some 6 million. Moreover, the special ties between the Arab populations on both banks of the River Jordan are anything but new; nor are they solely a consequence of the Arab-Israeli conflict and the birth of the Palestinian refugee problem.

The lie of the land has contributed to the merging of the peoples on both banks of the river since the earliest of times. Three rivers flow from east to west on the East Bank of the Jordan into the Jordan Valley, carving the East Bank into three distinct geographical segments: the Yarmuk in the north, along what today forms the border between Syria and Jordan; the Zarqa in the centre, flowing from its source near Amman into the Jordan Valley; and the Mujib in the south, flowing into the Dead Sea. On their way westwards, these rivers cut through the hilly terrain of the East Bank, creating deep ravines and gorges that are more difficult to cross than the river itself, which is easily traversed at most times of the year. Historically it was far less challenging for people and goods to travel along the east–west axis across the River Jordan than along the more daunting routes on the north–south axis.

It followed naturally that political, administrative, economic, social and family ties developed more intensively between the East and West Banks of the Jordan than between the northern and southern parts of the East Bank. Towns like Salt and Karak on the East Bank, which are part of the present-day Hashemite Kingdom of Jordan, were more intimately connected, through a web of historical family and commercial ties, with their sister towns Nablus and Hebron respectively on the Palestinian West Bank than they were to each other. In the administrative divisions of both banks of the river in biblical times, then again during the Roman era, at the time of the Arab conquest, thereafter under the Ottomans and finally with the initial formation of the British Mandate for Palestine, large areas on both banks of the river were united in the same provinces.

The Evolution of Polities and Collective Identities

It is frequently noted that the Middle East state order that came into being from the ruins of the Ottoman Empire was an artificial creation, designed to serve the imperial interests of Great Britain and France. While that is true, in the century that has passed new authentic territorial identities have been forged in these imperial creations. This is definitely the case in the Israel–Jordan–Palestine triangle. Despite the strong historical ties between the East and West Banks and even though the British Mandate for Palestine originally spanned both banks of the River Jordan, separate Jordanian and Palestinian identities were soon to develop. In 1922 the East Bank was formally separated from Western Palestine, as the Emirate of Transjordan was designated to become an Arab state where there would be no Zionist settlement or presence. This was seen at the time as a British concession to Arab nationalism in the form of a limitation on the Zionist enterprise.

As Zionist settlement was henceforth contained to Palestine west of the river, the conflict between Jews and Arabs was initially limited to this territory, where an indigenous nationalist movement began to develop as an outgrowth of the conflict with the Jews. However, up until 1948 the Arab nationalist movement in Palestine saw itself in the main as an extension of the general movement of Arab nationalism in the Middle East, of which the Palestinians were an integral part.

In the aftermath of the 1948 war, the major rump of Palestine that remained under Arab control, the West Bank, was annexed by Jordan with Israeli acquiescence (the Gaza Strip came under Egyptian military government). Neither Jordan nor Israel was interested in the creation of a separate Palestinian state or collective identity that might challenge either one or both of them. Jordan conducted a policy of 'Jordanisation' – that is, an effort to assimilate the Palestinians into the Jordanian state, in the name of Arab unity.

Following the defeat in 1948 the Palestinians generally adopted an Arab nationalist stance, but instead of standing behind the King of Jordan they tended to be enthusiastic supporters of Egypt's Gamal Abdel Nasser, in the belief that his more radical anti-Western form of Arab unity, coupled with an alliance with the Soviet Union, would eventually deliver Palestine. It was they who were the most ardent proponents of the dominant Arab nationalist discourse in the mid-1950s and early 1960s.[1]

After a decade of Palestinian nationalist decline and devotion to pan-Arabism in the wake of the *nakba* (catastrophe) of 1948, it was the identification with the *nakba* itself, as a formative traumatic collective experience, that was to become the core of a reconstructed Palestinian national consciousness. In the late 1950s the 'revival of the Palestinian entity' stemmed from two sources. One was within the Arab League, as the Arab states led by Egypt (then still the United Arab Republic, the UAR) and Iraq pressed for the creation of a representative Palestinian political framework. These efforts eventually culminated in the establishment of the PLO in 1964, in accordance with an Arab Summit resolution, as the organisational incarnation of Palestinian nationalism. The second source of the revival was the initially clandestine formation of a variety of organisations devoted to the idea of an independent Palestinian armed struggle. Of these Fatah turned out to be the most important and long-lasting.

After the war of 1967, when Jordan lost the West Bank to Israel, the policy of the 'Jordanisation' of the Palestinians came to an abrupt end. The war was also a catastrophic defeat for pan-Arabism, which gave way in its declining appeal to two competing forces: narrowly based territorial nationalism and Islamic politics. In the Palestinian domain this was translated into the takeover of the PLO by the formerly clandestine Palestinian fighting organisations led by Fatah. The newly constructed PLO promoted a particular independent form of Palestinianness that sought to mobilise the masses under the banner of armed struggle against Israel, waged in the late 1960s mainly from Jordanian territory. This soon led to Israeli retaliation against Jordan and to an eventual decision by the Jordanians to oust the PLO from their territory in September 1970.

The civil war of 1970 was a traumatic and formative experience for the Jordanians. The policy of assimilation of the Palestinians had obviously failed. The Palestinians in Jordan were henceforth increasingly seen by the Jordanian political elite as a potential threat. From the 1970s onwards Jordan has consequently undergone an intensive process of 'Jordanisation', which now meant the almost total exclusion of Palestinians from positions of influence in the bureaucracy and the military, and the calculated promotion of a sense of Jordanianness. Thus, from the top down by the regime and from the bottom up by segments of the East Bank population, an exclusive Jordanianism was fostered, defined implicitly and at times explicitly against the Palestinian 'other', with occasionally vicious anti-Palestinian overtones.

Jordan has weathered many storms, regional and domestic, and has undeniably acquired a Jordanian collective identity and stateness of its own. The Bedouin tribes in Jordan were well integrated into the state and gradually emerged as the key standard bearers of this newly articulated Jordanianness.

So, with the passage of time since the early days of the British Mandate – that is, for nearly a century – the conflict between Zionists and Arabs has produced modern vibrant and authentic collective identities, among nationalist Israeli Jews and equally nationalist Jordanians and Palestinians. These have resulted in conflict not between rival tribes, sects or ethnic groups within one single state, but rather between new competing national movements and polities that have culminated in the formation of two states, Jordan and Israel, and one in the making, sandwiched between them, Palestine. In each of these three national polities some people, some of the time, may wish for one or both of the other two to disappear into thin air, but that is not about to happen. These three identities and polities have come to stay, albeit with alternating measures of collaboration, competition or conflict between them.

Historical Fault Lines: Israel–Palestine and the Conflicting Narratives

As already stated, there is an unbridgeable divide between the Zionist and Arab Palestinian narratives. Zionism, in the widely held Jewish perspective, is a heroic project of national revival, restored dignity and self-respect. The rise of Israel as an act of defiance against the miserable predicament of the European Jewish diaspora is deeply imbedded in the Jewish collective consciousness – a sentiment that has been cultivated for decades by the scathing critique of Jewish hopelessness and helplessness that was the precursor to the catastrophic destruction of the Jews in the Holocaust. Jewish national liberation, statehood and sovereignty were therefore the literal rising from the ashes, in self-defence against the Jewish historical fate, to finally attain political independence and historical justice for the most oppressed of all peoples.

For the Palestinians, obviously, the complete opposite is true. Zionism, in their view, had nothing to do with self-defence or justice. It was the epitome of aggression from the start. The Palestinian *nakba* or catastrophic defeat, loss of homeland and refugeedom are at the core of the Palestinian collective identity and their self-perception of victimhood. The 1948 war had ended not only in their military defeat, but in the shattering of their society and the dispersal of half their number as refugees in other parts of Palestine and the neighbouring Arab states.

The 'shared memories of the traumatic uprooting of their society and the experiences of being dispossessed, displaced, and stateless' were to 'come to define "Palestinian-ness"'.[2] The traumatic and formative series of events leading up to the outbreak of war in 1948 and its tragic consequences for the Palestinians carried with them a powerful and pervasive sense of historical injustice to the innermost depths of the Palestinian collective soul.

The Palestinians yearn, therefore, to return to an earlier time. But is that to 1967 or to 1948? The resolution of the so-called '1967 file' relates to the outstanding issues of borders and settlements on the West Bank and to the final status of Jerusalem. As thorny as these matters may be, they do not impinge upon Israel's existence, or conflict with the principle of partition and a two-state solution – that is, the creation of two independent states within the boundaries of British Mandatory Palestine as initially proposed by the UN Partition Resolution of 1947. The '1948 file', however, relates to two existential matters: first, the question of refugee return to Israel proper; and second, the issue of the national rights of the Palestinian Arab minority in Israel itself. Both could severely undermine Israel's viability as presently constituted – that is, as the state of the Jewish people – precisely because it is these issues that might irreversibly derail the inner logic of a two-state solution.

It is the intractable nature of questions such as these in the 1948 file that have put an 'end of conflict' settlement out of reach. This was highlighted once again in the crisis between Israel and the Palestinian Authority on the recognition of Israel as a *Jewish* state in the run-up to the Annapolis meeting between Prime Minister Olmert and President Abbas under the auspices of US President Bush in November 2007, and again after Prime Minister Netanyahu made a similar demand in his Bar Ilan University speech in June 2009. Israel's demand that the Palestinians issue a binding statement to that effect was firmly and flatly rebuffed by all Palestinian spokesmen from Mahmud Abbas and Saib Arikat down.

An article in the semi-official Palestinian daily *al-Ayyam* summed up the matter thus: 'Such demands by Olmert and others coming from Israeli politicians … can only push the Palestinians with their backs to the wall … [which] would prompt them to redouble their efforts to regain at least the bare minimum of their legitimate rights as enshrined in the resolutions of international legitimacy [UN resolutions], which totally contradict Olmert's recent provocative and impossible demand.'[3]

But to the Jewish Israeli mind, Olmert's conditions were neither provocative nor impossible, nor did they contradict the relevant resolutions of the UN. This was simply an attempt to obtain from the Palestinians assurances that a two-state solution would remain the foundation for the peace process, and that all outstanding questions, including the refugee issue, would be resolved in accordance with the symmetrical two-state logic. Israel was to be the homeland of the Jewish people and Palestine would be the homeland of the Palestinian people. It followed that Jews would have the right to return to Israel and not to Palestine and Palestinians would have the right to return to the state of Palestine and not to Israel. For the Israelis this would ensure that the turning back of the clock would stop at 1967, with the undoing of the occupation, and not proceed further to 1948, to undo the very existence of the State of Israel.

Historical Fault Lines: 1967 v. 1948 – Oslo and Back Again

The Oslo Accords created a new political dynamic. In accepting them the PLO leadership gained access to the West Bank and Gaza, creating the Palestinian Authority (PA) here, ostensibly on the way to the attainment of a final status agreement with Israel that would lead to the establishment of a Palestinian state. This led to the formation of new, elected Palestinian institutions: the presidency of the PA and the Legislative Assembly. These changes portended great historical significance. The new institutions were elected solely by the people of the West Bank (including Arab East Jerusalem) and Gaza and thus represented only them, as opposed to the PLO, which claimed to represent all Palestinians everywhere, including in Israel and the Palestinian diaspora.

The PLO represented the claim to all historical Palestine and was an organisation that had functioned from the outset in the diaspora. It therefore had also tended to give high priority to the diaspora constituency and its aspirations – above all, the demand for refugee return.

The PA, on the other hand, represented the West Bank and Gaza and focused on their most immediate concern, which was liberation from the Israeli occupation. This meant a certain downgrading, though by no means an abandonment, of the primacy of the refugee question. The issue of Palestine, or so it seemed momentarily, was actually being reduced to the West Bank and Gaza and to the 1967 questions, at the expense of the 1948 file.

Israel sought to achieve finality on that basis – that is, that the Palestinians would agree to an end of conflict on the basis of a grand historical trade-off. Israel would concede on the 1967 questions, including Jerusalem, in exchange for closure of the 1948 file. But that was not to be. The Palestinians, and first and foremost Yasser Arafat, would not agree to an 'end of conflict' unless the 1948 primary issues and grievances were also addressed to their satisfaction.

The Camp David summit in the summer of 2000, therefore, failed and no agreement on an 'end of conflict' was actually reached. Instead Israel and the Palestinians were locked in the worst round of bloodshed they had ever experienced since 1948, with suicide bombers attacking Israeli towns and the Israeli military targeting the PA and the Palestinians in return. The weakening of the PA, the general degeneration of Palestinian governance and the disintegration of the peace process all served to strengthen the hand of Hamas, which reached a new peak of power in Palestinian politics in January 2006, when it handsomely won the elections to the Palestinian Legislative Assembly.

Hamas had never accepted the Oslo dynamic of ostensible prioritisation of the 1967 file. In the years since the failure of Camp David, Hamas has made a concerted effort to reverse the Oslo dynamic and refocus the Palestinian cause on the 1948 file and the diaspora concerns to ensure that no finality could possibly be obtained on the basis of a resolution of the 1967 issues. Palestinian documentation, formulated with Hamas input in recent years, reveals a deliberate inversion of the Oslo dynamic, from the narrowing down to the West Bank and Gaza to the broadening out again to the diaspora constituency and to a concentration on the primacy of the refugee question.

In June 2006, in what became known as 'The Prisoners' Document', Fatah and Hamas representatives, as well as representatives from other minor organisations, who were serving sentences in Israeli jails on a wide variety of security-related offences, signed a Document of National Reconciliation. The parties emphasised the need not only to defend the rights of the refugees but also to reorganise them and to 'hold a popular representative conference' that would create organisations 'that would demand the right of return and adherence to it, urging the international community to implement Resolution 194 [of the UN General Assembly of December 1948] stipulating the right of the refugees to return and [their right] to compensation'.[4]

The policy statement of the Hamas-led Government of National Unity, which was formed by Isma'il Haniyya in March 2007, similarly emphasised the right of return, and the implementation of Resolution

194, specifically noting the 'the right of the Palestinian refugees to return to the lands and properties that they had abandoned' – that is, to Israel proper. The statement also specified that any agreement reached by the PLO (which formally conducted the negotiations with Israel, not the PA) would have to be approved by the Palestinians in the West Bank and Gaza *and in the diaspora*. Any such agreement would have to be brought before a new Palestine National Council (the PLO's quasi-parliamentary body, which represented all Palestinians everywhere, and would now have to include a significant representation of Hamas itself) or alternatively 'a general referendum [on the agreement] would be held by the Palestinian people inside [the occupied territories] and outside [in the diaspora] ...'[5]

Even the Arab Summit, in its approval of the Arab Peace Initiative as passed in March 2002 and reaffirmed in March 2007, followed suit in this regard. The Arab Peace Initiative called for comprehensive peace between the Arab states and Israel on the basis of an Israeli withdrawal to the 1967 boundaries and for an agreed solution to the refugee question based on Resolution 194 and upon 'the rejection [of] all forms of resettlement' of refugees outside of Palestine.[6]

In the last two decades of negotiation between Israel and the Palestinians, on the various issues contained in the 1967 file, such as borders, settlements and even Jerusalem, the gaps have narrowed significantly. At the same time, however, on the two truly existential 1948 issues – refugees and the status of the Palestinian-Arab minority in Israel and the consequent Israeli demand of the Palestinians to recognise Israel as the nation state of the Jewish people – positions have hardened and the gaps between the parties are as wide as ever, if not wider.

The Newly Emphasised Religious Fault Lines

The rise of Hamas is transforming the Israeli-Palestinian divide from a nationalist conflict, which at least in theory could one day be reduced to a conflict over boundaries (the 1967 file), to an insoluble clash over religions and belief in the holy word of God Almighty. For Hamas, Palestine was not the land of national liberation but of the eternal struggle of the believers against the infidels (matched on the Israeli side by the extreme right-wing ultra-nationalist religious fringe, which had a virtually identical world view). In the Hamas world view not an inch of Palestine could be conceded to the Zionists. Moreover, since Palestine did not belong exclusively to the Palestinians, but to all Muslims, not in this, nor in any future generation, did the Palestinians or the Arabs have a right to concede any territory to an alien entity in Palestine.

Since for Hamas the Palestinian cause was a struggle not between two nationalist movements but between two rival religions, Islam and Judaism, the Palestinian cause was driven by an 'Islamic essence' and was part of the larger war between Islam and Western civilisation.[7] Just as the PLO and Fatah had nationalised religion for their more secular vision, so Hamas Islamised nationalism. For Hamas, the first and second Intifadas were part of a jihad that emanated from the mosques and embodied the return of the Palestinian people to their 'authentic Islamic identity and belonging',[8] a line of argument that was bound to resonate positively with a sizeable constituency.

Fault Lines and Common Ground between Jordanians and Palestinians

Much is usually said, justifiably, about the contemporary nationalist division between East Bank Jordanians and Palestinians and especially their suspicions towards their Jordanian compatriots who are of Palestinian origin. The original Jordanians are obsessed by the fear of their country being taken over by the Palestinians and transformed into an 'alternative homeland' (*al-watan al-badil*) to Palestine. Therefore, as of the mid-1980s, they became supporters of the creation of a Palestinian state in the West Bank and Gaza, so that it should be clear that Jordan was Jordan, on one side of the river, and Palestine was Palestine, on the other.

At the same time, however, not enough attention is paid to the common ground between Jordanians and Palestinians. The great majority of Jordanians and Palestinians are Sunni Muslim speakers of the Arabic language, a collective cultural and religious identity which has bound them together for centuries. In this sense they are united more significantly than they are set apart by their relatively new and more shallow modern national identities, however real and authentic they may be. Marriage is a useful barometer to identify critical social fault lines. Jordanians and Palestinians marry each other as a matter of course. The decisive fault line in these matters is religion rather than national identity, so Jordanian Muslims invariably marry their Palestinian co-religionists, as do Jordanian and Palestinian Christians.

There is no similar common ground between the Jews of Israel and either the Palestinians or the Jordanians. While the Jordanians and the

Palestinians have had their bouts of conflict, these pale in comparison to the virtually incessant bloodletting between Israelis and Palestinians. It is difficult to imagine Israeli Jews and Palestinians, after decades of horrific conflict and profound mutual distrust, sharing a confederation or any other form of bi-national state. It is extremely difficult to imagine Israeli Jews submitting to any political order in which they were not protected solely by their own independent military power.

Confederation between Jordan and Palestine, however, would seem to be a more realistic proposition. First of all, it is an idea that has been part of Jordanian and Palestinian political discourse since the early 1970s, and it has enjoyed considerable support by many if not a majority of Jordanians and Palestinians. There are, of course, various conditions that would have to be met for such a confederation to be accepted, and even then there will certainly be those in the Jordanian political elite and in certain parts of the intelligentsia who continue to strongly reject the idea. Those in Jordan and Palestine who agree on confederation also agree that an independent Palestinian state must be established first. Palestinians want to guarantee their independent statehood and Jordanians do not want to be dragged into Palestine prematurely. Nor do they want to undercut Palestinian independence and leave Jordan vulnerable to an overly intimate relationship with Palestine that might eventually threaten the Jordanianness of the East Bank of the river.

However, if and when Israel disengages from the West Bank, that territory, landlocked between Israel and Jordan, will become more dependent on Jordan and the Arab world beyond. There are some Jordanian nationalists who instinctively reject any close association with Palestine as a potential threat to their political patrimony, but there are others, equally nationalist, who see in confederation an opportunity to create a political order between Jordan and Palestine that will enable Palestinians in Jordan to exercise their political rights in Palestine rather than in Jordan, even though they will most probably continue to be residents of Jordan. The confederation could provide new formulas for citizenship and civil rights that would allow the Jordanians to feel more secure in their homeland on the East Bank by having Palestinians on the East Bank participate in the politics of the West Bank rather than the politics of Jordan.

Conclusion

Foreign powers would do well to come to terms with Middle Eastern realities rather than trying to engineer the peoples of the region to become what they are not. The failed attempts by outsiders to reshape Iraq and Afghanistan in their own image are good examples of what not to do and how not to do it. One cannot cease to be amazed by the capacity of people to ignore the realities on the ground and to believe that culture does not matter and that all nations at all times are all the same. Crushing Iraq at the beginning of the twenty-first century was expected to produce the same results that were seen with the defeat of Germany and Japan more than half a century ago – that is, to turn Iraq into a vibrant capitalist democracy and bastion of the West.

That Iraqi society is for the most part not secular but religiously sectarian to the core, in total contrast to Germany and Japan, was not factored into the equations of the those who set forth to push over the first domino in the democratisation of the entire Middle East. That Iraq degenerated into horrific sectarian strife, taking the lives of tens of thousands of people,[9] should not have surprised anyone, except those who chose to ignore the realities that were plain for all to see. Those who fail to take cognisance of the critical role of religious forces or of the importance of the sectarian and/or tribal fault lines in the most recent upheavals of the Arab world (between Muslims and Copts in Egypt, Sunni Muslims and Alawis in Syria, Shias versus Sunnis in Bahrain, or the tribal divisions behind the troubles of Yemen and Libya) are en route to repeating the errors of the past yet again.

Setting timetables for the locals to start behaving themselves is as patronising as it sounds. If negotiations between two rivals have a good chance of succeeding, one does not need a timetable. If the chances of success are low, no timetable is going to make any difference. The parties will not overcome their historical grievances and mutual suspicions and abide by these timetables just because they were set by someone. Nor can they be compelled to do so.

A timetable is usually just a predetermined date upon which failure to keep to it will be solemnly pronounced. So why court failure? Failure is worse than not trying at all. Great-power intervention sends messages of hope to the local players that their aspirations will be met. Failure by the supreme umpires of the universe leads the parties to despair and to revert to the battlefield and to more bloodshed. Israelis and Palestinians have already been there – unfortunately, only too often.

All those involved should make it their business to study the limitations, constraints, desires, aspirations and red lines of the players and make their best effort to help them get to where they would like to go. That would be preferable to trying to coerce the locals to do what they have no intention of doing in accordance with a timetable set by the political exigencies of the external powers, not the real interests of the protagonists.

There is a tendency to overestimate the power of external players and to underestimate the power and resilience of local players, their traditions and cultures. The conflict in the Middle East is driven more by considerations of history, communal identity, collective dignity and other socio-cultural factors than by socio-economics or political economy. This was as true of the Zionists as of the Palestinians. Had the Zionists been driven by mainly economic considerations, they would never have been quite as obsessed as they were with matters of identity, cultural revival and collective dignity. Their problem as individuals could have been resolved in America. The same is true of the Palestinians. Had economics driven their behaviour they could have conceded to the Zionists and profited accordingly rather than resisting them with all the suffering that their struggle eventually entailed. The causes of the conflict are not economic, nor will the solutions be founded on either largesse or economic retribution.

The Israeli-Palestinian conflict has its very specific causes and consequences. Israel–Palestine is not Northern Ireland or South Africa. False analogies obfuscate the specificity of every case and lead to misperceptions of the facts on the ground. Unfounded universalisms, or the idea that one size fits all, lead to the making of these false analogies, which may serve the propaganda machines, but make real and realistic solutions that much harder to find. They introduce a host of new obstacles that result in peace-making becoming much more difficult by creating paradigms that do not relate in the slightest to the realities at hand.

CONCLUSION

Jeffrey Herbst, Terence McNamee and Greg Mills

T HE LEGEND OF CAMELOT has had lasting appeal. The idea is that long ago enlightened humans were able to create a perfect society, free of divisions and tensions, mystically aware of their collective identity as they advanced towards a shared destiny. Through the ages the legend has been embroidered and recast for different eras in the hope that a new Camelot could be created. The increasing complexity of states has rendered that hope ever more illusory but the legend persists, mostly as allegory, in films, books and occasionally political speeches.

The contributors to this book show conclusively that modern statecraft is not about establishing a new Camelot but more about carefully and pragmatically *managing* the fault lines which exist within *all* societies. Fault lines, as noted in the Introduction, are universal. They have existed if not from time immemorial then most certainly, and conspicuously, from the advent of the modern state system in the mid-seventeenth century. The character and evolution of fault lines across societies are, however, highly distinct.

Among our selection of case studies we have examined fault lines that are relatively straightforward, as in the case of Canada, whose politics has turned on French–English relations for 250 years; and Northern Ireland, even though its sectarian divide has never been quite as clear-cut as it seems. In other countries they are dizzyingly complex, as in Nigeria, which has overlapping fault lines rooted in ethnicity, religion, geography and wealth; and Ethiopia, whose myriad fault lines mirror and criss-cross divisions found throughout the wider Horn of Africa region. Within some states different fault lines have taken radically different trajectories, as in Indonesia, where the seemingly intractable struggle in Aceh has abated but the spectre of renewed violence and instability in its former territory East Timor, now Timor-Leste, looms ominously; and South Africa, which forged a remarkable reconciliation between blacks and whites in the face of dire predictions of cataclysmic racial conflict, yet today contends with deepening fault lines over income inequality and ethnicity.

In considering their particular areas of interest, the authors have put forward recommendations aimed at both governments and the international community. Their objective – and the main impetus behind the project which gave rise to this book – is to help leaders and decision-makers convert fault lines from security problems to political problems, and in rare instances perhaps even resolve them.

Of all the critical eruptions along societal fault lines that occurred in the 2000s, none attracted more international attention than the sectarian violence which engulfed Iraq during the middle of that decade. In the weeks following the toppling of Saddam Hussein's regime in April 2003 Iraq was chaotic and traumatised, but commentators unfamiliar with the country's internal dynamics generally assumed the worst was over. Instead, the number of dead increased more or less steadily month on month for four years. Only then, as Chris Brown's chapter on Iraq explains, did the tit-for-tat violence abate, owing largely to a dramatic shift in tactics by the occupying forces. Yet it is now an article of faith, even among supporters of the US-led invasion, that in the planning and preparations for the war due consideration was not given – at least by those responsible for managing 'post-war' Iraq – to the forces that could be unleashed in its aftermath. Had the key decision-makers (in this case non-Iraqis) fully grasped the fault lines that had been partially obscured under Saddam's tyranny – between Sunni and Shia, Arab and Kurd – would so many have perished? Would the tensions and divisions have been managed more effectively?

The violence which can erupt along fault lines within states can be particularly brutal and catastrophic, although not every outbreak of domestic conflict is attributable to the kind of societal divisions analysed in this book. In December 2010 a Tunisian vegetable seller immolated himself in protest at his ill-treatment by the local police. His act set in motion a wave of unrest and rebellion across North Africa and the Middle East, aptly described as the Arab Spring. The mainly young protesters who took to the streets had multifarious grievances, but in general they were united by a common desire to destroy the autocratic Arab order.

The first victims of the Arab Spring were the long-ruling presidents of Tunisia and Egypt. But the revolutions which swept these leaders from power in 2011 were not, principally, the result of fault lines erupting within these two societies, which are largely homogeneous. People across the political and social spectrum had for years felt terrorised and abused by their respective governments. The historic shifts in power in Tunis and Cairo were in part made possible by people setting aside their political differences in order to oust despised dictatorships. Only time will tell how long the concord lasts.

Fault lines were central, however, to the civil uprisings that occurred in some countries affected by the Arab Spring. The violence which erupted in the small island kingdom of Bahrain in the Persian Gulf was sparked by long-held discontent among the state's Shia Muslim majority towards the Sunni royal family, whose members occupied all senior positions of government. Bahrain's leaders blamed the Shia-dominated regime in Iran for stoking up sectarian tensions. In Syria, the initial uprising was widely portrayed as a rebellion against another ruling family, also from a minority community, the Alawites. This view varied somewhat from perceptions inside the country that the main fault line generating the violence was between the long-marginalised provinces and the regime in Damascus.

As for other regimes threatened by the popular revolts in the Arab world, their fate rests on a complex interplay of factors specific to those societies. No one can reliably forecast how it will all pan out. At the start of 2011, who would have predicted that civil war would break out in Libya and the longest-serving ruler in Africa and the Arab world, Muammar Gaddafi, would be forced from power and later dragged through the streets of his home town before being ruthlessly executed? A salutary reminder, if any was needed, that events have a way of building on themselves.

Should the Arab Spring result in the establishment of nascent democracies, however, then the findings of this book do permit us to draw some conclusions. More representative and accountable governments in the Middle East and North Africa will not eradicate the manifold fault lines which exist within and across the region's twenty or so countries. On the contrary, it is probable that long-suppressed fault lines will come to the surface and new ones emerge because democracies allow different groups freedoms and forms of expression that are prohibited in autocratic systems. It was the justification used by former Egyptian president Hosni Mubarak's retinue during his final days in power: remove the strongman and the country's intrinsic divisions will explode into open conflict. Iraq after Saddam, Yugoslavia after Tito, Congo after Mobutu – if the scale of violence is your only yardstick, then it seems a credible argument.

Yet the corollary to that assertion, that autocracies can manage fault lines better than democracies, is not borne out by the evidence. The countries that have managed their fault lines most successfully *over the long term* have been democracies. That holds as much for less populous countries like Belgium and Canada, which have clear schisms, as for huge states like India and Brazil, which possess numerous intricate fault lines. To be sure, neither India nor Brazil has been free of violence across its fault lines. India has experienced savage bouts of religious-inspired bloodletting and Brazil has struggled to prevent outbreaks of violence over indigenous rights and between the state and slum-dwellers. Yet considering the scale of the challenges facing both countries, it is clear that the inclusion of ordinary citizens – of every race, caste, class and so on – in multiple forms of political participation has blunted the forces of violence. Democratic institutions – the rule of law, free and fair elections, an independent judiciary and so on – provide real opportunities for these groups to safeguard their interests and seek redress when their rights have been infringed. What 'success' means in the context of fault-line management is not that groups will always get what they want from the state, but rather that they don't resort to violence when they fail to get what they want because they believe that their interests are still best served by working through state institutions. Contrast that with the behaviour of both groups and governments in states that have experienced long periods of authoritarian rule – Sudan, Congo, Ethiopia, Nigeria, Iraq, Iran, Indonesia, to name only cases examined in this book. In some the resort to armed conflict has been the first option nearly as often as the last, but all their post-colonial histories have been marred by recurrent bouts of violent unrest and bloodletting. The one exception that might have broken the cycle is Indonesia, whose vigorous democratic transformation following Suharto's downfall in 1998 has reduced, although not eliminated, the potential for strife along the country's numerous fault lines.

It will take at least as long for democracy to establish firm roots in the Arab world, if that is the way history unfolds. Even then progress is bound to be uneven across the region and vulnerable to major setbacks, perhaps more civil wars and state failures, too. Building and entrenching democratic institutions in societies that have only experienced dictatorship and dynastic rule will be a formidable challenge. Add in the prospect of simultaneously managing emergent or renewed fault lines in an environment where popular expectations are rising, not least in terms of economic benefits, and the task facing the region's next generation of leaders becomes more daunting still. What remains to be seen is how salient certain fault lines are for the region's technologically savvy and media-aware youth who have led the charge for more freedoms and accountable governments. They are increasingly part of a globalised community for whom some of the traditional divisions between states and peoples have become less resonant.

One country that is, in some key respects, outside this global community is China, a case which is not addressed in this book but nevertheless poses vital questions for future research on societal fault lines. Han Chinese are the dominant majority in China but the country has fifty-six ethnic groups or nationalities that are officially recognised by the government and nearly 300 languages. The best-known restive minorities, the Muslim Uighurs in the north-west corner of the country and the Buddhist Tibetans in the southern plateau north of the Himalayas, comprise only a fraction of China's total population but still number together about 15 million people. Within China the gap has widened between rural and urban areas, creating a new set of class divisions and growing disparities in life opportunities and political rights. Opinions vary on how well the government has managed these fault lines. In so far as ethnic groups are concerned, Beijing frequently trumpets the success of its 'regional autonomy' strategy for the minorities clustered in different parts of the country, although its critics tell a different story. What is not disputed is the fact that China's fault-line management strategy is executed within a non-democratic context.

China is a notable outlier in the democracy–economic growth correlation that has been the subject of considerable quantitative research.[1] In short, China proves that you can have sustained growth without democracy, even though evidence otherwise points to a strong positive correlation between growth and democratic institutions when compared to autocratic systems of rule. The reasons postulated for China's economic success in a non-democratic setting might also be germane to its capacity to manage its fault lines, especially when contrasted with autocratic regimes in Africa. First, China has created more accountability structures in its collective leadership systems than the patronage-based, highly personalistic forms of rule that historically have enfeebled attempts to manage fault lines in so many African countries. It has also made some strides in the rule of law and even to a certain extent (provided the stories are not directly targeting the political system) press freedoms, evident in reports on official corruption and incompetence in Chinese media. China has also permitted much greater decentralisation than is typical of autocracies on the African continent, thereby creating a degree of accountability at the local level. How China's fault-line management strategy fares in the coming decades, as the internal social and regional pressures on Beijing inevitably mount, will no doubt determine whether its model is replicated in other parts of the world.

China is unlikely ever to call on international assistance to help manage its fault lines, but nearly all the cases examined in this book have been subject to outside involvement of one kind or another, including in recent times Britain's long-running sore, Northern Ireland. That particular engagement comprised key local leaders, the 'parent' governments (London and Dublin) and the diplomatic might of Washington. It has proved largely successful and set in train a process that appears less and less likely to be fatally derailed with each passing year, for all the sporadic attacks by dissidents who seek to foment renewed sectarian conflict.

All too often, however, foreign interveners have made the signal error of not recognising peoples and the fault lines which sometimes divide them for who and what they are. This proclivity has been eloquently described by several authors here, though Asher Susser's advice is especially universal: 'All those involved should make it their business to study the limitations, constraints, desires, aspirations and red lines of the players and make their best effort to help them get to where they would like to go.' This book has chronicled several examples, such as Somalia and Sudan, where the failure of foreign mediators to take cognisance of the realities on the ground has exacerbated fault lines, with disastrous consequences for the populations in those countries. The record of foreign involvement in Congo this past century – in all its forms – has been so appalling that Pierre Englebert describes Congo starkly as 'a crime of a country'. Though not for a second excusing the Congolese for their role in this tragedy, he outlines one possible route out of the abyss: '[the future is] not for any outsiders to decide but for the Congolese. The impetus to reform that is currently necessary is one whereby the presence and the authority of sovereign Congolese institutions across the territory are deflated and diluted so as to give local communities (defined here regionally and not ethnically) a voice and a chance to settle their conflicts. They must be given the tools to produce their own sovereign institutional solutions, based on local social contracts.'

The message from Englebert and other chapter authors is that outsiders may have a role in managing fault lines when it is called for, but the most efficacious assistance they can provide will mostly be on the edges; only very rarely can it be decisive. Locals must be allowed to own their own problems as well as the solutions.

The thorniest and most potentially significant issue raised in the Introduction pertains to national boundaries. Throughout this book authors have assessed the merits of different management tools to alleviate divisions within societies. Federalist-type arrangements were subjected to scrutiny in a number of cases. Done well, with the appropriate processes and institutions, in particular viable revenue-sharing arrangements, federalism can produce successful long-term responses. This may be especially so in relation to the ethnic-type conflicts that have scarred parts of Africa. Yet central authorities in countries such as Ethiopia and Uganda, which have adopted federal arrangements, have been highly reluctant to empower their regions and peripheries in ways that enable grievances and societal fissures to be managed effectively at their source. When pressures along these fault lines become extreme, some perennially marginalised groups may conclude that secession is the only option left.

The South Sudanese did exactly that in January 2011. It is somewhat paradoxical to argue that the formal slicing of Sudan in two on 9 July 2011 constituted a successful management of a fault line, since it represented the failure of a state, but maybe it was. Although it is hard to imagine how the war-ravaged and grossly underdeveloped south could be worse off as an independent state, the final verdict can't be delivered for many years, perhaps even a generation, by which time we'll know how the new government in Juba has tackled the formidable divisions left unresolved by secession.[2]

The term 'fault lines' evokes frontiers and borders on the ground, but the divisions in societies are rarely so neat. The contributors to *On the Fault Line* paint a compelling picture of a world riven with complex fault lines that often cannot be traced on a map. Nevertheless, it seems likely that in the future new boundaries may have to be drawn in some parts of the world to manage tensions between groups that would probably be better off on their own. This book shows how governments and the international community can help prevent fault lines from erupting and ensure that fewer and fewer groups seek this option.

NOTES AND FURTHER READING

Introduction: Managing Fault Lines in the Twenty-first Century

1. Interview, Juba, 3 November 2010.
2. The complete list of papers commissioned for this project by region is Afghanistan, India and Sri Lanka; Canada; Balkans and Northern Ireland; Congo, Ethiopia, Kenya, Liberia, Nigeria, Rwanda, Somalia/Somaliland, South Africa, Sudan, Tanzania and Uganda; Brazil, El Salvador and Guatemala; Indonesia and Malaysia; Iran, Iraq, Israel, Jordan and Lebanon. A number of thematic papers were also commissioned.
3. David D. Laitin, *Nations, States and Violence* (Oxford, Oxford University Press, 2007), p. 11.
4. Daniel N. Posner, 'The Political Salience of Cultural Difference: Why Chewas and Tumbukas are Allies in Zambia and Adversaries in Malawi', *American Political Science Review*, Vol. 98, November 2004, p. 529.
5. Andreas Wimmer and Lars-Erik Cederman, 'Ethnic Politics and Armed Conflict: A Configurational Analysis of a New Global Data Set', *American Sociological Review*, Vol. 74, April 2009, p. 318.
6. The authors are grateful to Stephen Chan, one of the project's participants, for this observation.

1   Boundaries and Bargains: Managing Nigeria's Fractious Society

1. Crawford Young, 'The Impossible Necessity of Nigeria: A Struggle for Nationhood', *Foreign Affairs*, November/December 1996, p. 139.
2. The concept of deeply divided societies is applied by Arend Lijphart, *Democracy in Plural Societies: A Comparative Exploration* (New Haven, Yale University Press, 1977).
3. Nigerian federalism is elaborated by Rotimi Suberu, *Federalism and Ethnic Conflict in Nigeria* (Washington, DC, United States Institute of Peace, 2001).
4. For a discussion of distributional politics in oil states, see Peter M. Lewis, *Growing Apart: Oil, Politics and Economic Change in Indonesia and Nigeria* (Ann Arbor, University of Michigan Press, 2007).

5. James S. Coleman, *Nigeria: Background to Nationalism* (Berkeley and Los Angeles, University of California Press, 1958), p. 15.

6. Pew Forum on Religion and Public Life, *Tolerance and Tension: Islam and Christianity in Sub-Saharan Africa*, p. 20, http://pewforum.org/uploadedFiles/Topics/Belief_and_Practices/sub-saharan-africa-chapter-1.pdf.

7. David Laitin, *Hegemony and Culture: The Politics of Religious Change among the Yoruba* (Chicago, University of Chicago Press, 1986).

8. Michael Crowder, *West Africa under Colonial Rule* (Evanston, Northwestern University Press, 1968).

9. See Billy J. Dudley, *An Introduction to Nigerian Government and Politics* (Bloomington, Indiana University Press, 1982).

10. The political history is summarised by Larry Diamond, 'Nigeria: The Uncivic Society and the Descent into Praetorianism', in Larry Diamond, J. Linz and S. M. Lipset (eds.), *Politics in Developing Countries: Comparing Experiences with Democracy*, 2nd edn (Boulder, Lynne Rienner Publishers, 1995).

11. See Tom Forrest, *Politics and Economic Development in Nigeria*, 2nd edn (Boulder, Westview Press, 1995).

12. See Ukoha Ukiwo, 'Politics, Ethno-Religious Conflicts and Democratic Consolidation in Nigeria', *Journal of Modern African Studies*, Vol. 41, No. 1, 2003, pp. 115–38.

13. These dynamics are analysed well by Suberu, *Federalism and Ethnic Conflict in Nigeria*.

14. The January 1966 coup briefly abolished the federal system and declared a unitary state. Gowon's intervention in July quickly restored federalism, but changed boundaries several months later.

15. The term 'elite cartel' was deployed by Arend Lijphart in discussing the bargaining process surrounding consociational democracies: see Lijphart, 'Consociational Democracy', *World Politics*, Vol. 21, No. 2, January 1969, pp. 207–25. My usage varies, referring to a collusive political-economic ruling group.

16. Richard Sklar has conceptualised Nigerian politicians as a 'class' grouping with comparable interests, access to resources and self-interested behaviours. See Sklar, *Nigerian Political Parties* (Princeton, Princeton University Press, 1963).

2 The Democratic Republic of Congo: Fault Lines and Local Fissures

1. Adam Hochschild, *King Leopold's Ghost: A Story of Greed, Terror and Heroism in Colonial Africa* (New York, Houghton Mifflin, 1998).

2. Herbert Weiss, *Political Protest in the Congo* (Princeton, Princeton University Press, 1967); Crawford Young, *Politics in the Congo* (Princeton, Princeton University Press, 1965).

3. René Lemarchand, *The Dynamics of Violence in Central Africa* (Philadelphia, University of Pennsylvania Press, 2009); Gérard Prunier, *Africa's World War: Congo, the Rwandan Genocide, and the Making of a Continental Catastrophe* (Oxford, Oxford University Press, 2009); Filip Reyntjens, *The Great African War: Congo and Regional Geopolitics, 1996–2006* (Cambridge, Cambridge University Press, 2009).

4. J. Gérard-Libois, *La sécession katangaise* (Brussels, CRISP, 1963).

5. Isidore Ndaywel è Nziem, *Histoire générale du Congo: de l'héritage ancien à la République Démocratique* (Paris and Brussels, De Boek/Larcier, 1998).

6. Crawford Young, 'Nationalism and Ethnicity in Africa', *Review of Asian and Pacific Studies*, Vol. 23, 2002, pp. 1–19; Herbert Weiss and Tatiana Carayannis, 'The Enduring Idea of the Congo', in Ricardo Larémont (ed.), *Borders, Nationalism, and the African State* (Boulder, Lynne Rienner Publishers, 2005); Pierre Englebert, *Africa: Unity, Sovereignty and Sorrow* (Boulder, Lynne Rienner Publishers, 2009).

7. See Theodore Trefon, 'The Political Economy of Sacrifice: The Kinois and the State', *Review of African Political Economy*, Vol. 29, Nos. 93/94, 2002, pp. 481–98.

8. Jean-François Bayart, *The State in Africa: The Politics of the Belly* (New York, Longman, 1993).

9. Mahmood Mamdani, *When Victims Become Killers* (Princeton, Princeton University Press, 2002).

10. Ibid., p. 238.

11. ICG (International Crisis Group), 'Congo's Transition is Failing: Crisis in the Kivus', Africa Report No. 91, Washington, DC, 2005, p. 9.

12. Pole Institute, 'Est de la RDC: le crime banalisé', Regards Croisés, April 2009, p. 23.

13. Denis M. Tull, 'Troubled State-Building in the DR Congo: The Challenge from the Margins', draft manuscript, July 2009.

14. Crawford Young, *The Politics of Cultural Pluralism* (Madison, University of Wisconsin Press, 1976).

15. Séverine Autesserre, 'The Trouble with Congo: How Local Disputes Fuel Regional Conflict', *Foreign Affairs*, Vol. 87, No. 3, May/June 2008, pp. 94–110.

16. Crawford Young, 'Zaire: The Shattered Illusion of the Integral State', *Journal of Modern African Studies*, Vol. 32, No. 2, 1994, pp. 247–63.

17. Tull, 'Troubled State-Building in the DR Congo'.

18. Marina Ottaway, 'Keep out of Africa', *Financial Times*, 25 February 1999; Jeffrey Herbst and Greg Mills. 'There is No Congo', *Foreign Policy*

(online edition), March 2009, http://www.foreignpolicy.com/story/cms.
php?story_id=4763.
19. Englebert, *Africa*.
20. Hernando De Soto, *The Mystery of Capital* (New York, Basic Books, 2000).

3 Overcoming the Past: War and Peace in Sudan and South Sudan

1. A detailed chronology of Sudanese history from the Middle Ages to 1995 is
available at http://www.sudanupdate.org/HISTORY/chron.htm (accessed
23 September 2011).
2. Douglas H. Johnson, *The Root Causes of Sudan's Civil Wars* (Oxford, James
Currey, 2003; revised edition, 2011), p. 7.
3. Peter Woodward describes how there was little mass participation in the
nationalist movements of the north, and describes the southern movement
as less 'nationalist' in its demands than focused on regional recognition:
Woodward, 'Nationalism and Opposition in Sudan', *African Affairs*, Vol. 80,
No. 320, 1981, pp. 380–82.
4. Atta el-Battahani, 'A Complex Web: Politics and Conflict in Sudan',
Conciliation Resources, 2006.
5. The mutiny of soldiers in the Equatorian town of Torit on 18 August 1955
was the trigger for the Anya Nya rebellion, and is commemorated as a
veterans day in South Sudan.
6. Heather J. Sharkey, 'Arab Identity and Ideology in Sudan: The Politics of
Language, Ethnicity, and Race', *African Affairs*, Vol. 107, No. 426, 2008, pp.
21–43.
7. Sudan Update in note 1.
8. Nevertheless, successive administrations in Khartoum sought to bolster their
ruling credentials by emphasising Arabness and Islam (enduring features
of northern rule) in the absence of democratic legitimacy: Sharkey, 'Arab
Identity and Ideology in Sudan'.
9. US Committee for Refugees, 'Sudan: Nearly 2 Million Dead as a Result of
the World's Longest Running Civil War', April 2001 (archived web content).
10. Johnson, *The Root Causes of Sudan's Civil Wars*, p. 63.
11. Ibid.
12. Douglas H. Johnson has suggested that the destructive factional infighting
of the first civil war led the SPLM leadership to suppress dissent via a
heavily militarised structure that rewarded complacent regions with civil
administration (such as Bahr al-Ghazal and Upper Nile), but mimicked
occupation in remote or stubborn regions (such as the Nuba Mountains
and Eastern Equatoria): ibid.

13. Robert O. Collins, 'Africans, Arabs, and Islamists: From the Conference Tables to the Battlefields in Sudan', *African Studies Review*, Vol. 42, No. 2, 1999, pp. 108–9.

14. See Adam Branch and Zachariah Cherian Mampilly, 'Winning the War, but Losing the Peace? The Dilemma of SPLM: A Civil Administration and the Tasks Ahead', *Journal of Modern African Studies*, Vol. 43, No. 1, 2005, p. 10.

15. Mohamed Suliman, 'Resource Access: A Major Cause of Armed Conflict in the Sudan: The Case of the Nuba Mountains', International Workshop on Community-Based Natural Resource Management, Washington, DC, 10–14 May 1998.

16. Efforts by Equatorians in the south of the country to redress the imbalance in the 1970s were unsuccessful. The proposed 'redivision' of the south did not give the non-Dinka tribes enhanced autonomy vis-à-vis the centre, but in fact strengthened central power: Johnson, *The Root Causes of Sudan's Civil Wars*, p. 55.

17. The Intergovernmental Authority on Drought and Development (IGADD) was formed in 1986 as a regional response to the Horn of Africa's recurring environmental disasters. It evolved into a forum for political and security dialogue and in 1996 became the Intergovernmental Authority on Development (IGAD). Its members are Djibouti, Ethiopia, Kenya, Somalia, Sudan and Uganda; Eritrea has also been a member.

18. See Collins, 'Africans, Arabs, and Islamists', pp. 115–16.

19. Peter Kok, 'Sudan: Between Radical Restructuring and Deconstruction of State Systems', *Review of African Political Economy*, Vol. 23, No. 70, 1996, pp. 555–62.

20. 'Sudan: The IGADD Peace Process', *Review of African Political Economy*, Vol. 22, No. 63, 1995, pp. 137–8.

21. The Intergovernmental Authority on Development led the peace efforts of the 1990s, in particular through the high-level contribution of member states Ethiopia, Kenya and Uganda. IGAD mediated the CPA, with the involvement of the UN Security Council, the UN Secretary-General and his Special Representative for Sudan, and the African Union. The US, UK, Italy and Norway also played important roles in backstopping the process. The US, Norway and China remain significant players in Sudanese affairs.

22. For more on the terms of the CPA, see 'The Background to Sudan's Comprehensive Peace Agreement', UNMIS, http://unmis.unmissions.org/Default.aspx?tabid=515 (accessed 29 July 2011).

23. There is not space to discuss the UN peacekeeping forces, the international community's largest and most high-profile resource investment in Sudan. Suffice to say that the missions are largely considered to be constrained and ineffective: UNMIS has been unable to protect civilians because of its weak mandate, logistical challenges and low capacity; and UNAMID, the mission

in Darfur, has had no peace to keep. See the report of the UK Associate Parliamentary Group for Sudan, 'On the Brink: Towards Lasting Peace in Sudan', March 2010, pp. 19–21.

24. Toni Johnson and Stephanie Hanson, 'Sudan's Fractured Internal Politics', Council on Foreign Relations, 7 October 2010.

25. Knox Chitiyo, 'The Horn of Africa: A Changing of the Guards?', *RUSI Newsbrief*, March 2010.

26. In 1993 the US designated Sudan a state sponsor of terrorism; in October 1997 the US imposed comprehensive sanctions. This was followed by the destruction of the al-Shifa pharmaceutical factory outside the capital by a US missile strike in 1998 because of alleged links to al-Qaeda, which had claimed responsibility for the embassy bombings in East Africa two weeks earlier. See 'US–Sudan Relations', Embassy of the United States in Khartoum, Sudan, http://sudan.usembassy.gov/ussudan_relations.html (accessed 29 July 2011).

27. Colonel Garang was killed in a helicopter crash six months after the peace accords were completed, having briefly served as First Vice-President of Sudan.

28. See International Crisis Group (ICG), 'Sudan's Comprehensive Peace Agreement: The Long Road Ahead', Africa Report No. 106, 31 March 2006.

29. The US State Department announced a new Sudan policy in October 2009 that focused on Darfur, CPA implementation and preventing Sudan from becoming a haven for terrorism. The US had previously seen Darfur and the CPA as separate policy issues, but renewed attention, together with the promise of full diplomatic relations, was designed to build political resolve in Khartoum: Johnson and Hanson, 'Sudan's Fractured Internal Politics'.

30. ICG, 'Sudan's Comprehensive Peace Agreement', p. 29.

31. During the 1930s and 1940s, the nascent nationalist movement embraced the notion of the 'Arab Sudanese', appropriating the folk culture of the Bedouin Arabs in order to 'invent tradition' and thus bolster the Arab credentials of a group that in the main had no genealogical ties to Arab culture: Sharkey, 'Arab Identity and Ideology in Sudan', p. 32.

32. Francis M. Deng, *War of Visions: Conflict of Identities in Sudan* (Washington, DC, Brookings Institution Press, 1995), p. 4.

33. For a discussion of regional marginalisation as the basis of conflict, see Alex Cobham, 'Causes of Conflict in Sudan: Testing the Black Book', QEH Working Paper No. 121, January 2005. The Black Book is an anonymous assessment of the disproportionate political control of northerners in Sudanese life and its implications for development indices in the rest of the country.

34. Douglas Johnson described Sudan as a collection of regions, rather than a nation: Johnson, *The Root Causes of Sudan's Civil Wars*.
35. Ann Mosely Lesch, *The Sudan: Contested National Identities* (Bloomington, Indiana University Press, 1998).
36. Suliman, 'Resource Access'.
37. Mosely Lesch, *The Sudan*.
38. African Rights, *Facing the Genocide: The Nuba of the Sudan*, 2005, cited by Suliman, 'Resource Access'.
39. 'Sudan's Invisible Citizens', *Review of African Political Economy*, Vol. 22, No. 63, 1995, pp. 136–7.
40. Anna Rader, 'Sudan: The Trouble Ahead', RUSI.org, 30 June 2011.
41. See Laurie Nathan, 'No Ownership, No Peace: The Darfur Peace Agreement', Crisis States Research Centre Working Paper 5, 2006, p. 1.
42. For a discussion of 'South-on-South' conflict in the Western Upper Nile Province after 1991, see Sharon E. Hutchinson, 'A Curse from God? Religious and Political Dimensions of the Post-1991 Rise of Ethnic Violence in South Sudan', *Journal of Modern African Studies*, Vol. 39, No. 2, 2001, pp. 307–31.
43. Mareike Schomerus and Tim Allen, 'Southern Sudan at Odds with Itself: Dynamics of Conflict and Predicaments of Peace', Development Studies Institute, LSE, 2010.
44. ICG, 'Jonglei's Tribal Conflicts: Countering Insecurity in South Sudan', Africa Report No. 154, 2009.
45. Suliman, 'Resource Access'.
46. It is for these reasons that a soft border has been advocated: The Brenthurst Foundation, '"Everything is at Zero": Beyond the Referendum – Drivers and Choices for Development in Southern Sudan', Discussion Paper 2010/05, November 2010.
47. The CPA built on the 1994 IGADD Declaration of Principles and the 1995 Asmara Declaration, which had acknowledged the importance of local autonomy and self-determination, and also took into consideration intra-south dialogues such as the 2001 and 2002 conventions that addressed calls for Equatorian self-rule and decentralised government within the south. See Branch and Mampilly, 'Winning the War, but Losing the Peace?', p. 5.
48. Edward Thomas, 'Decisions and Deadlines: A Critical Year for Sudan', Chatham House, London, January 2010.
49. Low domestic consumption has meant that approximately 300,000 barrels of oil a day are exported to China, Japan and Indonesia. See US Energy Information Administration, http://www.eia.doe.gov/emeu/cabs/Sudan/Oil.html (accessed 20 January 2010).

50. Douglas H. Johnson, 'Why Abyei Matters: The Breaking Point of Sudan's Comprehensive Peace Agreement?', *African Affairs*, Vol. 107, No. 426, January 2008, p. 18.

51. The ABC was supposed to define and demarcate the area of the nine Ngok Dinka chiefdoms transferred to Kordofan in 1905. For the final decision see http://www.pca-cpa.org/upload/files/Abyei%20Final%20Award.pdf (accessed 16 June 2011).

52. Neither side could agree on whether the seasonally migrant, cattle-herding, north-associated Misseriya tribe should be allowed to vote; the SPLM argued that only the permanently residing Ngok Dinka should be registered.

53. Denis M. Tull, 'Sudan after the Naivasha Peace Agreement: No Champagne Yet', *SWP Comments*, February 2005, p. 2.

54. The unanimous adoption of resolution 1990 (2011) formally established the United Nations Interim Security Force for Abyei (UNISFA), comprising a maximum of 4,200 military personnel, fifty police personnel and appropriate civilian support. See UN, 'Deeming Need for "Urgent" Response to Situation in Abyei, Sudan, Security Council Decides to Deploy Peacekeeping Force to Area, Unanimously Adopting 1990 (2011)', SC/10298, 27 June 2011.

55. Alan Boswell, 'Sudan's Conflict Spreads: Is This the Start of a New Civil War?', *Time*, 2 September 2011.

56. Branch and Mampilly, 'Winning the War, but Losing the Peace?', p. 1.

57. Sara Pantuliano, 'The Land Question: Sudan's Peace Nemesis', HPG Working Paper, Overseas Development Institute (ODI), 2007, p. 5.

58. Ibid., p. 9.

59. Reuters/Alert Net, 'Timeline – Violence Spirals in South Sudan', 7 January 2010.

60. Returnees need to be allocated both residential and agricultural land, which brings local tribal governance and national policy into competition; until issues relating to citizenship and land tenure are resolved, reintegration and return remain potential flashpoints for violence and will impede nation building in South Sudan. See Internal Displacement Monitoring Centre, 'Briefing Paper on Southern Sudan: IDPs Return to Face Slow Land Allocation, and No Shelter, Basic Services or Livelihoods', 30 May 2011; and Sara Pantuliano, Margie Buchanan-Smith and Paul Murphy, 'The Long Road Home: Opportunities and Obstacles to the Reintegration of IDPs and Refugees Returning to Southern Sudan and the Three Areas – Report of Phase 1', ODI, August 2007.

61. See Christopher Zambakari, 'South Sudan: Nation in the Post-CPA Era – Prospects and Challenges', *Pambazuka News*, 28 July 2011, for a discussion

on the difficulty of reconciling ethnic and residential notions of citizenship in South Sudan.

62. See David Hoile, *Darfur: The Road to Peace* (London, European-Sudanese Public Affairs Council, 2008), p. 4.

63. Nathan, 'No Ownership, No Peace'.

64. ICG, 'Darfur's Fragile Peace Agreement', Africa Briefing No. 39, 2006, p. 1, cited in Nathan, 'No Ownership, No Peace', p. 2.

65. Jeffrey Gettleman, 'Fragile Calm Holds in Darfur after Years of Death', *New York Times*, 2 January 2010.

66. See Hoile, *Darfur*.

67. Julie Flint, 'All This Moral Posturing Won't Help Darfur', *Independent*, 31 July 2007; Hoile, *Darfur*, also cites Mark Malloch-Brown, former UN Deputy Secretary-General, p. 10.

68. See ICG, 'Rigged Elections in Darfur and the Consequences of a Probable NCP Victory in Sudan', Africa Briefing No. 72, March 2010, and IDP Action, 'IDPs and Elections in Sudan', March 2010, for an account of the census and voter registration processes for displaced people.

69. In particular in its relationship with the US, which has retained sanctions against Khartoum for its continued support for international terrorism (1997) and its complicity in violence in Darfur (2007).

70. Maya Mailer and Lydia Poole on behalf of Oxfam International, Christian Aid, Cordaid, Handicap International, Save the Children, ICCO & Kerk in Actie, the International Rescue Committee, Secours Catholique/Caritas France, Tearfund and World Vision, 'Rescuing the Peace in Southern Sudan', Joint NGO Briefing Paper, Oxfam International, January 2010.

71. 'South Sudan Army Clashes with Renegade General Athor Kills 92', *Sudan Tribune*, 2 March 2011.

72. See ICG, 'Sudan: Regional Perspectives on the Prospect of Southern Independence', Africa Report No. 159, 6 May 2011.

73. Deng, *War of Visions*.

74. A. H. Abdel Salam and Alex de Waal, *The Phoenix State: Civil Society and the Future of Sudan* (Lawrenceville, NJ, Red Sea Press, 2001).

4 Somalia and Somaliland: State Building amid the Ruins

1. BBC News, 'Living in Somalia's Anarchy', 18 November 2004, http://news.bbc.co.uk/go/pr/fr/-/2/hi/africa/4017147.stm (accessed 1 June 2011).

2. Eugene Robinson, 'Down the Wrong Path in Afghanistan', *Washington Post*, 4 December 2009.

3. Abdinasir Mohamed and Sarah Childress, 'Suicide Bombing Kills Somali Ministers, Students', *Wall Street Journal*, 4 December 2009.

4. Robert I. Rotberg, 'The Failure and Collapse of Nation-States: Breakdown, Prevention, and Repair', in Robert I. Rotberg (ed.), *When States Fail: Causes and Consequences* (Princeton, Princeton University Press, 2004), pp. 9–10.

5. Peter D. Little, *Somalia: Economy without State* (Oxford, James Currey, 2003), p. 192.

6. See I. M. Lewis, *A Pastoral Democracy* (London, Oxford University Press, 1961).

7. I. M. Lewis, *Blood and Bone: The Call of Kinship in Somali Society* (Lawrenceville, NJ, Red Sea Press, 1994), p. 20.

8. See Maria H. Brons, *Society, Security, Sovereignty and the State in Somalia: From Statelessness to Statelessness?* (Utrecht, International Books, 2001), pp. 99–113.

9. I. M. Lewis, 'Visible and Invisible Differences: The Somali Paradox', *Africa*, Vol. 74, No. 4, November 2004, p. 492.

10. See Lewis, *Blood and Bone*, pp. 221–2.

11. Terrence Lyons and Ahmed I. Samatar, *Somalia: State Collapse, Multilateral Intervention, and Strategies for Political Reconstruction* (Washington, DC, Brookings Institution Press, 1995), p. 14.

12. See David D. Laitin, 'The Political Economy of Military Rule in Somalia', *Journal of Modern African Studies*, Vol. 14, No. 3, September 1976, pp. 449–68.

13. See Peter Woodward, *US Foreign Policy and the Horn of Africa* (Aldershot, Ashgate, 2006), pp. 22–7.

14. I. M. Lewis, *A Modern History of the Somali*, 4th edn (Oxford, James Currey, 2002), p. 263.

15. See I. M. Lewis, 'Nazionalismo frammentato e colasso del regime somalo', *Politica Internazionale*, Vol. 20, No. 4, 1992, pp. 35–52.

16. See John L. Hirsh and Robert Oakley, *Somalia and Operation Restore Hope: Reflections on Peacemaking and Peacekeeping* (Washington, DC, US Institute of Peace, 1995).

17. See Virginia Luling, 'Come Back Somalia? Questioning a Collapsed State', *Third World Quarterly*, Vol. 18, No. 2, June 1997, pp. 287–302.

18. Lewis, *Blood and Bone*, p. 167.

19. See I. M. Lewis, *Saints and Somalis: Popular Islam in a Clan-Based Society* (Lawrenceville, NJ, Red Sea Press, 1998).

20. See Michael van Notten, edited by Spencer Heath MacCallum, *The Law of the Somalis: A Stable Foundation for Economic Development in the Horn of Africa* (Lawrenceville, NJ, Red Sea Press, 2006).

21. See Roland Marchal, 'Islamic Political Dynamics in the Somali Civil War: Before and After September 11', in Alex de Waal (ed.), *Islamism and its Enemies in the Horn of Africa* (Addis Ababa, Shama Books, 2004), pp. 114–45.

22. Abdurahman M. Abdullahi, 'Recovering the Somali State: The Islamic Factor', in A. Osman Farah, Mammo Muchie, and Joakim Gundel (eds.),

Somalia: Diaspora and State Reconstitution in the Horn of Africa (London, Adonis & Abbey, 2007), pp. 196–221.

23. See Shaul Shay, *Somalia between Jihad and Restoration* (New Brunswick, NJ, Transaction Publishers, 2007), pp. 93–127; see also Kenneth J. Menkhaus, 'Somalia and Somaliland: Terrorism, Political Islam, and State Collapse', in Robert I. Rotberg (ed.), *Battling Terrorism in the Horn of Africa* (Washington, DC, Brookings Institution Press, 2005), pp. 23–47, and 'Risks and Opportunities in Somalia', *Survival*, Vol. 49, No. 2, Summer 2007, pp. 5–20.

24. See Medhane Tadesse, *Al-Ittihad: Political Islam and Black Economy in Somalia. Religion, Money, Clan and the Struggle for Supremacy over Somalia* (Addis Ababa, Meag, 2002), pp. 16–24.

25. It is significant that while the TFG and its predecessor entities have received various expressions of support from the international community, other states have been rather reluctant to actually accord it formal recognition. The United States, for example, never formally severed relations with Somalia after the collapse of the Somali state in 1991, though neither has it officially recognised any of the fifteen transitional governments, including the current TFG. The State Department website merely states: 'The United States maintains regular dialogue with the TFG and other key stakeholders in Somalia through the U.S. Embassy in Nairobi, Kenya.' In fact, the lack of affirmative de jure recognition for the TFG is presumed by the introduction in October 2009 of a Congressional Resolution by the chairman of the Africa Subcommittee of the US House of Representatives urging 'the Obama administration to recognise the TFG and allow the opening of an official Somali Embassy in Washington'. The clear implication is that the United States government accords the TFG something less than normal diplomatic recognition as a sovereign. Indeed, this point was formally conceded in early 2010 by the Obama administration when, in a brief filed with the US Supreme Court, the Solicitor-General of the United States and the Legal Advisor of the State Department acknowledged that 'since the fall of that government, the United States has not recognized any entity as the government of Somalia'. Similarly, the British Foreign and Commonwealth Office's website states: 'Since the fall of the Siad Barre regime in 1991 there have been no formal diplomatic links between the UK and Somalia.' See *Mohamed Ali Samantar* v. *Bashe Abdi Yusuf, et al.*, Brief of Amici Curiae Academic Experts in Somali History and Current Affairs in Support of the Respondents, 27 January 2010, http://www.abanet.org/publiced/preview/briefs/pdfs/09–10/08–1555_RespondentAmCuSomaliExperts.pdf (accessed 1 June 2011); also see *Mohamed Ali Samantar* v. *Bashe Abdi Yusuf, et al.*, Brief of the United States as Amicus Curiae Supporting Affirmance, January 2010, http://www.abanet.org/publiced/preview/briefs/pdfs/09–10/08–1555_AffirmanceAmCuUSA.pdf (accessed 1 June 2011).

26. See Ken Menkhaus, 'The Crisis in Somalia: Tragedy in Five Acts', *African Affairs*, Vol. 106, No. 204, 2007, pp. 357–90; see also Gerrie Swart, 'Somalia: A Failed State Governed by a Failing Government?', in Abdulahi A. Osman and Issaka K. Souaré (eds.), *Somalia at the Crossroads: Challenges and Perspectives on Reconstituting a Failed State* (London, Adonis & Abbey, 2007), pp. 109–21.

27. US Department of State, Office of the Coordinator for Counterterrorism, 'Designation of al-Shabaab as a Specially Designated Global Terrorist' (Public Notice 6137), 26 February 2008, http://www.state.gov/s/ct/rls/other/des/102448.htm (accessed 1 June 2011).

28. Commonwealth of Australia, Joint Media Release of Attorney-General Robert McClelland, MP, and Minister for Foreign Affairs Stephen Smith, MP, 'Listing of Al-Shabaab as a Terrorist Organisation', 21 August 2009, http://www.foreignminister.gov.au/releases/2009/fa-s090821.html (accessed 1 June 2011).

29. The Terrorism Act 2000 (Proscribed Organisations) (Amendment) Order 2010, No. 611, 4 March 2010, http://www.opsi.gov.uk/si/si2010/uksi_20100611_en_1 (accessed 1 June 2011).

30. Government of Canada, Ministry of Public Safety, News Release, 'The Government of Canada Lists Al Shabaab as a Terrorist Organization', 7 March 2010, http://www.publicsafety.gc.ca/media/nr/2010/nr20100307-eng.aspx?rss=false (accessed 1 June 2011).

31. See CNN, '21 Killed in Suicide Attack on African Union Base in Somalia', 18 September 2009, http://edition.cnn.com/2009/WORLD/africa/09/18/somalia.suicide.attack/index.html (accessed 1 June 2011).

32. See Stephanie McCrummen, 'Bombing Kills 19 in Somali Capital', *Washington Post*, 4 December 2009.

33. J. Peter Pham, Testimony before the US House of Representatives, Committee on Foreign Affairs, Subcommittee on Africa and Global Health, 25 June 2009, http://foreignaffairs.house.gov/111/pha062509.pdf (accessed 1 June 2011).

34. International Crisis Group, *Somalia: The Transitional Government on Life Support*, Africa Report No. 170, 21 February 2011, p. i.

35. Ibid.

36. Bronwyn E. Bruton, *Somalia: A New Approach*, Council Special Report 52 (New York and Washington, Council on Foreign Relations, 2010), p. 10.

37. See Nathan Mugisha, 'The Way Forward in Somalia', *RUSI Journal*, Vol. 156, No. 3, June/July 2011, pp. 26–33.

38. See Elizabeth Dickinson, 'How Much Turf Does the Somali Government Really Control?', *Foreign Policy* (online version), 23 September 2010, http://www.foreignpolicy.com/articles/2010/09/23/how_much_turf_does_the_somali_government_really_control (accessed 1 June 2011).

39. See J. Peter Pham, 'Somali Stability Still Poses Threat Even After Successful Strike on Nabhan', *World Defense Review*, 17 September 2009, http://worlddefensereview.com/pham091709.shtml (accessed 1 June 2011). The price of AK-47 rounds, for example, fell over 50 per cent to approximately $0.30 each.

40. See J. Peter Pham, 'Peripheral Vision: A Model Solution for Somalia', *RUSI Journal*, Vol. 154, No. 5, October 2009, pp. 84–90.

41. See I. M. Lewis, *The Modern History of Somaliland: From Nation to State* (New York, Frederick A. Praeger, 1965).

42. See Anthony J. Carroll and B. Rajagopal, 'The Case for an Independent Somaliland', *American University Journal of Law and Politics*, Vol. 8, Nos. 2/3, 1993, pp. 653–62.

43. See Mark Bradbury, *Becoming Somaliland* (Oxford, James Currey, 2008), pp. 77–136.

44. African Union Commission, Report of the AU Fact-Finding Mission to Somaliland (30 April to 4 May 2005).

45. See Iqbal Jhazbhay, *Somaliland: An African Struggle for Nationhood and International Recognition* (Johannesburg, South African Institute for International Affairs/Institute for Global Dialogue, 2009).

46. Abdi Ismail Samantar, 'Somali Reconstruction and Local Initiative: Amoud University', *World Development*, Vol. 29, No. 4, April 2001, p. 654.

47. See Kinfe Abraham, *Somalia Calling: The Crisis of Statehood and the Quest for Peace* (Addis Ababa, Ethiopian International Institute for Peace and Development, 2002), pp. 445–63.

48. While the region's constitution still formally commits it to being a part of a future federal Somalia, the lack of progress in the southern and central parts of Somalia and the lacklustre performance of the TFG have caused Puntlanders to edge closer to outright secessionism. In late December 2009 the regional parliament voted unanimously to adopt a distinctive flag (hitherto the flag of Somalia had been used), coat of arms and anthem.

49. Raymond Gilpin, *Counting the Costs of Somali Piracy* (Washington, DC, US Institute of Peace, 2009), p. 3.

50. Ken Menkhaus, 'Dangerous Waters', *Survival*, Vol. 51, No. 1, February–March 2009, p. 24.

51. See Brian J. Hesse, 'Lessons in Successful Somali Governance', *Journal of Contemporary African Studies*, Vol. 18, No. 1, January 2010, p. 79; see also J. Peter Pham, 'Putting Somali Piracy in Context', *Journal of Contemporary African Studies*, Vol. 28, No. 3, July 2010, pp. 325–41.

52. Report of the Special Adviser to the Secretary-General on Legal Issues Related to Piracy off the Coast of Somalia, S/2011/30 (25 January 2011).

53. Bruton, *Somalia*, pp. 33–4.

54. See www.galmudug.com (accessed 1 June 2011).

55. See Aggrey Mutambo, 'Somalis Swear in the President of Jubaland', *Daily Nation*, 3 April 2011, http://www.nation.co.ke/News/Somalis+swear+in +the+president+of+Jubaland/-/1056/1138186/-/m66vqdz/-/index.html (accessed 1 June 2011).

56. See Jeffrey Herbst, 'War and the State in Africa', *International Security*, Vol. 14, No. 4, Spring 1990, pp. 117–39.

57. Iqbal Jhazbhay, 'Islam and Stability in Somaliland and the Geo-politics of the War on Terror', *Journal of Muslim Minority Affairs*, Vol. 28, No. 2, August 2008, p. 198.

58. Lewis, 'Visible and Invisible Differences', p. 508.

59. See Abdiaziz Hassan, 'Somali Legislators Flee Abroad, Parliament Paralysed', Reuters, 24 June 2009, http://uk.reuters.com/article/idUKL0890231 (accessed 1 June 2011).

60. See Ken Menkhaus, 'Somalia: What Went Wrong?', *RUSI Journal*, Vol. 154, No. 5, August 2009, pp. 6–12.

61. UN Security Council, Report of the Monitoring Group on Somalia pursuant to Security Council Resolution 1853 (2008), S/2010/91 (10 March 2010), p. 4.

62. Ibid., p. 12.

5   *From Bombs to Ballots: The Rise of Politics in Northern Ireland*

1. For example, the Spanish enclaves of Ceuta and Melilla on the North African coast.

2. 'The opposite of a culture of violence is … what? It is not easy to move from a culture of violence, especially a long-established one, to a culture of coexistence – a state where conflicts are resolved in ways that are generally acceptable through discourse, compromise, politics. For many, the ending of violence is a sufficient objective. Only when it is achieved do its limitations and the obstacles to a more stable peace become apparent': John Darby, *Scorpions in a Bottle: Conflicting Cultures in Northern Ireland* (London, Minority Rights Group, 1997).

3. An issue resurrected in Iraq from 2003.

4. Almost 30,000 at its peak.

5. And its successor, the Royal Irish Home Service Force.

6. This requirement for continuity in a counter-insurgency campaign was a lesson the British failed to transfer to Afghanistan and Iraq.

7. For a fuller account of this negotiation, read Jonathan Powell, *Great Hatred, Little Room: Making Peace in Northern Ireland* (London, Bodley Head, 2008).

8. For example, the Reverend Ian Paisley, who led the DUP throughout the Troubles.

9. 'The Independent Monitoring Commission ... admitted in its most recent report that the threat level is "very serious" and at its highest in six years': reported in *The Times*, 23 November 2009, p. 5.

10. Principally the Continuity IRA (CIRA), the Real IRA (RIRA) and Oglaigh na hEireann (ONH).

11. Such as the murder of two soldiers on 7 March 2009 and a policeman on 9 March 2009.

12. This dilemma has been at the heart of the recent debate on devolution of policing and justice from Westminster to Stormont.

13. It is, nevertheless, not lost on both sides of the community that the demographic balance is increasingly shifting in favour of Catholics. That is not to say, however, that a Nationalist majority will emerge in time, as a significant percentage of Catholics have traditionally voted Unionist.

14. The Alliance Party, the largest of such coalitions, currently holds eight out of the 108 seats in the Northern Ireland Assembly.

15. In the same way that continuity and coherence of security forces proved key to the counter-insurgency campaign, as discussed above, the focus provided by a single UK government ministry (the Northern Ireland Office) has proved successful in a way in which the UK's 'comprehensive approach' to overseas insurgencies (e.g., Iraq and Afghanistan, where at least three ministries – FCO, DfID and MoD – are equal partners) has yet to gel.

16. 108 members: DUP (38), Sinn Fein (29), UUP (16), SDLP (14), Alliance Party (8), Green Party (1), Traditional Unionist Voice (1), Independent (1). The allocation of the recently devolved Ministry of Policing and Justice to the Alliance Party, giving them two ministries rather than one, is an exception to the D'Hondt system, agreed by the main parties to allow non-partisan tenure of this politically contentious position.

17. See, for example, *The Times*, 23 November 2009, p. 5: 'the Province's First Minister, the Democratic Unionist Leader Peter Robinson, admitting for the first time that he cannot guarantee the future of the power-sharing structures. The DUP and Sinn Fein ... are at loggerheads over the devolution of policing and justice ... Sinn Fein demands their immediate transfer, a move it says that will demonstrate that the 1998 Good Friday Agreement is delivering a Republican agenda.'

18. Effectively abandoning the Republic's claim to a united Ireland.

19. This, in turn, has cemented the links between the PSNI and An Garda Siochana which had steadily improved since the 1970s, making the border less porous and facilitating the sharing of intelligence.

20. Friedrich Engels to Karl Marx, Manchester, 23 May 1856, www.marxists. org/archive/marx/works/1856/letters/56_05_23.htm.

21. Net receipts from the EU averaged 4 per cent of GDP between 1973 and 1986.

22. By 2007 Irish GDP was 140 per cent of the EU average.
23. For example, the shipbuilding industry of Belfast was typically and almost exclusively manned by Protestant workers from east Belfast.
24. A recent Deloitte study put the wasted cost of segregation in Northern Ireland at 1 billion pounds per year.
25. John Hume, together with his Unionist counterpart David (now Lord) Trimble, was awarded the Nobel Peace Prize for commitment to the 1998 Good Friday Agreement. Interestingly, in 1976 Mairead Corrigan and Betty Williams, leaders of the Community of Peace People, had received the same award for their efforts to unite the females of Northern Ireland's divided society: 'The voice of women has a special role and a special soul-force in the struggle for a non-violent world.'
26. The hackneyed tale of Catholic schoolchildren visiting a Protestant church and, on being shown the Bible on the lectern, asking, 'Why do Protestants need Bibles?' is all the sadder for its proximity to the truth.
27. Less than 10 per cent of which have been completed.
28. The terrorist weapons were procured from a variety of sources, including Libya. Stopping the influx of weaponry coming through the Irish Republic into the hands of PIRA became an increasing priority for An Garda Siochana, whose complementary efforts to seal the north–south border are not to be underestimated.
29. Interestingly, Senator Mitchell failed to repeat his Northern Ireland success in the Middle East.
30. Including an ex-CIA Deputy Director and an ex-Metropolitan Police Assistant Commissioner.
31. Source: M. Bhatia, K. Lanigan and P. Wilkinson, 'Minimal Investments, Minimal Results: The Failure of Security Policy in Afghanistan', Afghanistan Research and Evaluation Unit, June 2004. Note that the figures for Afghanistan have since changed fourfold.
32. Dame Glynne-Evans's valedictory dispatch, British Ambassador, Lisbon, 2004.
33. 'In a struggle for legitimacy, politics is paramount', *The Economist*, 17 October 2009, p. 34.
34. If anything the east–west or city–rural divide within Northern Ireland is now more worrying than the traditional economic divide along sectarian lines, but it is not a show-stopper.

6   *Indonesia: Long Roads to Reconciliation*

1. For a detailed study on the shaping of Indonesia's geostrategic outlook, see Michael Leifer, *Indonesia's Foreign Policy* (London, The Royal Institute of International Affairs, 1983).

2. For masterly treatment of the Aceh conflict, see Kirsten E. Schulze, 'The Free Aceh Movement (GAM): Anatomy of a Separatist Organization', Policy Studies No. 2, Washington, DC, East-West Center Washington, 2004; Edward Aspinall, *Islam and Nation: Separatist Rebellion in Aceh, Indonesia* (Stanford, Stanford University Press, 2009).

3. In 1953 many of the ulama and other leaders who had led the Acehnese during the 1945–9 period led their followers into the Darul Islam (Abode of Islam) revolt. This revolt was aimed at establishing Aceh as an autonomous region within an Islamic Indonesia. They were quite explicit about these aims, declaring themselves part of the Negara Islam Indonesia (Indonesian Islamic State) earlier declared by Kartosuwirjo, another Darul Islam leader in West Java. This revolt continues to be important simply because the response of the Indonesian government since then has mostly been to address the demands of this revolt – that is, autonomy and the power to implement aspects of sharia or Islamic law. For example, in 1959 the Indonesian government responded by giving Aceh the status of a 'special territory', which ostensibly confers some degree of autonomy in religious, educational and cultural matters.

4. There were several rounds of talks in Helsinki: the first on 28–9 January 2005, the second 21–3 February 2005, the third 12–16 April 2005, the fourth 26–31 May 2005 and the fifth 12–17 July 2005.

5. Ian Robinson, 'The East Timor Conflict' in Michael Cranna (ed.), *The True Cost of Conflict* (New York, The New Press, 1994), pp. 11–12.

6. These actions are documented in Ben Kiernan, *Genocide and Resistance in Southeast Asia: Documentation, Denial, and Justice in Cambodia and East Timor* (Piscataway, NJ, Transaction Publishers, 2008).

7. Robinson, 'The East Timor Conflict', p. 14.

8. The East Timor situation attracted global attention when Indonesian troops opened fire on pro-independence demonstrators at the Santa Cruz cemetery in Dili, the capital of East Timor, on 12 November 1991, killing about fifty and wounding twice that many civilians. Further to that, the international media reported the torture of another 300–400 political dissenters arrested on this occasion at the hands of Indonesian security forces. The estimated 3,500 demonstrators had marched peacefully to the cemetery to commemorate a student killed in clashes with the police on 28 October. When the Nobel Peace Prize was awarded in 1996 to José Ramos-Horta and Carlos Belo, the resistance movement gained even more international recognition and legitimacy.

9. Jacques Bertrand, *Nationalism and Ethnic Conflict in Indonesia* (Cambridge, Cambridge University Press, 2004), pp. 159–60.

10. Ibid., p. 135.

11. The following points are drawn from Kirsten Schulze, 'Internal Conflicts in Southeast Asia', in Sumit Ganguly, Joseph Chinyong Liow and Andrew Scobell (eds.), *The Routledge Handbook of Asian Security Studies* (London, Routledge, 2010), pp. 253–4: Under the terms of the MoU, everything except foreign affairs, external defence, national security and fiscal matters would be devolved to Aceh. Aceh would be consulted with respect to international agreements and had the right to use regional symbols including a flag, a crest and a hymn. The Indonesian government would facilitate the establishment of Aceh-based political parties within eighteen months from the signing of the MoU. All Acehnese would be issued with new identity cards. With respect to the economy, the MoU granted Aceh the right to raise funds with external loans and to set interest rates beyond those set by the Central Bank. Aceh could raise taxes and seek foreign direct investment. It also had jurisdiction over living natural resources in its territorial sea, as well as being entitled to retain 70 per cent of the revenue from all current and future hydrocarbon deposits and other natural resources. GAM would nominate representatives to participate fully in the commission established to conduct the post-tsunami reconstruction. The legal code for Aceh would be redrafted on the basis of the universal principles of human rights and Aceh would receive its own independent court system. The appointment of the regional police chief and prosecutors would require the consent of the Aceh administration. Moreover, all civilian crimes committed by military personnel in Aceh would be tried in Acehnese civil courts. Regarding human rights, the MoU stipulated that Aceh would receive a human rights court as well as a truth and reconciliation commission. GAM members would be granted amnesty and those imprisoned would be released within fifteen days of the signing of the MoU.

12. Consent for international intervention was obtained from Indonesia as a result of pressure from international financial institutions as well as bilateral defence partners with whom Jakarta enjoyed long-standing cooperative arrangements.

13. Elizabeth F. Drexler, *Aceh, Indonesia: Securing the Insecure State* (Philadelphia, University of Pennsylvania Press, 2008), pp. 17–18.

7   *Managing the Two Solitudes: Lessons from Canada*

1. For the purposes of this paper 'independence', 'secession' and 'sovereignty' are used interchangeably, although in the Canada/Quebec context, the third term encompasses different forms of statehood from full independence to sovereignty association or sovereignty partnership, under which Quebec

would still retain some form of economic and political relationship with Canada.

2. Less significant but nevertheless important, and increasingly so, in the political development of modern Canada has been the fault line which has separated aboriginal peoples from English and French Canadians. More recently, some scholars and commentators have suggested that Canada's four western provinces collectively harbour growing resentment at their exclusion and alienation from mainstream Canadian political affairs, which are perceived as heavily weighted towards the concerns of Canada's two biggest provinces, Quebec and Ontario – in effect creating another fault line, separating 'the west' from the rest of Canada. See, for instance, Robert Lawson, 'Understanding Alienation in Western Canada: Is "Western Alienation" the Problem? Is Senate Reform the Cure?' *Journal of Canadian Studies/Revue d'études canadiennes*, Vol. 39, No. 2, 2005, pp. 127–55.

3. Pierre Trudeau was Canada's prime minister from 1968 to 1984 (save a nine-month period). Arguably the most influential and divisive leader in the country's history, Trudeau was widely acknowledged as the pre-eminent champion of the 'one-nation' or unified vision of Canada comprising ten equal provinces. Charles Taylor is widely regarded as Canada's foremost political philosopher. Among numerous contributions to political philosophy, he is best known in Canada for his call for recognition of Quebec's particularity within Canadian federalism and his critique of Trudeau-ian liberalism.

4. Stéphane Dion (2006–8) and Michael Ignatieff (2008–11).

5. Of the more popular and accessible writings on Canada's main fault line are John Ralston Saul, *Reflections of a Siamese Twin: Canada at the End of the Twentieth Century* (Toronto, Penguin/Viking, 1997), and Mordecai Richler, *Oh Canada! Oh Quebec!: Requiem for a Divided Country* (Toronto, Knopf, 1992).

6. See David Philip, 'Canada Undone? Signals from Quebec Referendum', *Economic and Political Weekly*, 30 December 1995, pp. 3354–6.

7. The title of Hugh MacLennan's 1945 novel *Two Solitudes* has become emblematic of the often uneasy relationship between English and French Canadians.

8. According to Statistics Canada (2003), since 1971 the population of Quebec has experienced a reduction to just under 600,000 of those Quebecers whose mother tongue was English, a drop in its share of the Quebec population from 13.1 to 8.3 per cent. In 2001 Quebec's total population was roughly 7.3 million.

9. In 2006 the federal government passed the 'Québécois nation motion', which recognised that 'the Québécois form a nation within a united Canada'. But this was widely seen as a political gesture supported by all

parties to draw support from Quebec voters in the run-up to an election. It did not have fundamental consequences, as would a constitutional amendment to recognise Quebec's 'distinct' or 'special' status.

10. Emphasis mine.

11. David Kaplan, 'Two Nations in Search of a State: Canada's Ambivalent Spatial Identities', *Annals of the Association of American Geographers*, Vol. 84, No. 4, 1994, p. 592.

12. Ibid.

13. Philip Resnick, 'Civic and Ethnic Nationalism: Lessons from the Canadian Case', in Ronald Beiner and Wayne Norman (eds.), *Canadian Political Philosophy: Contemporary Reflections* (Toronto, Oxford University Press, 2001), pp. 282–97 (version supplied by author, p. 10).

14. See Kenneth McRoberts, 'Canada and the Multinational State', *Canadian Journal of Political Science*, Vol. 34, No. 4, 2001, p. 700.

15. Philip Resnick, 'Hubris and Melancholy in Multinational States', *Nations and Nationalism*, Vol. 14, No. 4, 2008, pp. 789–807 (version supplied by author, p. 6).

16. Stéphane Dion, 'Why is Secession Difficult in Well-Established Democracies? Lessons from Quebec', *British Journal of Political Science*, Vol. 26, No. 2, 1996, p. 277.

17. Resnick, 'Civic and Ethnic Nationalism', p. 8.

18. Ibid., p. 18.

19. McRoberts, 'Canada and the Multinational State', p. 713.

20. Ibid., p. 700.

21. Resnick, 'Civic and Ethnic Nationalism', p. 12.

22. Marcel Adam, 'Le multiculturalisme nuit à la cohesion sociale en cultivant les différences', *La Presse*, 26 November 1994, cited in Guy Bouthillier, *L'obsession ethnique* (Montreal, Lanctot, 1997), p. 56, translation by Resnick, 'Civic and Ethnic Nationalism', p. 13.

23. See, for instance, Neil Bissondath, *Selling Illusions: The Cult of Multiculturalism in Canada* (Toronto, Penguin, 1994).

24. Dion, 'Why is Secession Difficult in Well-Established Democracies? Lessons from Quebec', *British Journal of Political Science*, Vol. 26, No. 2, 1996, p. 279.

25. Philip, 'Canada Undone?', p. 3356.

26. Philip Resnick, 'Recognition & Ressentiment: On Accommodating National Differences within Multinational States', in Ramon Maiz (ed.), *Democracy, Nationalism, Europeanism* (London, Frank Cass, 2004) (version supplied by author, p. 6).

27. Saul Newman, 'Nationalism in Post-Industrial Societies: Why States Still Matter', *Comparative Politics*, Vol. 33, No. 1, 2000, pp. 21–41.

28. I discovered this quip in Robert Vipond, 'Seeing Canada through the Referendum: Still a House Divided', *Publius*, Vol. 23, No. 3, 1993, p. 39.

29. John Ibbitson, 'Quebec's Profound Isolation', *The Globe and Mail*, 3 August 2011.
30. Resnick, 'Recognition & Ressentiment', p. 10.
31. Ibid., p. 9.
32. See, for instance, Mark Redhead, 'Charles Taylor's Deeply Diverse Response to Canadian Fragmentation: A Project Often Commented on but Seldom Explored', *Canadian Journal of Political Science/Revue canadienne de science politique*, Vol. 36, No. 1, 2003, pp. 61–83.
33. Dion, 'Why is Secession Difficult in Well-Established Democracies?', p. 281.
34. See Peter Russell, *Constitutional Odyssey: Can Canadians Become a Sovereign People?* (Toronto, University of Toronto Press, c. 1993), p. 75.
35. William Johnson, 'The Fragmentation of Quebec', *The Globe and Mail*, 26 August 2011.
36. Dion, 'Why is Secession Difficult in Well-Established Democracies?', p. 279.
37. Hudson Meadwell, 'The Politics of Nationalism in Quebec', *World Politics*, Vol. 45, No. 2, 1993, pp. 221–2.
38. As recast by John Mueller, 'Policing the Remnants of War', *Journal of Peace Research*, Vol. 40, No. 5, 2003, p. 514.

8 Ethiopia: the Perils of Reform

1. Emperor Menilek of Ethiopia to Queen Victoria, 21 April 1891 (PRO/FO 95/751 No. 100).

Many scholars have sought – with varying degrees of success – to understand and explain the fault lines of Ethiopia and the wider Horn. The following are among the more useful works for further reference.

Historical Background

Bahru Zewde, *A History of Modern Ethiopia, 1855–1974* (London, James Currey, 1991)

Richard J. Reid, *Frontiers of Violence in North-East Africa: Genealogies of Conflict since 1800* (Oxford, Oxford University Press, 2011)

The Haile-Selassie Era

John Markakis, *Ethiopia: Anatomy of a Traditional Polity* (Oxford, Oxford University Press, 1974)

The Derg Era

Christopher Clapham, *Transformation and Continuity in Revolutionary Ethiopia* (Cambridge, Cambridge University Press, 1988)

John Markakis, *National and Class Conflict in the Horn of Africa* (Cambridge, Cambridge University Press, 1987)

The EPRDF Era

Lovise Aalen, *The Politics of Ethnicity in Ethiopia: Actors, Power and Mobilisation under Ethnic Federalism* (Leiden, Brill, 2011)

David Turton (ed.), *Ethnic Federalism: The Ethiopian Experience in Comparative Perspective* (Oxford, James Currey, 2006)

Sarah Vaughan and Kjetil Tronvoll, *The Culture of Power in Contemporary Ethiopian Political Life* (Stockholm, SIDA Studies, 2003)

The Ethiopia–Eritrea Conflict

Dominique Jacquin–Berdal and Martin Plaut (eds.), *Unfinished Business: Ethiopia and Eritrea at War* (Lawrenceville, NJ, Red Sea Press, 2004)

Kjetil Tronvoll, *War and the Politics of Identity in Ethiopia: The Making of Enemies and Allies in the Horn of Africa* (Oxford, James Currey, 2009)

9　*Ethnic Fractionalisation and the Propensity for Conflict in Uganda, Kenya and Tanzania*

1.　Leo Kuper and M. G. Smith (eds.), *Pluralism in Africa* (Berkeley, University of California Press, 1969).

2.　For the purposes of this chapter 'Africa' means sub-Saharan Africa.

3.　Michael Crowder, *West Africa under Colonial Rule* (Evanston, Northwestern University Press, 1968), pp. 163–238.

4.　In a typical British colony, two to four elections were usually held before independence. The number of directly elected seats in the Legislative Council (the colonial legislature) increased at each election until the body arrived at its full complement of members prior to independence. At this point the British invited the leader of the majority party to form a government responsible for the internal affairs of the colony for a period of six months, after which all power was turned over to that government and the colony declared an independent state. In the case of the French territories, elections were first held for seats in the French National Assembly, beginning in 1954, but not for territorial legislatures until 1960. The transition was more abrupt than in the British colonies, but the overall process was the same – legislative elections were held in a series of single-member districts that put a primacy on the ability of politicians reaching out to the electorate on the basis of local and thus often ethnic appeals.

5.　Daniel N. Posner, 'The Political Salience of Cultural Difference: Why Chewas and Tumbukas are Allies in Zambia and Adversaries in Malawi', *American Political Science Review*, Vol. 98, No. 4, November 2004, pp. 529–45;

Shaheen Mozaffar, James Scarritt and Glen Galaich, 'Electoral Institutions, Ethnopolitical Cleavages and Party Systems in Africa's Emerging Democracies', *American Political Science Review*, Vol. 97, 2003, pp. 379–90.

6. Both Posner, 'The Political Salience of Cultural Difference', in his discussion comparing the salience of ethnicity in Malawi and Zambia, and Mozaffar et al., 'Electoral Institutions, Ethnopolitical Cleavages and Party Systems in Africa's Emerging Democracies', emphasised that while the configuration of ethnicity is important, ethnicity per se is not the only determinant of political conflict. Rather it is when ethnicity becomes mobilised through the efforts of political elites that it becomes a potent force in a nation's politics.

7. The post-election violence in Kenya following extraordinarily close elections in December 2007 is but one example. Inter-ethnic violence also occurred in the run-up to multiparty elections in 1992 and 1997.

8. The Kikuyu account for 22 per cent of Kenya's population. Together with the Meru and Embu, to which they are culturally and linguistically related, the Kikuyu account for 30 per cent of all Kenyans.

9. The Baganda are 17 per cent of Uganda's population.

10. The Kingdom of *Bu*ganda is headed by a hereditary monarch, the Kabaka, and populated by the *Ba*ganda people, who speak *Lu*ganda. The Baganda are now, of course, citizens of the larger former colonial protectorate of Uganda, a name the British derived from the kingdom and its most populous group.

11. Obote's party, the UPC, won a plurality of the vote and seats in the election held immediately before independence in 1962, but not a majority. He became prime minister in a strange alliance with Kabaka Yeka, or 'Kabaka Only', a party of Baganda royalists that formed a coalition government with the UPC. However, that coalition broke down in early 1966.

12. It is important to remember that the number of Ugandans who died during Obote's second presidency almost equalled the number who died during the rule of Idi Amin.

13. The Duke of York School is now Lenana School and the Prince of Wales School is now Nairobi School.

14. With this system of administration, Kenyatta governed Kenya like the colonial governors who had preceded him – via a group of eight provincial commissioners, who were given substantial powers, and via them with the support of forty-three district commissioners at the district level. Students of the period often refer to Kenyatta as 'the last of the colonial governors'.

15. The 'Mafia' also included several prominent politicians from Meru and Embu, whose peoples were closely related to the Kikuyu. A key lieutenant was Kiraitu Murungi, the Minister of Justice, who soon became deeply involved in the Anglo-Leasing scandal.

16. Although Tanzania's official capital is Dodoma, a sleepy town in the middle of the country, 360 kilometres from the Indian Ocean coast, the country's commercial capital remains Dar es Salaam and most government ministries, including the Office of the President, operate out of the city.

17. Julius K. Nyerere, *Nyerere: Freedom and Unity/Uhuru na Umoja* (Nairobi, Oxford University Press, 1966), pp. 195–203.

18. CCM stands for Chama cha Mpinduzi, which means the Party of the Revolution in Swahili.

19. Joel D. Barkan (ed.), *Politics and Public Policy in Kenya and Tanzania*, 2nd edn (New York, Praeger Publishers, 1984).

20. For example, competence in English was no longer required to obtain admission to the University of Dar es Salaam if one could demonstrate a high level of competence in Swahili, and competence in English generally declined. This has created other problems with respect to the ability of Tanzanians to communicate at a commercial and professional level with the rest of East Africa and especially with the world community. The impact of Swahili usage on national cohesion, however, is undeniable. Although literacy rates in Tanzania have fallen in recent years, literacy means literacy in Swahili.

21. Republic of Kenya, *The Proposed Constitution of Kenya*, Office of the Attorney General, 6 May 2010.

10 *From Districts Six to Nine: Managing South Africa's Many Fault Lines*

1. Antony Altbeker, *A Country at War with Itself: South Africa's Crisis of Crime* (Johannesburg, Jonathan Ball, 2007). The numbers of people killed due to political violence in South Africa since the National Party election victory in 1948 vary considerably, but are generally accepted to be in the order of 20,000. The SIPRI figure, for example, is 18,997. Around seventy were reportedly killed in government detention, 600 in the Soweto uprising in 1976, around 500 additionally by SA government security forces, and the bulk of the rest from internecine political violence. The number of murders, by comparison, in South Africa today is between 20,000 and 30,000 annually, depending on which statistics one uses. See, for example, http://gunowners.org/fs0304.htm.

2. For an excellent summary of the challenges confronting South Africa, see Alec Russell, *After Mandela: The Battle for the Soul of South Africa* (London, Hutchinson, 2009), esp. p. 46.

3. Thabo Mbeki, Progressive Governance Conference, 28 July 2005. At http://www.dfa.gov.za/docs/speeches/2005/mbek0802.htm.

4. The 2006 population breakdown of South Africa's 50 million people was: Blacks 79.5 per cent, Whites 9.2 per cent, Coloureds 8.9 per cent

and Indians/Asians 2.5 per cent. The population can be further broken down into the following language/ethnic categories (according to the 2001 census): IsiZulu 23.8 per cent, IsiXhosa 17.6 per cent, Afrikaans 13.3 per cent, Sepedi 9.4 per cent, English 8.2 per cent, Setswana 8.2 per cent, Sesotho 7.9 per cent, Xitsonga 4.4 per cent, other 7.2 per cent (see CIA World Factbook, https://www.cia.gov/library/publications/theworld-factbook/geos/sf.html). According to South Africa's National Planning Commission, some major fault lines include divisions of gender, language, ethnic groups and class. For more information see www.npconline.co.za/pebble.asp?relid=84.

5. Tutu in 1993, as quoted in Allistair Sparks, *Tomorrow is Another Country: The Inside Story of South Africa's Negotiated Revolution* (London: Heinemann, 1995).

6. Thabo Mbeki, opening the debate in the National Assembly on 'Reconciliation and Nation Building', National Assembly, Cape Town, 29 May 1998, http://www.dfa.gov.za/docs/speeches/1998/mbek0529.htm.

7. United Nations Development Programme, *Overcoming Barriers: Human Mobility and Development* (New York, UNDP/Macmillan, 2009), p. 177.

8. Places 159 to 182 (the category classified as 'Low Human Development') are virtually all African: Togo, Malawi, Benin, East Timor, Ivory Coast, Zambia, Eritrea, Senegal, Rwanda, Gambia, Liberia, Guinea, Ethiopia, Mozambique, Guinea-Bissau, Burundi, Chad, DRC, Burkina Faso, Mali, CAR, Sierra Leone, Afghanistan, Niger.

9. United Nations Development Programme, *Human Development Report 2007/8* (New York, Oxford University Press, 2008), and Natalia Dinella and Lyn Squire (eds.), *Globalisation and Equity* (Edward Elgar, Cheltenham, 2005), p. 45, http://books.google.co.za.

10. Latin America is the world's most unequal region, with a Gini coefficient of around 0.5; in developed countries the figure is closer to 0.3, with the least unequal countries, in order, Denmark (24.7), Japan (24.9), Sweden (25), Czech Republic (25.4) and Norway (25.8). Of the larger countries measured, Brazil (57), South Africa (57.8) and Colombia (58.6) are clustered just above the bottom five. The Gini coefficient is most often used as a measure of income distribution or wealth distribution. It is defined as a ratio with values as represented here between 0 and 100: a low Gini coefficient indicates more equal income or wealth distribution, while a high Gini coefficient indicates more unequal distribution. The number 0 corresponds to perfect equality (everyone having the same income) and 100 corresponds to perfect inequality (where one person has all the income, while everyone else has zero income). World Bank, World Development Indicators 2007, http://hdr.undp.org/en/media/HDR_20072008_EN_Complete.pdf.

11. At http://www.earthscan.co.uk.
12. See 'Winners and Losers: South Africa's Changing Income Distribution in the 1990s', cited in *South Africa Survey 2000/01* (Johannesburg, SA Institute of Race Relations, 2001), pp. 374–5. At the same time there was an overall rise in inequality in South Africa between 1995 and 1998, with the Gini coefficient rising for whites from 0.55 to 0.67 and for blacks from 0.70 to 0.81. The predominantly rural Northern Province and Eastern Cape had the highest levels of poverty registered, at 78 per cent and 74 per cent respectively.
13. It is estimated that in 1900 about 9.5 per cent of sub-Saharan Africa's inhabitants lived in urban areas. By the 1970s this had risen to 25 per cent and to 37.2 per cent by 2000. It is expected to rise to 45.3 per cent by 2015 and to over 50 per cent by 2025. See http://bic.cass.cn/english/InfoShow/Article_Show_Conference_Show.asp?ID=360&Title=Africa%20Beyond%20 2000&strNavigation=Home-%3EForum&BigClassID=4&SmallClassID=11.
14. Moeletsi Mbeki, 'The Oligarchs are Still in Place', *Sunday Independent*, 14 June 2009, http://www.africafiles.org/article.asp?ID=21064. See also his *Architects of Poverty: Why African Capitalism Needs Changing* (Johannesburg, Picador Africa, 2009).
15. See Michael Hamlyn, 'Race, a Social Barricade', http://news.iafrica.com/sa/2104441.htm.
16. At http://www.sacp.org.za/pubs/umsebenzi/2009/vo18-13.html.
17. United Nations Development Programme, *Overcoming Barriers: Human Mobility and Development* (New York, UNDP/Macmillan, 2009), p. 190.
18. Ibid., p. 185.
19. Afrikaans, English, Ndebele, Northern Sotho, Sotho, Swazi, Tsonga, Tswana, Venda, Xhosa and Zulu.
20. At http://www.sairr.org.za/press-office/archive/201cillega1201d-immigrants-are-a-permanent-feature-of-southafrica2019s-population-13th-may-2008.html/.
21. At http://www.irinnews.org/Report.aspx?ReportId=87562.
22. At http://www.mg.co.za/article/2009-12-10-mantashe-anc-must-remain-political-centre.
23. Zuma was interviewed on Radio 702 (Johannesburg) on 14 December 2009, as reported in *Business Report*, 15 December 2009.
24. At http://www.engineeringnews.co.za/article/unctad-2011-07-26.
25. The mining industry is South Africa's biggest employer, with around 460,000 employees and another 400,000 employed by the suppliers of goods and services to the industry in 2008, http://www.southafrica.info/business/economy/sectors/mining.htm.
26. Such as the Harvard group of economists invited by President Mbeki's South African government to analyse the country's economic constraints.

See, for example, Dani Rodrik, 'Understanding South Africa's Economic Puzzles', *Economics of Transition*, Vol. 16, No. 4, September 2008, pp. 769–97; and Ricardo Hausmann and Bailey Klinger, 'South Africa's Export Predicament', *Economics of Transition*, Vol. 16, No. 4, September 2008, pp. 609–37.

27. See, for example, Patrick Bond, 'SA Political Power Balance Shifts Left – Though Not Yet Enough to Quell Grassroots Anger', 13 June 2009, http://www.zmag.org/zspace/commentaries/3895.

28. For example, Bond writes: 'The SA economy is likely to shed a half-million jobs in 2009, especially in manufacturing and mining. January 2009 alone witnessed a 36 per cent crash in new car sales and 50 per cent production cut, the worst ever recorded, according to the National Association of Auto Manufacturers. The anticipated rise in port activity has also reversed, with a 29 per cent annualized fall in early 2009. Repossessed houses increased by 52 per cent in early 2009 from a year earlier, as house prices are down 11 per cent with much greater falls ahead. Most minerals are 70 per cent off their peak of a year ago. The stock market lost nearly 50 per cent last year' (ibid.).

29. The mid-2006 population estimates for all nine provinces were: Eastern Cape, 6.9 million; Free State, 2.9 million; Gauteng, 9.5 million; KwaZulu-Natal, 9.9 million; Limpopo, 5.6 million; Mpumalanga, 3.5 million; Northern Cape, 1 million; North West, 3.4 million; Western Cape, 4.7 million. See http://www.southafrica.info/about/geography/provinces.htm.

30. South Africa's National Assembly consists of 400 members elected by proportional representation from party lists. Of these, 200 members are elected from national party lists; the other 200 are elected from provincial party lists in each of the nine provinces.

31. Roger Southall, 'Introduction', in Sakhela Buhlungu, John Daniel, Roger Southall and Jessica Lutchman (eds.), *State of the Nation: South Africa, 2007* (Pretoria, HSRC Press, 2007), p. 6.

32. Ibid., p. 7.

33. *Sunday Times* (Johannesburg), 19 September 2004.

34. Southall, 'Introduction', p. 9.

35. Involving the purchase of 3 submarines, 3 frigates, Gripen and Hawk jet-fighters, and helicopters.

36. Cited in Russell, *After Mandela*, p. 8.

37. At http://www.timeslive.co.za/Politics/article1005234.ece/Vavi-tells-ANC-to-stop-scoring-own-goals.

38. At http://mg.co.za/article/2011–04–12-corruption-the-biggest-service-delivery-bugbear.

11   *Out of the Ashes: Progress in Iraq 2003–11*

1. Nevertheless, the Shia tolerated a significant amount of violence until their patience broke.
2. The total number of deaths and casualties resulting from the invasion and subsequent sectarian conflict is hotly disputed. See, for instance, the Iraq Body Count http://www.iraqbodycount.org.
3. For some Shia elements, de-Ba'athification came to be, and be seen as, de-Sunnification. This trend is still evident in Iraqi politics.
4. In such situations, external military intervention in the classic UN peacekeeping interposing model frequently becomes both an artificial barrier to peaceful bilateral solutions and a common whipping boy on which both sides take out their frustrations.
5. In 2011 Iraqi Security Forces numbered approximately 650,000, with 450,000 police and 200,000 Iraqi army plus a small navy and air force.
6. Through a process known as Provincial Iraqi Control (PIC).
7. A similar process has been adopted in Afghanistan.
8. This success contrasts with the British 'accommodation' with Jaysh al Mahdi militia in Basra in 2006, which was conducted from a position of weakness and led to a loss of visibility of a deteriorating security situation which required substantial reinforcement to resolve.
9. See Linda Robinson, *Tell Me How This Ends* (New York, Public Affairs Books, 2008), p. 36.
10. Mosul, the capital of Ninewa province, straddles the Kurd–Arab fault line.
11. The factions include Quietist (led by Grand Ayatollah Ali al-Sistani), Sadrist (led by Moqtadr al-Sadr) and Velayat-e faqih (led by Ayatollah Khameni) trends.
12. In October 2008, when thousands of Iraqi Christians fled their homes after a dozen had been killed, apparently by extreme Sunni Islamists, the government in Baghdad sent more than 100 extra police to protect the religious minority.
13. 'The Shia are afraid of the past, the Sunnis are afraid of the future, and the Kurds are afraid of the past and the future': Hoshyar Zebari, Iraqi Foreign Minister. As told by Zebari to the author at Maude House, Baghdad, in 2009, and more publicly as quoted in http://www.google.co.uk/url?sa=t&source=web&cd=10&sqi=2&ved=0CFIQFjAJ&url=http%3A%2F%2Fwww.humansecuritygateway.com%2Fdocuments%2FMIT_StrikingTheBalance_Iraq.pdf&ei=oZSNTqywNMzE8QPio-kU&usg=AFQjCNGY7ko35T-6gK53b59ncUxoJypLWQ&sig2=eI59E9gQ1hsjZQ28522 rmQ.
14. Under UNSCR 1770 dated August 2007.

15. Official comments, including those of General Ilker Basbug, Chief of the Turkish General Staff, reflect a growing understanding that resolution of Turkey's Kurdish fault line cannot be achieved on military lines alone.
16. Capital of the Kurdish region of Iraq.
17. The city is surrounded by an Iraqi army division and a Kurdish Peshmerga brigade that were invited by the coalition in 2003 to move forward to the outskirts of Kirkuk (and other areas in northern Iraq) in order to help maintain control. Neither army is allowed to deploy into the city, but soldiers from both forces live in the city.
18. Known as 'Anfal'. Kirkuk province was renamed Tameem ('Nationalisation') under Saddam's regime.
19. The coalition position is to support a confirmatory referendum on Kirkuk after a political agreement is reached, not a pre-emptive yes/no referendum as a substitute for political agreement.
20. Another option that has been considered is special status for Kirkuk, similar to the northern Bosnian town of Brcko, which was constituted as a neutral, self-governing administrative unit after the war in the former Yugoslavia in the early 1990s.
21. Kurdish intelligence service.
22. Under Article 107 of the constitution, the government of Iraq could insist that the Peshmerga withdraw to their pre-April 2003 positions and order the Iraqi army to move into the Kurdish region in order to protect Iraq's borders and defend the country.
23. The Patriotic Union of Kurdistan, the hard-line Sunni Tawafuq (Iraqi Accord Front) and the heavily Iranian-influenced Shia Iraqi National Alliance, comprising the Sadrists and the Islamic Supreme Council of Iraq.
24. Prime Minister Maliki's Dawa ('State of Law') alliance, Iyad Allawi's Iraqiya (Iraqi National Movement), comprising Sunni and Shia elements, and 'Unity', which likewise spans the Sunni–Shia divide, led by the current secular Shia Minister of the Interior, Jawad al-Bulani, with Ahmed Abu Risha, the Sunni tribal leader who was instrumental in the Sawat ('Awakening') in western Iraq.
25. In the results announced on 26 March 2010, Iraqiya secured ninety-one of the 325 parliamentary seats, Dawa secured eighty-nine and the Iraqi National Alliance secured seventy; 163 seats are needed for a majority in parliament.
26. With the emergence of a new Kurdish opposition group, Goran ('Change').
27. 'Chiarelli [US Multinational Corps – Iraq Commander] believed the US and the Iraqi governments had fundamentally different objectives and that it was critical to resolve this "endstate mismatch"': quoted Robinson, *Tell Me How This Ends*, p. 36.

28. Iraq is estimated to have the world's third-largest reserves of oil, but dropped to thirteenth place in the international production tables under Saddam.
29. In discussions with the author 28 April and 22 May 2009.
30. For example, the refurbishment of the Mosul dam and lining of canals to reduce water loss.

12 Iran: Foundering under the Weight of Its Own Contradictions

1. See, for example, Nikki Keddie, *Modern Iran: Roots and Results of Revolution* (New Haven, Yale University Press, 2003), pp. 240–84.
2. US support for ethnic militants in Iran is not only alleged by the Iranian government, but also reported by well-informed Western journalists such as Seymour Hersh.
3. See entry on Azeris in the Minorities at Risk Project, University of Maryland's Center for International Development and Conflict Management, http://www.cidcm.umd.edu/mar/assessment.asp?groupId= 63002.
4. Sonia Ghaffari, 'Baluchistan's Rising Militancy', *Middle East Report 250*, Spring 2009.
5. Amnesty International, *Defending Minority Rights: The Ahwazi Arabs*, 17 May 2006.
6. Amnesty International, *Iran: Human Rights Abuses against the Kurdish Minority*, July 2008, p. 6.
7. See, for example, Lionel Beehner, 'Iran's Ethnic Groups', *Backgrounder*, Council on Foreign Relations, 29 November 2006.
8. The UN statistics division figure for 2008 is 73.3 million.
9. Keddie, *Modern Iran*, pp. 240–84.
10. Jim Muir, 'Clashes Show Unresolved Iran Crisis', *BBC Newsonline*, 18 September 2009.
11. World Bank, *Iran Country Brief*, June 2009.
12. UN Division of Statistics.
13. Djavad Salehi-Isfahani, 'Economic Fears and Discontents', *New York Times*, 23 June 2009.
14. Djavad Salehi-Isfahani, 'Iran Sanctions: Who Really Wins?', *MRzine*, 15 October 2009, http://www.monthlyreview.org/mrzine/si151009.html.
15. Ali Ansari (ed.), *Preliminary Analysis of the Voting Figures in Iran's 2009 Presidential Election*, Chatham House, 21 June 2009.
16. Robert Dreyfuss, 'Iran's Ex-Foreign Minister Yazdi: It's a Coup', *The Nation*, 13 June 2009, http://www.thenation.com/blogs/dreyfuss/443348.
17. Amnesty International Report, *Defending Minority Rights*, pp. 1–2.
18. Transparency International, *Corruption Perceptions Index*, 2009.

19. Rafsanjani is a former conservative. His political realignment with the reformists in the 2009 election was an important indicator of the concern within the political elite at the radical direction in which Ahmadinejad has been taking Iran.

20. Fariborz Ghadar, 'Iran at the Crossroads', Center for Strategic and International Studies, 10 July 2009.

21. Human Rights Watch Report, *Iran: Freedom of Expression and Association in the Kurdish Region*, 2009, pp. 8–9.

22. Seymour Hersh, 'Preparing the Battlefield', *New Yorker*, 7 July 2008.

13 Israel, Jordan and Palestine: Linked Fates, Hard Realities

1. Musa Budeiri, 'The Palestinians: Tensions between Nationalist and Religious Identities', in James Jankowski and Israel Gershoni (eds.), *Rethinking Nationalism in the Arab Middle East* (New York, Columbia University Press, 1997), pp. 196, 199.

2. Beshara Doumani, 'Palestine versus the Palestinians? The Iron Laws and the Ironies of a People Denied', *Journal of Palestine Studies*, Vol. 36, No. 4, Summer 2007, p. 52.

3. Ali Jaradat in *al-Ayyam*, 19 November 2007.

4. *Wathiqat al-wafaq al-watani*, 28 June 2006, paragraph 9.

5. Policy Statement of Isma'il Haniyya Government, *al-Jazeera*, 17 March 2007.

6. Riyad Summit Resolutions as published in *al-Sharq al-Awsat*, 31 March 2007.

7. Meir Litvak, 'The Islamization of the Palestinian-Israeli Conflict: The Case of Hamas', *Middle Eastern Studies*, Vol. 34, No. 1, January 1998, pp. 148–50, 153–5.

8. Meir Litvak, 'Hamas: Palestinian Identity, Islam, and National Sovereignty', in Asher Susser (ed.), *Challenges to the Cohesion of the Arab State* (The Moshe Dayan Center, Tel Aviv University, 2008), pp. 156–8, 167.

9. Total number of deaths varies widely, but for an authoritative figure see Iraq Body Count http://www.iraqbodycount.org.

Conclusion

1. See, in particular, research by Joseph Siegle of the Washington, DC–based African Center for Strategic Studies, including 'Overcoming Autocratic Legacies', Development Outreach (World Bank Institute, 2007) and 'Explaining the Variation in Economic Performance of Developing Country Democratizers', prepared for the Community of Democracies Seminar on Democracy and Development: Poverty as a Challenge to Democratic Governance, Bamako, Mali, 29–30 March 2007.

2. For example, see the Brenthurst Foundation, '"Everything is at Zero":
    Beyond the Referendum – Drivers and Choices for Development in
    Southern Sudan', Discussion Paper 2010/05, November 2010.

AUTHOR BIOGRAPHIES

Joel D. Barkan is Senior Associate at the Center for Strategic and International Studies and Professor Emeritus of Political Science at the University of Iowa. A specialist on issues of democratisation, governance and political economy across anglophone Africa, he straddles the worlds of academe and the international donor community by consulting extensively for USAID and the World Bank. His latest book is *Legislative Power in Emerging African Democracies* (Boulder, Lynne Rienner Publishers, 2009).

Chris Brown retired from the British Army after thirty-six years with the rank of lieutenant general. He saw operational service in eight theatres, including Northern Ireland where he ended up as General Officer Commanding, Bosnia, Kosovo, Afghanistan and Iraq, where he was Deputy Commander of Coalition Forces and Senior British Military Representative. His final military appointment in 2010 was leading the UK MoD's analysis of lessons from the Iraq campaign. In 2011 he was senior military adviser to the African Union High-Level Implementation Panel for Sudan. He read law at University College, Cardiff, and International Relations at Peterhouse, Cambridge.

Christopher Clapham is Editor of the *Journal of Modern African Studies* and is based at the Centre of African Studies at Cambridge University. From 1989 until his retirement in 2002, he was Professor of Politics and International Relations at Lancaster University, and he was President of the African Studies Association of the United Kingdom from 1992 to 1994. His main interests lie in the politics and international relations of Africa, with a particular focus on the Horn of Africa. He has also worked on Liberia and Sierra Leone.

Pierre Englebert is Professor of African Politics at Pomona College in Claremont, California. He is the author of *Africa: Unity, Sovereignty and*

Sorrow (Boulder, Lynne Rienner Publishers, 2009) and *State Legitimacy and Development in Africa* (Boulder, Lynne Rienner Publishers, 2000). He has done research in the Democratic Republic of Congo since 2001.

Jeffrey Herbst is President of Colgate University. He served for five years as Provost and Executive Vice-President for Academic Affairs at Miami University and before then as Professor of Politics and International Affairs at Princeton University. He is the author of several books on African politics, including *States and Power in Africa* (Princeton, Princeton University Press, 2002).

Peter Lewis is Director of the African Studies Program and Associate Professor at the Johns Hopkins University School of Advanced International Studies (SAIS). His work focuses on economic reform, democratisation, civil society and social identity in sub-Saharan Africa. His most recent book, *Growing Apart: Politics and Economic Change in Indonesia and Nigeria* (Ann Arbor, University of Michigan Press, 2007), is concerned with the institutional basis of economic development, drawing upon a comparative study.

Joseph Chinyong Liow is Associate Dean and Professor of Comparative and International Politics, S. Rajaratnam School of International Studies, Nanyang Technological University, Singapore. His research interests are in the areas of Muslim politics in South-East Asia, armed resistance movements in South-East Asia and the international politics of the broader East Asian region.

Terence McNamee is Deputy Director of the Brenthurst Foundation. Educated at universities in Canada and the UK, Dr McNamee was Director of Publications at the Royal United Services Institute (RUSI) in London and Editor of the *RUSI Journal* from 2002 to 2010. He has conducted research on security and development issues in numerous fragile states. His publications include *CENTURY* and *DECADE* (London, Phaidon, 1999, 2010) and *War without Consequences: Iraq's Insurgency and the Spectre of Strategic Defeat* (London, RUSI, 2008).

Greg Mills is Director of the Brenthurst Foundation. From 1996 to 2005 he served as the National Director of the South African Institute of International Affairs. Dr Mills has lectured at universities and institutions in Africa and abroad, from the Pentagon to the Peruvian and Chilean Naval

Staff Colleges, and is on the visiting staff of the NATO Higher Defence College in Rome. He has been seconded three times to the NATO mission in Afghanistan (2006, 2010) and to the Office of the President of Rwanda (2008). He is the author most recently of *Why Africa is Poor – and What Africans Can Do about It* (Johannesburg, Penguin, 2010).

J. Peter Pham is Director of the Michael S. Ansari Africa Center at the Atlantic Council of the United States. He currently also serves as Vice-President of the Association for the Study of the Middle East and Africa (ASMEA), an academic organisation representing over 1,000 scholars of Middle Eastern and African Studies at more than 300 universities and colleges across the United States and Canada, and Editor-in-Chief of ASMEA's refereed *Journal of the Middle East and Africa*.

Tom Porteous is Deputy Program Director at Human Rights Watch. He has worked as a journalist in the Middle East, Africa and Europe and in UN peacekeeping operations in Somalia and Liberia. A conflict management adviser for sub-Saharan Africa at the UK Foreign and Commonwealth Office, his book *Britain in Africa* (London, Zed Books) was published in 2008.

Anna C. Rader is an Associate Fellow of the Royal United Services Institute in London. She was an international observer of the Sudan general elections in April 2010, based in Bentiu, Unity State. She is the former editor of the *RUSI Journal* and a contributing author of DECADE (London, Phaidon, 2010) and *VII: Questions without Answers* (London: Phaidon, 2011). She is currently conducting research on political consolidation in Somalia, focusing on identity and citizenship in Puntland.

Asher Susser is Senior Fellow at the Moshe Dayan Center for Middle Eastern Studies at Tel Aviv University (TAU). Professor Susser was the Director of the Center for twelve years and has taught for some thirty years in TAU's Department of Middle Eastern History. His most recent book is *Israel, Jordan and Palestine: The Two-State Imperative* (forthcoming, 2011).

INDEX